dance lest we all fall down

a journey of friendship, poverty, power and peace

MARGARET WILLSON

Cold Tree Press
Nashville, Tennessee

Library of Congress Control Number: 2007939965
Published in the United States by Cold Tree Press
Nashville, Tennessee
www.coldtreepress.com

Printed in the United States of America
ISBN 978-1-58385-222-4

Dedicated to

Rita Cassis dos Santos de Conceição
aka
Rita Cliff

All proceeds from the sale of
Dance Lest We All Fall Down
will go to Bahia Street.

This is a true story. Some names and incidents have been changed to protect the privacy of the people involved. Although some conversations are verbatim, taken from field notes, others have been constructed from memory. I have condensed various occurrences and occasionally shuffled the time line in order to create a more cohesive narrative.

The incidents and people in this book, however, are real. Likewise, the recording of the conversations and interactions reflect a reality that was sometimes painful for me to experience. I hope, through the words of this book, I have been able to convey some of the insights, struggles, and courage of these people I have been lucky enough to know.

table of contents

part one - learning to dance

part two - treading water

part three - laughter lessons

dance lest we all fall down

a journey of friendship, poverty, power and peace

2006
2006

Tropical nights fall quickly.

I stood alone on a curb in the city of Salvador da Bahia, Brazil. Rain, surprisingly cold against the warm night air, flattened my hair, soaked my scalp, and migrated through my shirt to the hollow of my spine. A man standing beneath the awning of a darkened store watched me. I had stayed too late at my appointment. Buses were no longer safe at this hour so I hailed a taxi.

The driver slowed, water spitting from beneath his wheels. He leaned over the passenger seat and opened the backseat door. I closed it gently so as not to batter the flimsy metal of his locally produced Brazilian car, then opened the front door and climbed in beside him. I checked him out: scruffy hair, gaunt cheekbones, a short beard. His long thin fingers lay lightly on the steering wheel. He took stock of my appearance: tall, white skin, light hair. A foreigner, or perhaps from Southern Brazil. Certainly middle-class. His eyes glinted, almost metallic in the dim reflection of the dashboard lights.

"Thanks," I said in Portuguese. "What a downpour! It's not supposed to rain like this in December." The driver visibly relaxed at the sound and slang of my lower-class Portuguese.

"Tell me about it," he said. "Bad for business, nobody's out. The weather's gone wacky lately, you can't count on anything. Where you going?"

"Carlos Gomes, near Dois de Julho."

"Right." He turned onto a dark side street, a shortcut I also knew. I acknowledged his street savvy with a nod. He smiled.

"Look at this kitchen store," I said. "About ten years ago it had only a few lights. Each year they keep adding more and more. Now it's a wall of illumination, a blazing beacon."

The driver glanced at the store and laughed. It occupied a corner lot. Row upon row of bright white lights fully covered one side. Fake green leaves, perhaps intended to represent ivy, were draped over one edge. These, in turn, were covered by a cascade of gold colored balls. At the front of the store, every limb of every bush was entwined with even more lights. As we passed, choral tones, seemingly varied renditions of Edelweiss, rang out at deafening decibels.

"Yes," the driver said. "The city and companies invest a great deal in all these Christmas lights and decorations. They think then we poor people won't notice the rotted walls they cloak, the decaying infrastructure. Personally, I think the money might be better spent on education and feeding people."

I glanced at him. "That's my thought," I said, "but I don't often hear people express it that eloquently."

He shrugged and skillfully maneuvered the taxi through spray and heavy traffic. "It's a fantasy set up to divert the population's attention from the horrors of living here. They think the starving residents of the city won't notice the darkness behind this blanket of light. The lights have no substance; they're a flimsy curtain balanced only on darkness and air." He paused while he steered into a deep gutter to pass a stalled truck.

"I've never been to Las Vegas," he continued, "but I think it must be similar. There the casinos lure people in to lose their money, to gamble it away until they have nothing. To encourage them, they and the local government make the entire city a fantasy, bright lights, pretend worlds. This is the same, only I suppose here people have no money to lose; they have nothing, only their connection to reality. And here, with their lights and foreign music, they're taking that away as well."

"And after Christmas is Carnival," I said.

The driver laughed. "Ah, now Carnival is an entirely different matter. These lights, these plastic Christmas trees, these Santas, they're a foreign invasion; they're a fantasy created from politician's glitter. But Carnival, it's our own fantasy, our own complicated past superimposed on a present that includes the rats, racism, death, love, sex, forgetfulness, and bliss. Carnival is our own rhythm. As the song says, sadness has no end, only happiness. That's Carnival."

"This is where I'm staying," I said.

"On the corner?" I nodded. "You're not from here, are you? Are you a foreigner or from the South?"

"A foreigner. My accent doesn't sound Brazilian, does it?"

"You have an accent, but your Portuguese is local. Why do you have such good Portuguese?"

I opened the door and glanced up to see the beloved face of my friend Rita. She waved from the balcony of the apartment she'd recently rented in this relatively safe corner of central Salvador. The rain had stopped. "Thanks for the conversation," I said to the driver. "You're a poet." He smiled and took the fare I held out for him.

"And you're easy to talk to."

"I have a history with Bahia," I said as I climbed from the car and waved back at Rita, "a long history."

part one | learning to dance

one
seduction

I had just boarded a Varig Brazilian Airlines flight from Brussels to Salvador. The year was 1991. I knew I had left European space and entered Brazilian almost as soon as I entered the plane. I walked to my assigned seat and found a nun sitting there. "Excuse me," I said. "You're in the wrong seat."

"No," she said. "This is my seat."

"May I see your ticket?" I said. The people in the adjoining seats were all listening; a child stared over the back of the next row. Who would harass a nun?

She handed me her ticket. It was for three rows back, a center seat. The plane was packed.

"See," I said. "Your seat is different." The annoyance around me thickened to hostility.

The nun looked at me, said nothing.

"Do you understand?" I asked.

"This is my seat," she said. "I'm sitting here." The man beside her placed a protective hand on her arm.

A man behind me took my hand luggage. "Let me help you with your bag," he said in Brazilian-accented English. He strode toward what was indisputably my new seat and placed my bag in the overhead.

Brazil-1, Margaret-0.

I was now squashed into my new seat between a fat man who was already snoring and a man whose foul breath rushed at me when he smiled. As I settled in, I contemplated the politics of the World Cup. If a game like that could invert power relations between G8 countries and countries struggling to pay off international debts, then what unbalancing experiences could I expect in Brazil?

I was only on this plane because of Alexandra. It was her fault. I was an anthropologist working in Amsterdam and had been awarded a year's fellowship position in Australia. Alexandra had somehow convinced me that from Amsterdam, Brazil was on the way to Australia, and, that being the case – particularly since she would be visiting herself

— I simply *had* to visit her family in Salvador, a major city in the state of Bahia, Brazil. Somehow I had conceded to this dubious plan.

"You'll love it," Alexandra had said to me only a few weeks before. We were sitting in her section of an illegal squat in the Red Light district of Amsterdam. She loaded more wood into the old, rusted barrel that served as her heating source. The building was in a state of disuse and disrepair, virtually abandoned by its owners, and it had been taken over by squatters. About twenty other people lived in this squat, but Alexandra had sectioned off this large room for herself, secured by a heavy wooden door, a bolt, and large lock.

Alexandra's room overlooked a canal. Its floors were wide sixteenth-century oak, the ceilings high and dark from centuries of life and grime. In one corner, Alexandra had built herself a bed of planks. Near the ancient glass-paned double door that lead to nothing but a view above the canal, she had placed two lumpy but serviceable sofas she had found in the street somewhere nearby. Across from the bed, fairly near the stove, she had set up a gas burner on a rough counter and connected it to a propane tank. Beside the burner stood a battered sink and a bucket to catch the water beneath. Everything was as tidy and spotless as cleaning could make it.

"You will love my family, my sisters," Alexandra said, handing me a steaming cup of tea she had poured from the pot that stood warm on a homemade shelf above the stove. "How long will you be able to stay?"

"I don't know," I said. "My position in Canberra doesn't start for two months, so I suppose I could stay as long as six weeks."

We settled into the sofas. Late afternoon sun shone across the dark planks, catching their soft, deep color, making them luminous. Alexandra opened the doors, and we heard the bells of bicycles and the conversations of people as they passed below.

We sat in silence for a moment, savoring the peace.

"When you get to Salvador," Alexandra said, "you will understand why I so love this place."

"I love this place too," I said.

"No, it's different for me. You'll see." She laughed. "You know, I wouldn't give this invitation to visit my family to just anybody. It's exactly because you see the beauty here, of this squat, this place most people wouldn't even want to set a foot in. This is why I know you'll rest fine with my family." Alexandra sighed. "A half an hour before my Dutch class. You know, it's funny. I'm learning to read and write English and Dutch, and I never really learned to read and write Portuguese." She laughed. "After I learn these other languages, maybe then I'll be able to learn the language I was born with."

"*Você pode dormir comigo!*" Andrea said. Andrea was Alexandra's thirteen-year-old sister. I wiped the sweat from my eyes and surveyed the narrow, low bed in front of me. From everyone's gestures, I gathered that she and I were supposed to share it. Alexandra had just escorted me from the airport by bus. The flight, on four different airplanes, had taken over twenty hours. In Salvador, it was now sometime in the evening after dark. I was in the bedroom of Alexandra's family home. Alexandra's family lived in a very poor part of Penambuas, a neighborhood at the periphery of Salvador. Inside their bedroom, a dim lightbulb hung above our heads. The single bed in front of me was about five inches from my shin, a bunk bed about five inches behind me. The only ventilation came from the door to the living room and a six-by-six-inch grated hole in the wall above our heads. I could hardly breathe. Alexandra watched me carefully for my reaction.

I laughed. I was an anthropologist. I had lived for months in the jungles of Papua New Guinea, subsisting on sago grubs. I could handle this.

"Thank you," I said to Andrea. "Tonight I could sleep on anything. But I'm a lot bigger than you. I will push you onto the floor!"

Alexandra translated and Andrea shook her head dismissively. "Would you like to take a shower?" Alexandra asked.

I nodded and she led me from the bedroom to a bare concrete box of a room. It contained only a toilet with no seat and a shower head with a drain near the center of the floor.

"The toilet doesn't work," Alexandra said. She gestured toward a bright red plastic bucket. "Just fill that with water from the shower, dump it into the toilet when you are done, and the water will just flush stuff down the drain." I nodded. "This towel is clean," she said handing me a towel that hung from a nail on the wooden door.

I thanked her, shut the door, and turned on the shower. The water came out surprisingly cold. Strange, I thought, I'm so hot, yet my skin still tenses at the anticipation of a cold shower. I stepped in, and, after a few seconds, my body adjusted and it felt fine. Then, as I was shampooing my hair, I saw a dark shadow on the wall. My eyesight has always been bad, and the only light in the room came filtered from above the short wall that separated the bathroom from the kitchen. I leaned closer for a better look, then jumped back.

It was a cockroach, at least three inches long. Once I'd seen the first one, I began to notice them everywhere: two in the corner, one by the ceiling.

I rinsed my hair, turned off the shower and, watching carefully where I stepped in my bare feet, quickly dried off and put on a sleeping shirt.

Alexandra's three younger sisters smiled at me as I reentered the bedroom—I now realized that all five of us were to be sleeping in here. Alexandra gave me a fierce glance. I toweled my hair and said, "I feel much better."

Andrea shoved my bag to the foot of the bed, the only space available for it, and shut the door. The temperature in the room immediately rose ten degrees. She lay down on the bed and I perched beside her. Alexandra, eighteen-year-old Ana, and sixteen-year-old Soraia took the two bunk beds.

The "mattress," I discovered as I lay down, was a flimsy plywood box with no padding whatsoever. It was covered only by a thin sheet. I raised myself onto my elbow and felt the wood begin to crack. This entire thing is going to collapse, I thought. I lay perfectly still.

After some time, Ana spoke. "*Está muito calor aqui,*" she said. "*Vou subir.*" She crawled from the top bunk bed, pointed toward the ceiling, and with a motion of her hand, invited me to join her. Andrea grabbed our sheets and bounded out behind us. We unbolted the back door, climbed a ladder made of wooden slats nailed into the crumbling concrete wall, and climbed onto the roof.

A warm night wind touched my face, and I breathed a grateful sigh. I curled up in the sheet and lay down upon the concrete roof. The night was not quiet; I counted at least five radios blaring competing music stations at full and tinny volume. A mosquito bit my elbow, so I covered my arms with the sheet. Another mosquito landed near my eye. I pulled the sheet over my head. Then from below, something bit me. I jumped.

Andrea said something I didn't understand. Then she made a crawling motion with her hand. "Ant," I said copying the motion. She nodded. Another bite. How many hours before dawn?

I'm an anthropologist, I kept thinking. I can handle this. But I don't have to like it.

The next morning I discovered that what I had thought the night before to be an urban stream running past the front of their house was actually an open sewer. This sewer emptied into an even larger sewage canal at the bottom of the hill. Alexandra told me that their house now had a completed cement and tile roof and a partially-plumbed indoor toilet because of money she and her brothers had sent from Amsterdam. Despite the daily scrubbing that Ana and Soraia gave to their house, rats still lurked beneath the back washing trough. The girls washed the dishes immediately after we ate and placed them in tightly shut cupboards, yet, when I pulled out a coffee cup for morning coffee, I found a cockroach nestled cozily inside.

Their neighbor's home consisted of rubble piled into unstable walls, topped by a roof of broken boards. At the bottom of the hill, next to the larger sewer, young children, who seemed to have no parents, lived in a makeshift tent of torn blue plastic sheeting. These children came daily to beg at the door for food.

Everyone I saw in the area was part African descent, various shades of brown and black, often clearly mixed with indigenous or European ancestry. At five feet ten inches, I stood taller than anyone around me, except Andrea and Ana, who were both close to six feet tall with long, graceful limbs. Wherever I went, I was an object of curiosity.

Andrea, Ana, and Alexandra's father sold sugarcane juice, which he squeezed in a motorized cane-crusher, at the edge of the highway. Their mother, Tatiana, looked about sixty-five, but told me she was forty. She had given birth to fifteen children. Nine still lived. Tatiana sold *sonhos*, sweet, sugar-covered buns filled with guava paste, from the window of the house. Because the cement used to construct the house had been mixed with a great deal of sand, the sill crumbled beneath our elbows and fingertips. I learned to lean carefully against both sills and walls.

Tatiana awoke at four each morning to make the sonhos. Sonho, they told me, means dream in Portuguese. So each day, I stood beside

Tatiana as she sold dreams from the crumbling front window sill.

Of Tatiana's nine surviving children, five still lived at home—two boys and the three sisters. The brothers only came home late at night, and the father, when I saw him, was usually drunk. Alexandra only shrugged. "He beats us," she said.

After about three weeks, Alexandra returned to Amsterdam, leaving me in her sisters' charge. Andrea became my primary teacher of Portuguese and the ways of the streets. I nicknamed her *Ursinha* or "Little Bear" because of her bright eyes and fierce temper.

Over the following weeks, Andrea, Soraia, and Ana insisted I change my wardrobe; they replaced my one-piece swimsuit with a tiny bikini, refusing to appear on the beach with me otherwise. They tightened my clothes, shredded the hems of my shorts to create a fringe, and in various ways changed every piece of clothing I had into what they considered more beautiful.

These "remodeled" clothes, which were often revealing and explicitly sexy, I considered "cheap" or overly suggestive, going by the standards of the Northern, middle-class society in which I was raised. I tried to explain to the girls that in the United States and Europe, a woman who wore explicitly sexy clothing was perceived as being sexually available or "loose." I told them that in rape trials in the United States the way a woman was dressed at the time was often used as proof that she was "asking" for sexual violence.

Andrea and Ana told me that in Bahia, except in church or other places where one needed to show respect, this was not the case. A woman who wore sexy clothing was simply considered attractive. It was a woman's behavior, they told me, as well as her class in society, that determined whether she was considered "loose." During our evening chats, as we sat on the roof to catch the wind, Andrea and Ana instructed me that a woman was supposed to be sensual at all times and was expected by society at large to use her sensuality as a means to control men. But, they said, presenting a sensual image and actually being sexually available were morally and socially separate. Indeed, part of the derogatory image of the *gringa* or Northern female was that she was available, but not sensual. And such insults they certainly did not want said about their guest. I was, after all, their responsibility.

A few weeks after my arrival, the sisters set out to show me what they considered beautiful and important in their city. They took me to see a mall. In an instant we walked out of some of the worst poverty I had ever seen and into a designer shopping center. Light and clean hallways were flanked by inviting shops, sporting top-brand fashion and housewares. Music played from a high-tech sound system while escalators silently moved people from one well-lit floor to the next. In architecture and goods sold, this shopping center was equal to the best of its kind in the world. The majority of the people in this mall looked well-fed and well-dressed. And, like myself—and unlike my friends—they were all white.

The girls and I paused before shops that sold goods they could never buy and they smiled as if proud, showing off these stores to me and apparently wanting me to be as delighted as they were. Constantly they urged me to buy, something. I refused and grew increasingly uncomfortable, acutely aware that my ability to buy these goods underscored and reinforced the economic, class, and racial differences between them and me.

The longer we wandered the mall, the more my confusion and discomfort grew. I was no stranger to inequality and racism—I was, after all, from the United States. What I couldn't understand, though, was the girls' reaction to the mall. Why were they so eager to show me this hub of materialism that seemed to me a blatant symbol of their oppression? Why was their inclination not one of anger, to smash the colorful displays? And where was their anger at these light-skinned, well-dressed people who clearly had advantages so explicitly denied them?

Where was their anger at me?

A few days before I was supposed to leave Bahia, Ana and Andrea told me about a festival that coming weekend in Arembepe, a small fishing village about an hour north of Salvador.

"Is it beautiful?" I asked.

Andrea looked at the dust between her feet. "We've never been there," she mumbled.

"Really?"

"It costs extra on the bus," Ana explained, her eyes proud and defiant to belie the shame of this admission.

When I asked the price of the trip, she told me about 30 U.S. cents. I decided I wanted to visit the village as a goodbye to my time with them.

"How about you be my guides," I asked. "I'll pay our expenses. That'd be fair. I certainly wouldn't be able to go there alone."

Andrea and Ana looked at each other, then at me. "Really?" Andrea asked. "We can go?" She pranced in a circle around me, telling me everything she had heard about this town. She ran inside to ask Tatiana's permission. We left that evening.

Arembepe, Ana told me, had been made famous in the 1960s when it became a hippie haven for the likes of Mick Jagger and Janis Joplin. Some "hippies" still remained in a small community on the northern edge of the town. They lived in grass shacks and made a living selling jewelry and marijuana. A factory had also been built somewhere nearby. Because of the factory and the hippie influence, middle-class Brazilians avoided the place, going instead to Praia de Forte and other communities further north.

"So, that's why there're no big hotels there?" I asked.

"Yeah, there are some small *pousadas* where you can stay," Ana smiled, "but we can sleep on the beach or somewhere. The pousadas are too expensive."

I nodded. I wasn't sure of the best thing to do: offer to pay for a stay in a hotel or let them tell me how they would spend the weekend if I hadn't been there. I finally chose the latter because that seemed to sit the best with them. Although I was the foreigner, I was also just a part of their big adventure. I gave my money to Ana for safekeeping and asked her to spend it as she thought best. She nodded. "Good idea. A pickpocket is more likely to target you than me."

When we arrived, the streets were alive with music and people. Ana and Andrea stuck close beside me, both protective and watching for themselves. I was immediately struck by the beauty of the people. Alexandra had explained that people who lived near Salvador were mostly of African descent, mixed with Portuguese, Italian, Lebanese, German, Dutch, and the indigenous peoples. Each person embodied a colonial past transmogrified into this mixed and turbulent present. I kept smiling at people. Some smiled back and some did not.

Sometime during the evening, I smiled at a man dancing nearby.

He smiled back and continued to dance near us. The loose curls of his black hair fell to his shoulders, his eyes cobalt, his skin dark, high cheekbones, full lips and a narrow, proud nose. His smile seemed to light up the sky. I wasn't sure I had ever seen anyone so beautiful. By then, my skin was dripping sweat, my body spinning Carnival and heat. Ana and Andrea moved us away.

"We are poor and dark," Ana said, adjusting her shorts and middi top. "We dance only with people we know at *festas*. We are judged more harshly than others."

I followed their example, cast my eyes away, and wouldn't dance with him. But I kept seeing him in the surging crowd. When he smiled at me, I wondered if I could love someone with whom I had not exchanged a single word. I danced lambada with Andrea, close and sexy, giggling, knowing I was showing off, intoxicated by the assurance that this tall man watched me.

When I looked around, the crowd had taken him. Ana and Andrea wanted water, so we struggled out of the swell.

"Camila!" Andrea shouted. "Over there! She's selling water. That's our cousin!"

We all hugged, and when I tried to pay Camila for the water, she refused and laughed at me. After she handed us our waters, she quickly replaced the lid of her vendor's Styrofoam box. "The ice inside is expensive," she said.

We slid into the crowd again. I turned and saw the man dancing behind us again. I smiled at him and then looked away. He danced near Ana and began talking with her. I had begun using an infantile Portuguese, heavily supplemented by university French. Ana and Andrea spoke slowly for me, explaining things I didn't understand, seemingly clairvoyant in their ability to understand me. But I couldn't understand this man at all. His accent was completely different; he could have been speaking anything. Ana translated. He told them he was from Arembepe but had also lived in Penambuas, in the valley near the sewer canal where the wind never blew. He had stayed there three years, but couldn't find a job so he came back. Ana then told me I could dance with him.

The four of us danced together, then he showed us the special sights of Arembepe. We embroidered the night with joy, planted our feet wild in the street, ate from the mouth of the *trio elétrico*, the deep throb of the bands. The light of our smiles pulsed with reflections of the moon and popcorn machines.

Sometime, very late, when the crowd began to thin, we all walked to the beach. Ana took a candle from the small bag she carried and lit it. She and Andrea curled up in *cangas*, long pieces of cloth people often wore over their swimming suits, and tried to sleep. The man took my hand and led me to the sea. We waded in the low surf to soothe the cuts and bruises of our soles. He kissed me.

We sat on the sand near Ana and Andrea and tried to talk. He told me he had nine brothers and sisters, that he lived in a nearby village, that his father was dead, and that most of his family worked in the factory. When he told me his name, I couldn't understand him

"They get sick there," he said. "That's how my father died. I didn't want to work there, but...." He shrugged. "You're from São Paulo?" he asked, touching my sun-blonde hair.

"No," I said, "I'm a foreigner."

"You're a Spanish factory worker," he said, smiling.

"No," I said, "I'm an American."

"From where?"

"From the United States."

He took his hand from my hair. "Maybe I don't understand you. What's your native language?"

"English."

He crouched in the sand then, head between his thighs. I sat beside him and said nothing.

"America must be very beautiful," he said to the sand. His voice fell bitter like dead leaves. "What are you doing here?"

I wanted to lie, but didn't. "Visiting."

His laughter came, a burnt stick. "Don't you have family at home? Why have you left them?"

I touched his shoulder because I felt him shivering. "You're cold," I said.

He pulled my hand away, took my head between his fingertips and kissed me again, this time a strong and violent kiss, as if he wanted to suck my insides to the bottom of his throat. Did his soul reside there, I wondered, or did he want mine so he could spit it into the sand?

His hands moved gently across my belly and over my hips where my shorts had pockets. He was feeling for money. He shook, I was sure, not from desire, but because he didn't know what he would do if he found some. I took his hands in mine, glad for both of us that I had none.

He glanced over my shoulder. "Someone has stolen your shoes," he said. His voice sounded tired.

I glanced at the empty sand beside me. He had sat on his shoes. "I will dance barefoot," I said.

"Are you staying for the festa again tomorrow?" he asked.

"No," I lied. "Are you coming out tomorrow?"

"It's a festa. I dance every night."

I twined his hair between my fingers. "I'm going to join my friends. Will you come or stay?"

"I'll stay."

I kissed him again, on the mouth. Twice. I wasn't sure why. "Good bye," I said.

"Until later." His smile strained the skin below his cheekbones, but never got near his eyes.

We slept all day, Ana, Andrea, and I. At night, we danced again. In empathy, they wouldn't wear their shoes, the plastic ones they'd brought specially to show off. All night, with one eye, I watched for the man. I was edgy. Other people leapt in ecstasy to the music, but for me the dance never came inside. Arembepe was not large and he was tall. Had he come, I would have seen him.

The next week, Ana, Andrea, and Tatiana accompanied me to the Salvador airport. "It's the first time I've been here," Andrea said, gazing around her at the wide counters and high ceiling. We stopped for a fruit drink before I boarded my plane to São Paulo.

"We'll miss you," Ana said.

"I'm coming back." And as I said it, I knew it was true. Suddenly I realized that I couldn't imagine leaving this place forever. I didn't know how yet, but I was coming back. And this time, I'd stay.

two
the first return

I had a strange year in Australia. I spent my days busily researching a topic for which I had already received a grant. But I kept thinking of Salvador.

In the evenings, I read about the city and reflected on my impressions. Salvador was an old city, by New World standards, settled by Portuguese in the 1500s. Thinking of their Catholic roots, they named Salvador's remarkable turquoise bay Baía de Todos os Santos, or the Bay of All Saints. The graceful buildings they constructed were tinted the colors of southern Europe: deep rose, robin's egg blue, Seneca yellow. During my visit to Salvador, I had seen many of these buildings, now decayed, their colors softened by the centuries.

I reflected on the tourist brochures I had requested from local travel agencies. They were of a Salvador I had visited on outings with Alexandra and her sisters: brilliant white beaches shaded by tall palm trees bending to warm afternoon breezes. For a small fee, the brochures told me, beachside vendors would provide visitors with a comfortable chair on the sand and cold drinks—including beer or coconut juice iced in its shell and served with a straw. As an added service, vendors would even watch people's belongings while they frolicked in the waves or snorkeled in the tepid shallows. In these celebrated tourist areas, the night air carried the scent of the sea. Lovers and casual strollers leaned against the ancient railing of the promenade, struck silent by a glistening tail of moonlight snaking its way across dark water. Bars, open to the evening air, served local drinks made from limes, drinks strong enough to make anyone lightheaded and open to love.

I did not find in these brochures the Salvador I had mostly encountered: intrusive freeways, apartment blocks that already seemed in disrepair the year they were completed, vast shantytowns surrounding the city's tourist center and small middle-class neighborhoods. Most of the shantytown residents, I learned from more academic books on Brazil, had fled their homes in the countryside, forced off the land by drought, poverty, and unequal land laws. They flooded Salvador, looking for a better life, but they arrived with few city skills or city connections. In the shantytowns that I had seen, people had moved themselves and their belongings onto every unsupervised space. They had stacked shack upon shack to house arriving relatives and children, creating a honeycomb of disorder and distress.

Rubbish and sewage were constant roadside companions in these shantytowns. In some neighborhoods, I had seen residents collect their sewage in plastic grocery bags, in a faint hope of sanitation, and throw it into the major roadways. In Penambuas on rainy days, raw sewage cascaded over paving stones. Rat bites were not uncommon, and tuberculosis was endemic. Brazil was a rich country in terms of natural resources and gross national product, yet the economic chasm between the rich and the poor was greater than India.

In Canberra, I sat in my clean office, listening to the kookaburras, going out for lattes with new friends, and wondering why Salvador so intrigued me, why I found myself outlining possible research options that would take me back. I marveled at the strength of Salvador's African culture, transformed through the mixing of other societies and peoples. The culture was a multilayered one, created by African slaves who had obtained their freedom, returned to Africa, influenced society there, and then returned to Salvador. Now the city was at least 80 percent nonwhite, almost all of mixed African ancestry. It had become the center of African culture in Brazil, considered by many sources the largest African city outside Africa. In Salvador, one found samba, the *afro-blocos* of Carnival, and the African-Brazilian spiritist religion of *Candomblé*.

I had published earlier on topics related to race, class, and gender, so, after much deliberation, I decided to turn my academic interests to these issues in Bahia. I rang Alexandra for advice.

"Why don't you research *capoeira angola*?" she asked. "It's an African-Brazilian martial art form and dance, a symbol of male virility, but some women play. It was brought by the slaves, so it has lots to do with race and class—plus, I used to train with a group there. You can join my group."

I took Alexandra's advice. I studied Portuguese and dove into whatever materials on capoeira I could find. It had come to Brazil with the slaves in the sixteenth century and became a dance and form of defense for the slaves on the sugarcane plantations. In the nineteenth century, capoeira gangs protected their various territories in the streets of Rio de Janeiro, wearing specific colors to denote gang alliances. At the time, the *capoeiristas* were noted for the small, delicate shoes they wore. They flummoxed the police because although they did attack and kill people, they never stole from anyone.

Throughout the mid-1800s, more slaves were arrested for practicing capoeira than for any other activity, except escape attempts; yet capoeira was only made officially illegal in 1890. Punishment for practicing capoeira was brutal—four hundred lashes and imprisonment if you survived. But still men continued to train and to create social disorder through its practice.

Based upon the information I found, as well as my earlier anthropological work, I wrote a grant to do research for a year in Bahia. Then I waited with bated breath for the seven months until I heard back.

When I was awarded the grant, I could hardly believe it. It was, I knew even then, one of those occurrences that changes a person's life forever. I rang Alexandra in Amsterdam and told her to let her family know when to expect me.

When I arrived in Salvador, Alexandra's family greeted me as though I'd never left. I felt almost the same as they did. Two days after I arrived, on a Monday evening, I took the bus with Andrea to my first capoeira class.

The group trained at a neighborhood at the city's center, a neighborhood called Pelourinho. The name Pelourinho, Andrea told me, means "whipping post" and was named after the whipping post that once stood in its central plaza. Andrea smiled. "They don't talk about that now," she said.

We walked through cobbled streets dusted by late afternoon sun. Colonial Portuguese buildings with casement windows and gracious verandahs overlooked tree-lined plazas. Nearly all of these beautiful buildings were in various states of decay. But the decay of beauty creates its own beauty. These crumbling buildings shone gray-rose and umber in the hot afternoon sun. Strong Amazonian hardwood still held them together, but the membrane of walls, floors, and roofs hung on a cobweb of chipped plaster and mold. Andrea told me that most of the houses dated from the 1600s through the 1800s.

"How do you know all this history?" I asked. She shrugged and looked at the ground. "I like history," she said. She gave a small skip and glanced over at me shyly. "I'm writing about the history of the churches in Salvador. I want to show photos of the churches and then write about it. Maybe you would like to see it?"

"I'd love to."

When we entered the building where the capoeira group trained, I treaded lightly. In these buildings, to fall though a floor was to tumble into whatever horrors lay in the darkness below. Rats lived fat in every gutter. It seemed that literally hundreds of people lived in every house. Cockroaches, the most populous residents, were everywhere.

We walked up a dark wooden stairway to the second floor. When we entered the room, a group of people, mostly dark young men clad in white, fell silent and stared at me. Andrea walked over to a tall man in his early thirties with short dreadlocks and began talking with him. I stood by the door and waited for her to rejoin me.

"He says because you are Alexandra's friend he will try you out," she said when she returned. She glanced at my legs. "You're wearing shorts though. At least they're fairly long. He says you must never come back in shorts. Don't worry, we'll make you some white long pants at home if he lets you stay." She gave me a little push, and I walked toward the center of the room.

The teacher, as I now understood the dreadlocked man to be, motioned me to stand in front of him. He began to move gracefully back and forth, almost a dance move, very light on his feet. He motioned me to copy him. I did and soon we were moving together, facing each other, swaying. I tried to match his moves. He stared into my eyes; it was a gaze so intimate I blushed. I moved with him, looking only into his eyes, transfixed in their pull and their power.

Then, suddenly, he looked away. The release was so strong it felt as though I had been holding a taut rope that someone had just let go. I fell over. The teacher and the rest of the class laughed. The teacher turned to Andrea and said something I didn't understand.

"He says you can train with them," she said. "He says you move very strangely, but you can feel the energy and, for a woman, you're strong. That, he said, is at least a start."

The teacher motioned me to stand behind a line of other students, and I found myself performing a series of exercises: seemingly endless knee-bends and contorted push-ups. My head spun with the heat and exertion, but I was determined not to stop. My sweat formed a slippery pool around my hands and feet. Thank God I'm strong, I thought.

The building where we trained capoeira was as decrepit as the rest of the buildings in Pelourinho, but its second-story floorboards were wide and strong. Our training room had a twenty-foot ceiling of thick beams and two walls that were lined with high, arched casement windows from which hung heavy wooden shutters that we opened and closed when we came and went. The windows had no glass, only filigreed ironwork on the bottom third to prevent people who leaned out too far while watching street movement from crashing to the street below. It seemed to me that watching street movement was an honored occupation in Pelourinho.

We trained from five to seven, three nights a week. Each evening, as the sun began to set, long shafts of light stole through the window openings, joining us in our efforts, turning the walls a deep blue. Gradually, the shafts of light shaded pink, mixing with the dimness of the room to create a stillness that all our grunting and exertions could not disturb.

During the second training session, one of the better students came up to me and said hello. His skin was the color of light copper and his hair hung in loose curls around his shoulders. "I am studying English," he said in beautifully accented English. "May I practice with you?"

I smiled. "Of course. It sounds as though you know English pretty well though."

"Oh, no. I have few people who can talk with me. My name is Fernando. I am at university here."

"May I ask you questions about capoeira?" I asked.

He nodded. "I'd be delighted. I am not a teacher, of course, but I can share with you what I know." We walked together to a nearby cafe for fresh tropical fruit drinks that I had quickly grown to love. As we walked, I tried to ignore his remarkable beauty.

Fernando told me that it wasn't until the 1930s that capoeira began to acquire some standing as a valued traditional Brazilian art, and this was largely because of the efforts of a few powerful teachers in

Salvador. At that time, capoeira split into two loose groups. One, commonly known as capoeira regional, incorporated moves and practices from Eastern martial arts and other innovative practices. Capoeira regional was quickly adopted by the Brazilian middle class and was considered a "modernist" form of the art. The other major form, known as capoeira angola, was considered to have preserved the original African-Brazilian practices of capoeira and was the "traditionalist" form. Over the decades, Brazilian middle-class society had taken aspects of capoeira for themselves, transforming it in the process from a dangerous and mysterious practice that threatened social order into the National Brazilian Sport.

In Salvador, Fernando told me, capoeira angola was still practiced largely by the African-Brazilian lower-class. (He was an exception, Fernando said. "I'm middle class – no, lower middle-class, not really poor, but we aren't rich.") Despite cultural co-option, capoeira angola had remained, for all people who played and trained, a central part of their social and spiritual lives. And despite its lethal potential, capoeira angola was considered a "game" in Brazil and the verb used to describe its practice was to "play."

After about a week of talking with Fernando, I decided to ask him if he would like to work as my research assistant for a few hours a week. I reflected sadly that this relationship of employer-employee would stifle any potential romance, but I had determined before arriving in Salvador that I was not going to get sexually involved while in Brazil, anyway. Fernando accepted my offer with delight. "It'll help me pay for university," he said.

We wandered Pelourinho, and Fernando began to tell me about it as perceived through his sharp eye and knowledge. He said that at some point, the Portuguese upper classes moved away and the huge houses became tenements, inhabited by the descendants of the very people who had previously been subjected to the whipping posts. The area became a rough neighborhood the middle classes avoided.

It appeared that the major commerce in the area was drugs, alcohol, prostitution, and con artistry. The only tourists was young backpackers who hung out on street corners, lured by the music, beauty, drugs, and prostitution. The con artists pounced on them as everyone watched. We saw a tourist get robbed one day while I was with my capoeira group. Our teacher shrugged and looked at me.

"They can afford it," he said. "And they're stupid. They just come to take what they can and get it cheap."

As I began to get more and more involved with the capoeira group, I met few foreigners and found myself mostly in the company of young men. Nearly all foreigners playing capoeira angola in Salvador seemed to be with one very organized group that catered to them. I met almost no women players, Brazilian or otherwise. Of those few women who did play, I met almost none who were any good.

I became intoxicated by the training, play, and camaraderie; even as a novice player, I experienced a wonderful sense of joy, laughter, balance, and real play in every sense of the word within this practice that was also, as Alexandra had said, a symbol of African-Brazilian power and male sexual virility.

One Friday, about six weeks after I began training capoeira, I walked up the long hill to the Praça Sãnto Antônio, my leather-bottomed sandals sliding on the uneven cobblestones, my bare arms touched by an early evening breeze. This cobbled street climbed from the lower *praça*, or plaza, of Pelourinho along the upper sea cliff. It was lined with houses from past centuries, their upper stories encased with ornate iron latticework, the shuttered doors open in the early evening to the street below. One house was painted with blue and pink stripes, another checkered red and yellow. In the shadows of twilight, all were touched with blue. Along the road stood clots of friends and family. Bursts of laughter, the occasional radio, subdued sounds that were supported by connecting silences and rhythms of familiarity.

Suddenly, a huge rock whizzed past my ear and shattered on the paving stones in front of me. I leapt behind a pile of forgotten concrete. A small boy slid in beside me. The people on the street disappeared. Another rock crashed into our concrete shield like a small bomb while down the street a car window burst into spinning glass. I heard shouts, then silence.

Within seconds people stepped onto the street again and picked up the threads of their gossip. The small boy beside me glanced at me quickly and then shuffled away. I rose and, with my still halting Portuguese, asked a man what had happened.

He flicked a toothpick at his teeth. "A fight," he said. I nodded and continued on my way. I was not as accustomed as he to violence that erupted from calm and then, just as quickly, disappeared.

I reached the road's summit and the hilltop praça. On one side stood the church, decayed, plaster flakes dusting steps built to honor an immense doorway that had not been grand itself for a century. On the other side of the praça, the hill dropped away sharply, offering a view of the city and the darkening sea beyond. I loved this praça: the young boys playing soccer in their bare feet, lovers sitting together on low walls, exchanging touches and shy smiles.

At the far end of the praça stood the old Fort. Once a valiant protector of the city, it was now an unmaintained center for African-Brazilian cultural groups. An indeterminate number of people also lived there—street children and others who had nowhere else to stay. The Fort had no functioning sewage facilities (we always peed in the dark spaces behind walls) and only one spigot for running water. In the center of the central courtyard, people had ripped out a circle of stones and dug a pit. When I arrived, a fire burned there.

Every Friday at the Fort, we had our capoeira circles, or rodas. I entered the stone-walled room and blinked in the tenuous glow of a poorly connected light bulb. Before me sat my fellow capoeira players in a circle, all dressed in the white trousers and shirts that were considered the traditional garb of capoeira. At the far end of the circle, seven people played instruments: an African-style drum, two tambourine-like instruments called *pandeiros*, a cowbell-like *agogô* and three varied-toned *berimbaus*. The berimbau was a single stringed bow with a resonating gourd that had been developed in Brazil but was similar to musical instruments in Angola. It came to Brazil with the slaves, my teacher told me, and had changed over the centuries. For more than three hundred years it had been the central instrument of capoeira.

Jorge, about twenty, tall, dark, fine-featured with short hair, played the lead berimbau. He gave a long call that was half cry and half shout that began the chanting of capoeira angola. These chants were based on African rhythms and cadence, moving between set calls and response. When Jorge changed his lead call, those responding also changed their words and tones in a seamless stream, with no break in the rhythm between chants. This music had the intoxicating quality of a trance, and yet it was also the opposite of a trance: in capoeira angola, all nerves and sensibilities were focused, aware, and Zen-attentive.

I had begun to know my fellow players. Louis, a tall, broad-shouldered man, sold coconut juice on the beaches. He said that capoeira was what kept his insides from getting too hot. Luzia, an actress from the southern state of Minas Gerais, said it kept her equilibrium steady on those days when everything went wrong. Gato (Cat), our wonderfully lithe assistant teacher, said that being black and poor, he was everyday forced to eat the violence and aggression that society fed him. Capoeira angola, he said, was what prevented him from vomiting this violence back at someone. In a society where he had control of nothing else, capoeira angola gave him the possibility of internal control and self-respect. Fernando was at every practice, of course. And then there was Rita, dark with long dreadlocks, one of only two skilled female players.

At the center of the circle, Gato and Faísca (Spark) played together in a pair, rolling from their hands to their feet, swaying apart only to come together again, each with a devilish smile, balancing his play with the concentration of a chess game.

As I entered the roda, I thought about the rock that didn't hit my head, about the hand that threw it, and about how much I had to learn.

The next week, Jorge and Gato invited me to accompany them to one of the roughest rodas in Salvador, where players had been known in recent times to break each others' ribs in supposed play and where one person had reportedly been killed the year before. The single light bulb that lit the dark basement room there dimmed and brightened on an uneven pulse of electric current. It took a particular skill to keep track of the moving legs and heads in the spurts of this ill-timed strobe.

It was here that I saw Rita play for the first time away from our group. The only other women I had seen at these outside rodas merely watched the play from the back on the visitors' benches. Rita stood at the front of the roda holding the lead berimbau. The men standing beside her towered above her as she took up her bow and gave the beginning cry that drew the roda energy to her. As she began to play, the men fell in beside her. Her dreadlocks fell past her waist, a solid mass that, when she played, became a third, lethal leg that confused the eyes and the soul of the person who played with her. She played with a huge, wide smile.

Although Rita trained with the same teacher as I did, she had also studied for many years with other teachers before him. None of the men, including our teacher, dared cross Rita. They never mocked, flirted, or made passes at her as they did with all the other female players. She was the only woman I had seen who could (and would) lead the capoeira angola chants outside the safety of her own group. These chants were passed down orally and Rita had learned them in the shantytown where she was born. She knew chants dating from the time of slavery and she knew chants dating from the time of the military dictatorship from the 1960s to the 1980s. Her chants made a clear connection between the oppression of the past, the oppression of ten years ago, and the oppression she understood that day.

Rita had grown up in a Salvador shantytown and somehow managed to get though university to become a sociologist and professional photographer. She was the only Brazilian I met who, after completing the education that gave her a way out of her shantytown, chose to stay.

"If all of us who get educated leave," she said to me one day, "how are things to change? It has to start somewhere." Then she laughed, as though what she was doing was a perfectly ordinary choice that required no courage at all.

After a few months, I began to notice that in Salvador, everyone was into religion. Not that it was a spiritual city—quite the opposite in fact—but the presence of religion, the smell of it, was everywhere.

One afternoon, I was drinking a beer with Rita in a small praça that was really just a wide space where the street divided. An enterprising entrepreneur had filled the middle section of the street with tables and served beer to passersby. At one end of this praça was a kind of obelisk, a baroque blue and white spear with a wrought iron fence around the base. With my great anthropologist's eye, I had never noticed it.

"This praça is called Sainted Remains of St. Jill," Rita said.

"Why?"

Rita pointed to the obelisk with her glass. "That's her. She's here."

"What do you mean 'here'? Her corpse is in that—that thing?"

"Certainly. Go look. You can see her. In the glass window up at the top."

I circled the obelisk with trepidation, unsure if I wanted to see the remains—did that mean bones, bits of parched skin and hair?—of some woman who was probably mutilated to death if she had ascended to martyr status.

I needn't have worried. The window was so fogged over with pollution that no one had seen our sainted lady for probably a hundred years. I walked back to the table.

"It's all—" I waved my hands around trying to mime the word corroded. Rita nodded and shrugged.

"That's Bahia," she said.

three | agnaldo and *candomblé*

"Look!" Jorge nudged me. We were sitting in the circle of our weekly capoeira roda, chanting as we watched Gato and Fernando play. "It's Agnaldo!"

Agnaldo danced across the room, snapping his fingers as he came. About five feet eleven, Agnaldo was fairly tall for Salvador, with tufts of black-gray hair that stuck out in short, spiky dreadlocks. He had lost a few teeth along the way, and his smile, always generous, was gapped. His face was deeply lined. Now in his mid-thirties, he seldom came to practice; when he did, he arrived sometimes drunk, sometimes stoned. Now he pranced, performing impossible moves while wearing open-toed leather sandals.

"I thought our teacher said we always had to wear sneakers," I said to Jorge.

Jorge shrugged. "I think he's been drinking too, but are you going to say anything?" Agnaldo slid past us and our teacher shot us a stern look. We shut up.

Agnaldo moved to enter the play, and those sitting on the floor wiggled aside to make room for him. He glanced at our teacher who nodded that he could enter. He did, cutting Fernando out and turning to face Gato. He began making ridiculous faces at Gato while sneaking in truly devilish moves, spinning like a top, then sliding inches above the ground. His joy infected us all and we began to chant with more force. Our teacher, who was leading the chants, began improvising clever stanzas about Agnaldo, teasing him, harassing him about wearing sandals. If any of us had tried to enter play wearing sandals, he would have expelled us from the room. Seeing the kind of skill and effortless grace Agnaldo possessed, I figured he must have started playing when he was about two.

After Agnaldo played for a time, he went over to our teacher, who passed him the lead berimbau, teasing and poking him at the same time. Our teacher was a superb berimbau player, but from his first note, Agnaldo was electric. He brought to his playing a different intelligence, the hot winds of Africa, the pain of Brazilian inequality, a music that endured in the silence after he finished. He knew and could improvise indefinitely upon the traditional rhythms of capoeira and his gods, the *orixás*. When Agnaldo played the berimbau, I finally understood why it was considered a sacred instrument.

After the roda, our teacher corralled us all to join him and Agnaldo for drinks.

"I think Agnaldo makes our teacher happy," I said to Fernando as we watched them laughing on the rainy street.

Fernando nodded. "Yes," he said. "I think if our teacher loves anyone in this world, he loves Agnaldo."

At some point soon after I first met him, Agnaldo decided to teach me about his gods. I was not sure why; perhaps because he knew I loved his music so much. He told me that orixás were both saints and gods in his African-Brazilian religion of Candomblé. He taught me their names, male and female, their colors, their different personalities, and the protections they offered. He said I should learn their dances.

Agnaldo talked about the women, the Mothers of the Saints, who led his Candomblé community, his *terreiro*. The Mothers and initiates, the Daughters of the Saints, tended to the orixás, fed them and looked after their altars.

"All the leaders of your religion are women?"

"Of course," Agnaldo said. He laughed. "Or mostly. Women are much stronger for these kinds of things."

Agnaldo told me about the history of Candomblé, how it had come to Brazil with the slaves in the 1600s or earlier, and how it had been repressed.

"There's still oppression," he said. "Before it was the Catholics. Now, it's the evangelical Christians who think we worship the Devil. Recently, some Christian evangelicals burned a local terreiro and beat up a Mother so badly she died."

Agnaldo told me to look for the Candomblé subtext in the Catholic churches in Bahia. During the time of slavery, Catholics forced the Africans to worship the Catholic saints and god. "But, it's strange," he said. "Those Catholics didn't know that their saints were so connected to our African gods, the old gods from which their saints probably came. So we pretended to worship their saints, but instead, with the very same figures and altars, we worshiped our own. Saint Barbara is also Iansã, the protector of firefighters. The orixás are all like this. They are our guardian spirits." He smiled. "As you live here longer, you'll see. No matter the religion people say they have here, they're also Candomblé. It's a force they take care about; when people really need something— a lost lover to love them again, to cleanse themselves, to ward off the effects of Evil Eye, to take out bad spirits that are making them ill— when these things happen, they don't go to a priest or doctor, they go to the *mandingueira*, the Candomblé advisor, and then they know what they should do."

When I told Ana and Andrea of my talks with Agnaldo, they agreed. "If you're interested," Ana said, "next weekend, February second, is the day for Iemanjá, the goddess of the sea. Her house is on a promontory overlooking the sea. On Saturday, everyone will be there, making her offerings of flowers, perfume and pretty things that she likes. I always make an offering to her." She glanced at me. "We can go if you like. You can make her an offering."

When we arrived at the House of Iemanjá, the line of people waiting to present their gifts, all standing in the sweltering sun, extended a mile. Ana cheerfully directed us to the end of the line. While we waited, she described to me what I could expect at the end of the day. All the gifts to Iemanjá would be loaded onto a barge and floated out to sea. Groups of men would swim beside the barge, wishing to be close to her power and energy. If Iemanjá was pleased with the offerings, she would accept the barge and it would sink, taken by her beneath the waves.

The day was calm. I asked Ana if it were possible that people would rig the barge, put a hole in it or something to make sure it sank, since it was so important that Iemanjá accept the offerings. Ana looked at me in disgust, but she quickly softened her expression to a condescending smile. "No," she said. "Iemanjá's wrath against someone who did anything like that would be unspeakable."

In front of Her House, high on a raised dais, stood a statue of a mermaid, a representation of Iemanjá. Hundreds of people paid homage, kneeling before the statue, touching it lightly or bowing their heads as they passed.

Finally, after more than two hours, we reached the House and stepped inside. It was cool and seemed to have its own breath, deep and rich, dark, scented with flowers, and strangely still despite the hubbub outside. We made our offerings, then reemerged, blinking, into the bright sunlight. Several people played drums.

We noticed a group of foreigners speaking English with American accents. Two were white men—one with a fancy camera—and the third was a very beautiful Japanese woman. She wore a loose robe and sandals.

"So, great. We can get some great shots here," said the man without the camera. He looked around. "Oh, fantastic, fantastic!" He steered the woman forward. "Get up there by that statue. You'll look great. You, the metaphorical mermaid. Fantastic!"

The man with the camera set up a tripod, and the other man boosted the woman onto the dais surrounding Iemanjá. She looked behind her nervously. I felt a rising tension around me.

"Do you think this is OK?" the woman asked.

"Yeah, sure, honey, sure. It's just a statue of a mermaid." The man turned back to the cameraman. "Ready?" The cameraman nodded. "OK, then take off the robe and put your arms around the statue. Like that. Great!"

The woman now stood almost nude in a tiny bikini, her arms wrapped around Iemanjá's waist, her head nestled beneath the deity's breasts. The model did not look relaxed. "I don't like this," she said. "I don't think we should be doing this."

Beside me, Ana began looking around frantically. Two women ran into the House and the crowd began to surge toward the dais. Several men shouted and began pushing their way to the front of the crowd.

"It's OK, honey," the director told the frightened model, "it's just a Carnival thing."

Someone pushed the cameraman. His tripod tipped, but he managed to grab his camera before it fell. He looked behind him. "No, it's not all right, George." He rapidly folded up his tripod. The woman shimmied down from the dais, sliding her bum over Iemanjá's leg in the process. Andrea gave a small cry and started forward. The crowd closed around the three and began pushing them away from the dais.

George finally looked around. "Maybe we'd better go," he said. The model grabbed the cameraman's hand and began trotting, pushing through the crowd, slipping from view. George followed closely behind.

Everyone's attention turned back to Iemanjá. Two women in the white dresses of Daughters of the Saints came running behind an older woman who, by her dress and demeanor, was clearly the Mother. She ran to Iemanjá, crying loudly for forgiveness for not protecting her properly. She grabbed the dais edge, knelt before it, and immediately her body went rigid. She held on tightly while the rest of her body flew into the air, her feet and legs rising a good four feet from the ground. Then she slammed to the ground again, her face crushed against the stone. Again and again, her body flew up into the air, seemed to stay suspended for a second, and then was slammed to the ground. Everyone around began to murmur in distress and concern, but no one moved. All the time, the Mother begged for Iemanjá's forgiveness. She looked to be sixty. I wasn't sure how she could withstand this battering or how her hands continued to grip the sides of the dais. I worried that she had broken her nose, or worse.

Finally, after perhaps eight tosses into the air and smashes to the ground, the Mother lay still. Iemanjá was apparently satisfied and released her. The Mother was also unconscious. Now, people rushed into action. Two Daughters and several others from the House ran to her side. Vendors pushed forward and provided cold water to bathe her body and face. Six people lifted the Mother's limp body and carried her into the House.

I looked at Ana and Andrea. My stomach hurt from tension and incomprehension. "She's hurt," I said.

Ana nodded. "Yes. Those people were so stupid!" She tightened her lips in anger. "How could they not understand what they were doing?" I remained quiet. I certainly didn't understand.

That evening the barge went out as usual. People around the square whispered that after several hours the Mother had finally regained con-sciousness. In the long shadows of twilight, we watched the barge. Men jumped into the sea beside it, shouting blessings to Iemanjá. We all crowded toward the water, few talking, watching the barge float away. I began to pray to all the gods I knew that Iemanjá, or whatever force was involved here, accept the gifts.

We waited almost an hour, mostly in silence, the samba music stilled. Suddenly, the barge sagged on one side. Strangely, it then seemed to sag also on the other side. Then, as if the waters literally created a depression to receive it, the barge disappeared.

Men and women on shore burst into tears. Vendors shouted the attributes of their ice-cold beers. People beat samba on their drums and on the backs of the metal folding chairs where they sat.

We danced most of the night.

One day, I asked Agnaldo to play the rhythms of the orixás for me on his berimbau so I could record them.

"It's for my research," I said, although in reality I wasn't sure how I could use these recordings. I just wanted them; I wanted to remember the tones he played.

"This is good," he said. "We must record our stories, our music, because people are changing them. They don't know the true stories from before."

We sat in the capoeira practice room, alone in the quickly fading light of an equatorial evening.

"Rhythm: Oxum," Agnaldo said, naming an orixá. Then he played, the notes reverberating, fast and varied. Then, "Rhythm: Iansã," and Her rhythms echoed around the walls, sneaked into corners now lost to shadow.

The recording I made of Agnaldo's music was full of street noise that I hadn't noticed at the time, but Agnaldo's notes still come through pure and strong. Later, Agnaldo asked me to come visit him at his home to record the tales that his father, a "big African," had told him when he was a child.

Pelourinho's large stucco buildings created veritable walls along the area's narrow streets. To reach Agnaldo's house, I passed through a tunnel beneath one of these buildings and emerged on the other side to a country hillside. The cobbled city street became a dirt path lined by green grass and trees. One-room dirt and tin shacks dotted the hillside. The steep hillside offered a vista for miles across the city, which suddenly seemed silent and far way.

The huts were built one upon the other. They had dirt floors, no toilet facilities, and no running water. Most shared a common wall and some leaned precariously down the hillside. I imagined that in the rain, all the floors and the path itself became a single rushing sheet of water.

Agnaldo ushered me into his two-room house. I never saw the back room, but it was apparently a bedroom with only a doorway and no window. The front room, where the only light came from the doorway and front window, contained a small gas burner upon which he heated water for coffee. Also in the front room were scattered wooden boxes for sitting, some dishes, two pots, and a radio on a shelf. Boards had been laid between several boxes to create a table. There was a cupboard for food; it was tightly shut, I knew, to keep out cockroaches and rats. Everything looked spotless: the dirt floor was swept and a bucket of clean water stood near the stove. Agnaldo offered me thick sugared, coffee, and we drank it as we sat on wooden boxes in the shade in front of his house. He recited tale after tale, many in Iorubá, a Nigerian language which I did not understand, but most in Portuguese with Iorabá phrases. It was clear that Agnaldo remembered the tales exactly as his father had told them.

I made Agnaldo an extra copy of the tape I made because he said he couldn't get his children interested in memorizing the tales. He feared the tales would get lost when he no longer remembered them.

A month or so later, Agnaldo invited me to a Candomblé gathering.

"You need to find your orixá, your guardian spirit to protect you," he said. We were sitting on the front steps along the gutter in front of the old building where we had just finished capoeira practice. I kicked at a piece of rubbish with my toe.

"I don't know how to choose an orixá," I said.

"You don't choose the orixá. She or he chooses you."

"But, Agnaldo, this is not my religion. I'm not *baiana*. I don't want to be a tourist gawking at someone else's sacred space. I don't want to disrespect you that way."

Agnaldo laughed. "That's why I've invited you. To understand us, you must know our gods. And anyway," he stood and held out his hand to help me up, "you need a guardian spirit to protect you here. I wouldn't be a friend if I didn't introduce you."

I went to the gathering with Ana. Agnaldo told me not to wear black, to wear white if possible. When I told Ana about Agnaldo, I discovered that she knew who he was.

"He's a well known drummer in Candomblé," she said. She told me that people at these gatherings tended to go into trance and that a drummer had to be not only incredibly good, knowing the rhythms of all the orixás and many others besides, but also a person who is not "taken" by an orixá, who can resist trance. "Agnaldo connects with the orixás in a different way," she said.

On the night of the gathering, Ana guided us to a small house on a hillside—it seemed all of Salvador was either on a hillside or in a valley. As we approached, we encountered a man spinning in an almost dervish-like twirl outside on the grass. He suddenly vomited into a bucket. I paused and looked to Ana for direction. Ana said nothing and greeted the women standing beside the doorway. When they knew I was a friend of Agnaldo, they greeted us warmly. They invited us to join others who sat in folding chairs around the edges of the room, offering us plates of rice and beans. We sat for an hour while Agnaldo and some others played without a break or pause. Then people began to dance.

"These are the dances of the orixás," Ana whispered. One dancer was "taken" by an orixá and began to spin and dance faster and faster. I couldn't understand how she continued or how she moved so fast. Finally, the orixá let her go and she collapsed. Others picked her up and took her to the other room to care for her.

The music continued without pause, changing rhythms, undulating up and down, seeming to stretch fingers out to entwine us all. Dancers rose, became other beings, rode another current. Hours passed. The heat became insufferable. I felt short of breath. But I couldn't leave; I knew leaving was not permissible. Ana had told me this before we'd arrived. But also an energy coming from the circle of people kept me in. The heat grew more intense. Agnaldo played and his notes seemed almost to travel inside me now. Time became heat.

I watched as the people sitting beside me went into trance. One by one, their eyes glazed over and their bodies took on a different tension.

I wondered if I could move my own limbs. Probably not. The music had entered my organs now, melting them, removing whatever solid substance they once had. Heat, sound, and substance became one. I knew I was moving toward trance. I did not want to go into trance. I wasn't sure what I would do if an orixá took me, and I didn't like the looks of what happened to others. I knew too little of the religion. Which orixá was entering me? Some of them did not sound like the nicest gods. Fear crawled from my bowels to my throat.

With what part of my mind that still functioned, I began an internal mantra, "I will not go into trance. I will not go into trance." Chanting, chanting, on and on, keeping track only of those words and their repetition.

Only when I felt Ana helping me to my feet did I realize it was dawn. My legs wouldn't move properly, whether from the orixá's influence or from sitting for so many hours I didn't know. We stumbled to the front of the house and to the lane below.

"The Mother has invited you to come back," Ana said. "She's surprised the orixás would choose a foreigner, but you're open. She says she'll teach you how not to be afraid."

"I need a coffee," I said.

"Of course," Ana replied

I tasted the damp dawn air and let Ana lead the way home.

four
letting salvador inside

At capoeira practice one day, Rita asked me if I would like to come visit her at her home for Sunday lunch.

"You take the bus to the very end of the line. Don't get off until it stops for good and everyone else leaves. I'll meet you there at one."

So, Sunday noon I boarded the bus marked with the name of Rita's *bairro* and watched out the window as it passed neighborhood after neighborhood, uphill and down, along the seashore and inland again. I had no idea where I was and just trusted that, at some point, the bus would park at an obvious final stop and Rita would be waiting there. Finally, after about an hour, it did.

I descended the bus steps into a huge outdoor market. Five streets met to form a wide central area of road that was carpeted with mats and cloths covered with tomatoes, oranges, pineapples, bananas, jackfruit, carrots, and other fruits and vegetables I had never seen before. Everywhere people pushed between the piles of produce. Vendors shouted the qualities of their wares. At the corners of the market stood bars, cement rooms with an open wall at the front, where men packed inside drinking beer. I was the only white person there.

Where was Rita?

I had grown used to being a minority of one in Penambuas. At first the men in that neighborhood had watched me with hostile eyes from the doors of their homes. But gradually, as Andrea and Ana introduced me to their neighbors, the men began to acknowledge my presence. They began to shout, "*Oi*, gringa!" as I passed. As more time passed and they came to know me as a temporary resident of their neighborhood, they began to greet me by name.

This is good experience, I thought as I wandered around the market, feeling peoples' eyes on me, the obvious outsider. In the North, as a white person, I was nearly always in the majority. I almost never felt the discomfort of entering a room where everyone else was a different color than me. When I did anthropological fieldwork in Papua New Guinea, I had been different than the local population, but a strong colonial attitude amongst the indigenous people there, which persisted despite the relatively recent independence of that country, made the situation different. I was alien there, but my place was established: like it or not, I was a member of the colonial power group, a position that brought certain separation and a defined, if dubious, status. Here in Salvador, however, it was different. I was an outsider, pure and simple. Rita's neighborhood was not my place. Peoples' glances silently asked what I was doing there.

Then, from behind a horse tied to a truck, Rita came bouncing out along with a small slender woman. "Margaret!" she shouted. "You made it!"

The rush of relief I felt made my knees weak.

"This is my sister Norma," Rita said, indicating the woman beside her. She kissed Norma goodbye and turned to me. "She's staying at the market. Let's go buy some fish and cook lunch at my place." We headed through the market where it seemed that everyone shouted a greeting to Rita. As my presence faded into the background, I relaxed and began to smile. As I looked at people, they smiled back.

"It's a wonderful market," I said.

"As long as it lasts," Rita replied. She bent over some tomatoes, selected the four she wanted and handed the vendor some coins without asking the price. He seemed satisfied. "The city wants to close all the markets such as this one. They say it causes too much mess." We skirted a pile of oranges. "But that isn't really the problem. The big grocery chains here—they're mostly owned by one family— want to control the buying and selling of food so they can get all the profit. Markets take their money away, as they see it."

"But that's terrible, Rita! How long has there been a market here?"

"It was here as long as I can remember, and I grew up here. When I was a child, there were dunes here. Can you believe that?" I looked around at the urban landscape of hovel built upon hovel. "This whole area was full of dunes and grass and trees. We used to run down the hill and play in the water at the bottom, go swimming. This was a fishing village on the outskirts of Salvador."

We came upon three men sitting in the shade of a bar wall. Before them was a wooden crate covered with newspaper. Laid out on the paper were several fish. Rita squatted in front of them. "What kind of tuna is this?" she asked, picking up one of the fish. The man replied with a name I didn't understand. "That's good," Rita said. "I'll buy it."

"How's your brother?" the man asked as he began to wrap the fish.

"He's started university," Rita said.

"You sent him to school, didn't you? Paid for it, paid for him to take the university exam?"

"He wants to be a biologist," Rita said.

The man laughed as he wrapped the fish. "Your friend is a good person," he said to me. I nodded. "Does she understand?" he asked Rita.

"Yes, she can understand most things now."

The man nodded. "Maybe your brother can figure out why all the fish are disappearing," he said. "We only see a few varieties of tuna these days."

Rita laughed. "You ask him that," she said.

"How will these people make a living if they close the market?" I asked Rita as we walked away.

"They won't," she said. "It's up this way." We turned up a steep hill on a very narrow lane. "It's even worse than that. The market is open to everyone. People who have more money come first thing in the morning and buy the produce when it's very fresh. Then about noon, as it gets hot, the farmers begin to lower their prices—they have to sell everything before it spoils. So people who have less money, but can still afford to buy, come then. Then mid-afternoon, when things are beginning to spoil, the farmers lower their prices again and people with even less money can buy. Finally, in the evening, after the farmers have left, the people who have nothing, who live in the streets, come out and eat the fruit and vegetables left in the streets to rot. The food isn't such good quality then, but it is food and it doesn't make them sick. In that way everyone gets to eat. But grocery stores have just one price, and poor people can't even go in there, let alone buy anything."

The hill continued upwards. It was very hot. Rita was sweating, but she did not seem short of breath. She walked this hill every day to her home.

"Oh, well, it's life in Salvador." She laughed again. "See this *ladeira*?"

I nodded. Ladeira described a lane that goes up a hill. I had learned that from walking the many ladeiras in Penambuas.

"We have a saying here, 'a green ladeira.' It means hope or a dream of a better life. A green ladeira is beautiful, going upward to a sunny hill, like this one used to be. But ladeiras in Salvador aren't like that. Instead, garbage is everywhere, rats, sewage, shacks, people sitting on the side starving. It's the opposite of a green ladeira. So, people live beside ladeiras like this one and dream of the other one they have never seen." We had reached the top of the hill. "Until," Rita said, "they cease to dream." She smiled ironically, but I saw no bitterness in that smile. I wondered why.

We headed down the other side of the hill, turning into tangled streets and continuing until we stopped in front of a house with a single door and window. The upper story of the house seemed to be under construction. Beside the house was a high sheet metal gate.

"This is mine," Rita said as she unlocked the gate. We walked along a path perhaps three feet wide. "Be careful on the stairs," she said. "I'm constructing this as I get the money, and I haven't been able to fix the stairs yet." We ascended a set of narrow concrete stairs that had no wall or railing on either side. At the top was a door, which Rita also unlocked. We walked into a single room containing a kitchen, living room and eating area. Beyond this room were open doors to a bedroom and bathroom. Rita placed her groceries on the kitchen counter. "This is in progress. I'm building it on the top of my father's house."

"What do you mean?"

"My father built the place below, so I'm building my house on top. I was able to save the money to build this part last year and will begin to tile the floor next year. I should have asked you, do you like fish?"

"I love fish." I stared out the window, which opened onto a spectacular vista of the valley beyond, one vast series of shantytowns. "Great view," I said.

"Yeah. That all used to be forest down there."

"So people just came and built over it?"

"In the seventies—and from then until now. People keep losing their land, starving in the countryside, so they come here. Then they can starve here."

I watched Rita rub the fish with lemon and salt. "What do you do for a job, Rita?"

"I'm a video technician for the city. But we haven't been paid for five months."

"What?"

"Salvador is pretty leftist, you know. Last election we voted in a more leftist city government. But the right and the military are still really in control, so they've just withheld all the money to strangle the local government until the people all get tired of not getting paid. Then they'll have an election and everyone will vote out the leftist government. The rightist ones, the ones who control everything anyway, will take over the government again and we'll all get paid."

"So, will you vote for them?"

"No. But I don't have any children."

"Except for paying for your brother's education."

"We'll keep him in school." She began to chop up cilantro and onions. "Now, I am going to make you some real *baiana* food."

"Whatever happened with the history of churches you were doing?" I asked Andrea one day as we sat at the dining table. I was drinking medicinal tea because I had stomach cramps and diarrhea—again. Andrea had shown me her project some months ago. It had been about five pages, written in a round cursive hand, and—somewhat to my surprise given Andrea's obvious intelligence and expressive speech—it resembled the work of a first-grader. I, whose Portuguese was barely more than conversational, helped her with her grammar and tried to show her how to put paragraphs together. I told her about history projects I had done as a girl and told her we could use my camera to take pictures. She had seemed excited at the time, but never mentioned it again.

Now she picked at the plastic tablecloth. "Oh, I'm not doing it anymore," she said.

"Why not?"

"Don't know." She scrunched the tablecloth between her fingers. "Got bored, I guess. But did I tell you I won a samba contest?"

"Yes. That's great." I looked at her closely. "Did you show the project to your teacher?"

"Yeah. She wasn't interested." Andrea rose abruptly from the table. "They don't care anyway—the teachers. They don't even show up most of the time. Last week I went to school three days, and there wasn't anybody to teach our class!"

"So—how much are you going to school this week?"

"What's the point? Nobody cares. And why should I be interested anyway?" She glared at me, leapt away from the table, and stormed out into the street.

I sighed, picked up my pen and tried to write some research notes about capoeira in my field notebook. Ana came in and turned on their new and very small television to the first of three daily soap opera miniseries that everyone watched. Within minutes a few close neighbors had settled in to join her, and several others watched through the open window that faced the street. Once the miniseries started, Andrea crept in and sat beside her sister. She looked as though she'd been crying.

I had now been living with the family for about eight months. I had learned so much from them, but I wasn't getting my research done. I wasn't writing enough. I felt another stomach cramp coming on and excused myself from the room. Ana and a couple of neighbors smiled. Cramps and such sickness were normal in these shantytowns. How do they do it? I thought. I'm just exhausted all the time.

After another few months, I moved into an apartment with Luzia, from the capoeira group. I told the sisters and Tatiana to come visit me anytime. We hugged and cried. I felt desolate, but also relieved. I had grown to love the family, but I also wanted some space. I laughed ruefully to myself. I was a middle-class softie.

In many ways Luzia's apartment was not much better than the house in Penambuas. It was some twenty years old and built very cheaply. Here I still slept on a wooden box of a bed—on the floor this time rather than on a bunk. The toilet worked, about half the time, but the elevator never did. And we were on the tenth floor. "Good for our capoeira," Luzia said. The apartment was in the center of town, and although it did not have quite as many cockroaches as the Penambuas house, it was noisy, dusty...and noisy. One thing I could count on in Salvador was the noise: it never stopped.

The street in front of our apartment was an ocean of sound, a continuous cant punctuated by the louder noise of cars without mufflers, buses without mufflers, and whole orchestras of horns. I seldom noticed the bar music during the day, but at night the bars owned the sound waves. All four bars on our short street played popular Brazilian pop and Carnival beat at the highest possible decibel through the night. Then, around three in the morning, the street fights started. The fights were often between a transvestite prostitute and her client. Our street was a center for the transvestite prostitution scene in Salvador. The fights usually revolved around robbery: either a client thought that he'd been robbed (generally true) or a transvestite claimed she'd been robbed (almost never true—they were too street smart for that).

I now knew two other foreign anthropologists living in Salvador: Don and Cecilia. Don came to do research on these transvestites. He told me that the robbery game was routine: while the transvestite and client had sex in the back of the client's car, the transvestite casually removed the client's wallet, took whatever money she found there, and then replaced it, leaving behind all the client's credit and identity cards.

When the time came to pay, the client found he had no money. The transvestite became righteously indignant: she had fulfilled her part of the bargain, she trusted him, and he had assured her that he had money, which now—magically it appeared—had vanished. And yet, his cards remained. What was an honest businesswoman to think? As the volume and pitch of her protests increased, the client began to glance nervously up and down the street. These confrontations generally ended with the client apologizing and giving the transvestite his wristwatch.

The transvestites in Salvador injected silicone into their thighs, knees, and buttocks to give them what they considered a more feminine shape. The silicone they used was not medical silicone, but the substance used to mold car dashboards. According to rumor, some had as many as twenty liters (five gallons) of silicone in their bodies, but the norm was four to five liters (about a gallon).

I grew to know these transvestites, greeting them as I walked home late from a roda or evening gathering. Below our living room window often stood a transvestite who wore a beautiful dress, marine blue and flowing to her knees. Only when she turned did you realize that the dress had a front only; the back was two thongs and her bum provocatively bare. Nadia, a very tall, mocha-skinned transvestite with short, dark hair, hung out on the street above the bar that my capoeira group frequented. "You can send any of those boys my way anytime," she'd say to me, shaking her hand rapidly in an expressive and lewd manner. I was happy for her and her fellow transvestites' presence. They knew the streets well. I also felt they protected me.

But my tolerance for noise in Salvador usually lasted about two weeks. One Friday—after a night of particularly spectacular and loud fights and a day of climbing up and down ten flights of stairs because the elevator had broken again—I shouted at Luzia for no reason at all. She looked at me and smiled. "I think you need a change of energy," she said.

I shut up and called Cecilia, my other expatriate anthropologist friend, an Englishwoman who had gone "native" several years before and married Edilson, a local Bahia man. Cecilia read Portuguese with expert fluency and generously shared with me her extensive bibliographies. Bearing all this in mind, I invited myself along on her and her husband's weekend trip to Valença, a provincial riverside town three hours south of Salvador, famous in certain circles for having Brazil's first cotton gin. Cecilia and Edilson were going to participate in a *micareta*—a small local carnival. In the months preceding Carnival, many towns had micaretas to honor the orixás. The energy of the entire area grew with each micareta, culminating with the explosion of Carnival. I loved these smaller scale micareta festivals with their local color, meaning, and their intimacy of human connection. They reminded me of Arembepe.

Valença boasted three *trios elétricos* in its micareta parade. A trio elétrico was a huge, moving sound system housed on a cargo truck. The speakers amplified the rhythms of a band that played atop the truck. The music was so loud in Valença that the bands had to stop playing when they passed old buildings or crossed the antique central bridge, as it was feared their vibrations might destroy the structures.

When I arrived at the micareta with Cecilia and Edilson, I still felt fragile, assaulted by Salvador's destruction of any hope of silence or privacy. I walked alone, well away from the blast, rejecting any music as a continuation of the pure noise I'd been trying to escape. This samba beat was not my rhythm, I decided. I watched the quiet river, the fishing boats sitting on dark water, a silent space removed and yet beside the pushing, bounding human exhilaration that inhabited the streets.

Then, when my concentration wandered, when I forgot myself, I realized I'd begun to dance. A man with whom I'd exchanged smiles grabbed my hand, and we began some kind of samba-reggae. Then, Cecilia put her hands around my waist and we began a line dance: two steps to the right, back, forward, three slides to the right, one to the left.

By midnight I was dripping sweat, and like most of the women, had tied my T-shirt high under my breasts, leaving my waist bare to catch any passing breeze. Most of the men had removed their shirts altogether. At one point I looked up and saw the stars. No moon.

We caught an early bus back to Salvador, and I arrived at my apartment in time to see the sun rise. The transvestites were gone, the bars closed, the cars still in their garages. I sat outside in front of my apartment building for a few moments with Pedro, the security guard. He was out there every night, all night, making friends with people on the street, surveying whatever activity took place before him. He made about eighty dollars a month and traveled over an hour each way to work. He was in his mid-thirties, and his dream was to finish high school and get a job as a mechanic. He often brought books and studied during the night.

"This is my favorite time of the day," he said.

Yes, I thought. Across the street I heard a lizard sing.

five
learning to dance

I tried to stay connected with my close friends overseas through periodic telephone calls. It worked poorly. My life in Bahia was so different. The mundane details of my friends' daily lives became meaningless to me as more time passed. Their concerns often sounded petty and almost banal. And yet, these were people whom I loved, whom I missed—sometimes terribly. I was as elated as I had ever been while in Brazil, but also the loneliest I'd ever been.

I had left John behind when I came to Brazil. We agreed to be "free" while apart, but I think both of us had expected to get together again when I returned. The conversations with him were the most difficult. Because we no longer knew the intimate details of each other's lives, our conversations became increasingly superficial. One evening, despite our best efforts, we had a terrible fight born of disconnection. Somehow we weren't communicating, and the further we got from understanding each other, the less we told each other the truth.

I lay in bed that night, listening to the street noise, and thought about communication. The telephone is a dangerous way to try to resolve an argument because we share only words; things said are left in the air with nothing to support them but memory and uncertainty. Unlike the written word, the telephone presumes to emulate a physical connection; we are engaging in spontaneous exchanges in which the body is completely absent. So no matter what the intention, a tense telephone conversation leaves an electronic taste on the tongue. We rank such technology of communication high in our society, I thought as I tried to sleep. Our technology was supposed to elevate us into a communication revolution; we vicariously touch the world through the information highway. In Amsterdam, when we wanted to learn about a bomb in London, we turned on the computer. A colleague of mine wrote articles with someone by email for a year. Only when they finally met did he realize his colleague was deaf and dumb. So, they sat side by side and talked through their computer screens.

We have invented so many ways to try and understand each other better, but I wished I could have seen John's face as we talked, to have known what his eyes told me. Even more, I wished I could have felt the energy that came off his body, to have sat beside him, to have known what his body said. We have found no technology that helps to understand the communication of bodies, no technology that will dance with us, that can imitate what our bodies feel when they move and touch the world. Isadora Duncan once said, "If I could tell you what it meant, there would be no point in dancing it." There is meaning inherent in all movement whether it is in exertion, in anger, or in affection.

In Brazil, during Carnival, almost everyone danced, from children to the elderly. If one could walk, one could dance. Indeed, one could not escape Carnival. The dancers possessed the streets. During my first Salvador Carnival, I danced for five days, sleeping hardly at all, and as the nights passed, I danced for them to come again. Only in the dust of the last dawn, as we stood crushed on the bus homeward, sharing sweat and the surface of our skin, only then did I understand what exhaustion was.

People said Carnival was a time when society turned upside down, when the boundaries of ethnicity, wealth, and class crumbled under the resonance of a multitude of drums. But the dance of Carnival held more meaning than that. It also embodied poverty, death, and annihilation.

One night during this first Carnival, I danced joyously with Ana and Andrea. In Salvador's street Carnival, crowds of literally millions pushed you along the street, and you could not stop. If you didn't dance in the same rhythm as everyone else, you got smashed. Lines, ten people wide, passed each other, all dancing, all wearing very little clothing. This was a time to flirt. Men and women watched each other as they passed in the varied currents. I would see a beautiful man, or feel his eyes on me, and we would approach. Dancing slowly toward each other, staring into each others' eyes, promising everything, knowing we could not stop there in the street and could fulfill nothing. Then, as we passed, we would touch arms, and hands, feeling the slick of each other's sweat, the crackling intensity of the hour.

I would then turn my eyes again to the flowing current to watch the people coming toward me, to find the eyes of another and, for another five minutes, fall into whatever they held. The music, the heat, the touching, the rhythm, all came together to create an intoxicant beyond any of the beer sold on the streets. To scream with pleasure. And dance on.

Sometime around midnight of this first Carnival, a police van tore into the crowd and twenty or more police descended upon a man dancing near by. One pulled the man off his feet and the others beat him. I heard his bones crack under the force of their batons. His girlfriend, or perhaps his sister, screamed and tried to run to his side. Her friends held her back, pinning her arms and holding her head so she wouldn't bite them in her fight to escape. The man fell but the police kicked him long after he had ceased to move.

After they tossed his limp body into the back of the van, the police passed around a cloth with which they wiped his blood from their hands. I stood nearby, my body cold, the memory of his snapping bones a louder percussion than the blasting Carnival tune.

Andrea touched my shoulder. "Dance," she said.

I looked at her and turned my head away.

"Dance," she said. She began to push my hips with her hands.

"Didn't you see that? What are you doing? How can you possibly just forget it like that?"

"I don't forget anything," she said. "Dance."

I looked into her young eyes, eyes that had seen thirteen years of violence, starvation, and want. The power of a poem by Yeats from my childhood came to me.

"Come away O human child!
To the waters and the wild."

It is the song of the faery folk, calling us to dance, to go where time passes unnoticed and forgetfulness is bliss. I don't know if it is possible to transcend violence, but with Andrea's guidance, I began to understand that on this night, we danced for the pain of the tortured man, for those before him, and for those who, assuredly, would follow. Our dance was the equilibrium that kept the world from tipping over.

I placed my hands on her shoulders, and we began to move. After a time she smiled at me. After a longer time I smiled back.

Trying to develop a balance between the physical violence that confronted me and the violence of everyday life in Salvador—the starvation, the poverty, the lack, for many people, of any kind of escape from their daily struggle with mere survival—confused me. I was often in situations that could have escalated into violence in two seconds. When I first began playing capoeira angola, my teacher and friends nicknamed me "Danger," a name I didn't quite understand. But I gradually came to realize that it referred to the fact that I would go anywhere. And that I didn't quite understand fear.

Pelourinho, in the early 1990s, was full of bars that were simply dark rooms in the front or back of the old buildings. They had stone floors and stucco walls and were furnished with plastic crates, and rickety stools, ragged tables, and makeshift counters for selling drinks. The drinks were mostly soft drinks, beer, and *pingau*, a licorice-tasting liquor that was the common man's version of whisky.

Our capoeira group frequented one of these bars after training—and despite the teacher's admonishment not to drink, he usually joined us. He often drank a sweet black beer that no one seemed to consider real beer, even though it was just as alcoholic as regular beer. The bar attracted other regulars as well: Simon, with long dreadlocks who played the saxophone; Marcos, who wore bright African style clothing and who was a good capoeira player with a wicked sense of humor.

"Why is your nickname Gato?" I asked Gato one evening.

"Can't you tell?" the teacher responded. "How many questions he asks. He's just too curious, like a cat."

Gato gave me a disingenuously shy smile. "I'm curious what it would be like to make love with a North American woman," he said. The others laughed.

"If you've played capoeira with me in the roda," I replied, "then you already know."

"Good answer," Angela said, raising her glass in a salute.

"Does that mean," Gato said, looking deep into his beer, "that you kick a lot and fall flat on your face when you're trying to stand on your hands?" I laughed and lightly hit him over the head.

One discussion between the teacher and several students that occurred almost every night was whether they should grow dreadlocks or not. Dreadlocks and Africanist clothing represented a political statement. One was drawing attention to one's African descent, defining this as important. It was also connected to the Black Power movement in the United States. Brazil had an ethic, if not a reality, of racial harmony, an idea that there was no racism in Brazil, that all peoples were equal in race and only class made a difference to one's life chances. In such a country, then, to promote one's "difference" was an affront to the status quo. Our teacher, who had grown up in the slums, finished only the first grade and taught himself to read so he could learn about Bob Marley, thought racism did not exist in Brazil. He idolized Bob Marley but worried that dreadlocks might imply that he smoked marijuana, so he compromised and kept his dreadlocks short. Jorge, who was also from the Salvador slums, but finished the sixth grade and had parents who discussed politics at home, was certain of Brazil's racism. Jorge, however, did not wear dreadlocks because, he said, it was too much bother. Gato, who worshiped our teacher, echoed our teacher's political views and wore his hair in whatever style the teacher wore his.

The group may have argued about racism, but they all agreed on police and violence. The streets were considered dangerous in general, but the people these capoeiristas most dreaded and disliked were the police. It seemed that nearly every day in Pelourinho, I saw police beating residents. One night, as my capoeira friends walked me to my bus, we saw a group of police smashing a man's head against a wall.

Gradually, over conversations with the capoeiristas and others, particularly those who lived in the slums, I gained more insight into this brutality. I learned that during the Brazilian military dictatorship, from 1964 to about 1984, citizens were "disappeared" and tortured. Much of the torturing was done by police, many of whom came from economically impoverished backgrounds. In the early 1990s, many of the same police officers still held their original jobs. Being forced to torture their fellow citizens had brutalized them. I began to understand that in torture, the tortured was not the only victim. Those forced to perform the acts were damaged forever as well.

The men in the capoeira group always watched over my safety. For the first six months or so, two or three walked with me everywhere. They later relaxed somewhat, but when we went to the bars, they sat me beside the wall, sitting themselves protectively on the outside of the table. Angela, the teacher's "public girlfriend" or *amante*, was often the only other woman who went out with us, but she wasn't protected at all. It was apparently assumed she could take care of herself. (Our teacher was married. Most of the capoeira teachers had several girl-friends: one who accompanied them publicly and others with whom they had passing affairs.)

One night as we sat at the bar, a man came in, drunk and muttering swear words under his breath to no one in particular. He went to the bar and ordered a pingau. All the men in my group moved so none had his back to him.

"Off duty policeman," Jorge said to me in a low voice. Marcos walked in, also drunk, making his usual jokes. He accidentally bumped the policeman. In a second, the men at my table and Angela were up and out a side door I never knew existed. They dragged me beside them, running up the street. I heard the shot seconds after I was outside. Then I heard the fighting start. More shots. We continued to run.

"Did you see his gun?" I asked.

"Yeah," Jorge said. "He had it in his pants."

When we returned to the bar the next night, it was closed. Later, Jorge told me the policeman had somehow missed Marcos, but had pistol-whipped him and smashed his leg. The stories about Marcos were confused: he was in the hospital. No one seemed to know if he would live or not.

"He won't play capoeira anymore," our teacher said.

Away from the capoeira group, I spent increasing amounts of time alone, exploring, talking with people I didn't know. I learned a great deal about Salvador this way. I learned which drugs the prostitutes liked best, the way the kids sniffed glue. One night, very late, I was walking home and passed a group of about seven kids sleeping on the street. One moved in front of me and demanded money. I laughed while I watched for a knife. The street boys knew they could die any day and would easily slit your stomach if they thought you were pre-venting them from getting money for food or for glue, which made them crazy but stilled the hunger pains.

"I don't have any money," I said to the boy. "If I did, do you think I'd be walking? I'd be taking a taxi!"

To my surprise, the boy paused and slid back into his pocket what

I now saw clearly as a knife. "You're right," he said.

The next night I was walking along the same street at about the same time of night. I had been drinking. It was São João, a harvest festival, and I'd been drinking *genipapo* liquor with friends much of the evening. Genipapo liquor is special to São João and is made from the genipapo fruit that grows in the Amazon. It is delicious, seldom sold commercially and not a drink to waste. I still carried a nearly full cup in my hand that was definitely that last cup I shouldn't drink, but I couldn't quite bring myself to throw it away. The boys were in their accustomed place.

"Hey Amiga!" the same boy I'd confronted the night before shouted. "What you got for us?"

I crossed the street and held out the cup. "Take this," I said.

Three boys leaped up. "Genipapo!"

"Now you've got a drink," I said, "and a starry tropical night," indicating the cloud-heavy sky. It was sure to rain and they would get soaked. My drink gave them about a sip each. The kids laughed at my irony and began splitting the drink. I waved and continued on my way.

A few minutes later, a taxi cab slowed and pulled up beside me. "Hey girl," the driver said. "Where're you going? You want a ride?"

"No, thank you," I said. "I live only around the corner."

"Are you sure? I'm going the same way you are."

"No," I said. "Thank you," and I walked to the inside of the sidewalk. After a brief pause, he drove away. Five seconds later, I heard someone running up behind me. I consciously relaxed my body, waiting for whatever attack might come.

"Hey lady!" I heard someone shout.

I ignored it.

"Hey lady!" The person ran up beside me. I turned, poised to kick. Then I realized the person was a girl from the group of street children. She was barefoot, wore a ragged cotton skirt and T-shirt. She looked to be about twelve.

"What did that man want? Where did he say he was going?"

"He asked me if I wanted a ride."

"What did you say?"

"I said no thank you." I wondered if the girl thought I was a prostitute intruding on her territory.

"That's all you said?"

"Yes."

The girl paused for a moment, then walked with me a few feet.

"You know, he didn't want to give you a ride, he wanted sex." She looked at me, her mouth tight. "He didn't want to take you home."

I looked at the girl and tears welled in my eyes. She could hardly have survived this long on the street without being raped, probably several times. Her eyes had the look of someone who hasn't eaten enough for a long time. She was barefoot on this filthy street. If she looked to her future, she saw prostitution, begging, and death. I wore comfortable jogging shoes, fashionable shorts, a bright colored shirt. My belly was rounded with good food. I was the symbol of everything that oppressed her.

"I understood what he was saying," I said softly. But I wasn't sure I understood her.

six
a dangerous embrace

When I wrote my year-end report on my research and requested a renewal of my grant, I assumed Ferando would continue as my research assistant. I had come to rely heavily on his textual knowledge. We had spent months collecting capoeira chants, researching, and translating them.

One night after we had struggled for several hours transcribing some difficult chants relating to the time of slavery in Brazil, I threw down my pen and stretched.

"This is so complicated," I said. "Not straight resistance, not straightforward hatred of whites, shape-changing when captured by the police... How am I going to explain all this in English to a non-Brazilian audience?"

Fernando laughed. "Race and its history in Brazil is complicated. It's like that Black American guy we met last week."

"Yeah, what did you think of him?" An African-American who was learning capoeira from another teacher had joined us for drinks after a capoeira gathering. He'd been in Salvador a few weeks and did not speak Portuguese. He had ignored me.

"You're an American, so please excuse me if I insult Americans," Fernando said, "but he really annoyed me. He kept calling me and Gato and Jorge 'brother!' And Angela his 'sister.' He isn't our sibling. He's a middle-class American. We are Brazilians. And then—" Fernando tapped his pen on the table in irritation, "he had the audacity to tell Matthias—that white fellow visiting from Rio, the one who plays capoeira so well?—he told him that he had more right to play capoeira than Matthias because he is black and Matthias is white! He was trying to tell us that capoeira was from Africa not Brazil. What does he know about all this? Good thing only you, Matthias, and I could understand him."

"Well, African-Americans have a strong sense of their own identity as ex-slaves, the same as African-Brazilians are..."

"And there it stops! Our situation here was very different from that in the States. You don't call people from Holland—or wherever your

53

family originally came from—sisters, do you? And with Brazilians it's even worse than that. He has the power; he's from a First World nation; he knows nothing of having the sovereignty of his country questioned by others in the world, other people telling his government what they should do with their own land, with their own trade policies, their own social programs. No. It's the arrogance, Margaret. Matthias is a thousand times more my brother than that American could ever be. I don't even like most people from Rio and still I say that!"

I shuffled my feet uneasily. "Many Black Americans come down here to see another model, to see a country divided by class, not so much race, to see a place where race has some equality."

"And there you are wrong. You think Brazil has no racism? Look around you, Margaret. Who has the good jobs? Whites. Who do you see in the magazines, the newspapers? The only nonwhites are people being accused of crimes."

"But, Fernando, who actually is black here? Everyone seems to have a different name to describe themselves—mocha, mulatto, yellow, cinnamon—everything except black. I almost never hear anyone actually calling themselves 'black.'"

"The word 'black' is pejorative—most of the time. I think of that term for 'black,' *preto*, as a black object, not a person. Using that term, you're saying the person is not only dark in color, has kinky hair, but also is less than a person, almost like an object. That they are very poor and have no standing in society. No one wants to be called that." Fernando paused. "It is true that you in the States have your historic 'one drop rule,' that anyone with any 'black blood' in them is considered black, while here it is based on one's appearance, and how much money you have. As a rule though, the darker you are here, the poorer you are—and the more likely you'll stay that way."

I sat for a long minute in silence. "So, how did you get so political, Fernando? You're not considered black here; you're middle-class. In Bahia people consider you white. Why do you care?"

Fernando looked at me for a moment and then laughed. "Good one. I suppose I've learned through playing capoeira and becoming friends with the people there. Capoeira is Brazilian, but its roots are Africa. It's a space between one world and another. I have learned a lot about my spirit, particularly the African part of my spirit, through playing capoeira. With all its traditions and immediate reminders of oppression, I enter African-Brazilian culture. I become a part of it, and that part of me which is descended from Africa comes out; I understand it more." He paused, thinking. "But it comes out in white players too, even in you. I can see it, as you get better, as you sing and learn about the chants. There is Africa in all of us, in the way our feet touch the earth, in the way our souls breathe."

I said nothing.

"Does that make any sense to you, Margaret?"

"Yes. I think it does, but not in a way I could explain to anyone, or that would make sense in different words."

"You understand it," Fernando said. "In your body, in the way you play, in the way you drink beer with everyone, in the way you laugh. You don't need to say anything."

I rubbed the pen I was holding. "Shall I make us some tea?"

"No." Fernando sat back in his chair. He picked up my hand and began playing with my fingers. "I may be leaving."

"What? When?" I felt a pain of lose, and then, unbidden, came the thought what would I do for a reseach assistant?

"Soon." He turned my hand over and began tracing the lines that criss-crossed my palm.

"What about Theresa?" Fernando's girlfriend Theresa was a professional dancer in Salvador.

"Um...we may be breaking up anyway. I think she has another lover."

"She's being pretty dumb to lose you," I said. "Why do you think she has a lover?"

"She told me."

"Oh."

"Look how different our hands are." Fernando laid out his long, narrow hand beside mine and began to compare their length and size. "She said she has two lovers actually, a man and a woman. I guess I wouldn't mind if she wanted to experiment, but she wants to continue having sex with them." He looked at me, and I saw tears in the corners of his eyes.

I took his hand in mine and kissed it. "I'm sorry," I said. "You love her, don't you?"

"Yeah." Fernando pressed my hand against his cheek. "So, I've been accepted to do my master's degree down near São Paulo. I think I'll go."

"Everyone in the capoeira group will be sad."

"Yeah. But I'll come back." He looked at my fingers. "But you'll probably be gone by then, won't you?"

"Maybe. Are you excited about the program?"

"It's psychology. The program's supposed to be good. I got some funding from the government."

"Oh, Fernando." I gently pulled him toward me and hugged him. "You don't want to go, do you?" He nestled his face on my shoulder, and I felt his tears on my neck.

"In some ways. But I love Bahia. This is me. When I go south, people will make fun of my Northeastern accent. I don't know. Once I get there I'm sure it'll be good, but now, leaving, I feel so torn. I have this hole where my love for Theresa is supposed to be."

I took his head in my hands and looked into his eyes. "Fernando, you are a wonderful, beautiful man. You know how to love. And I shall come back to see your face full of light and you laughing again."

Fernando smiled. "And you will find another good research assistant."

I laughed and pretended to slap his cheek. "You are so bad! I am thinking only of you!"

Fernando pulled his face away and joined my laughter.

"Liar. You are not so simple as that. And you should ask me who I think would make a better research assistant than I could ever be."

"Who?"

"Rita."

"Rita?"

"You never thought of her, did you?"

"No." I looked down at my notes, scribbled absentmindedly on the margins of the typed pages, and then looked up. "You know, Fernando, I think she intimidates me. She's always doing so many things, I don't know how she would have time. She's a video technician, she does her photography, she does all this political work, she seems to be on all these committees. Do you think she'd want to work with me?"

Fernando gathered up his papers. "You pay in American dollars, Margaret. And after this last election...." He paused. "You know the old party got back in, don't you? You understand what that means?"

"It means people will start getting paid again."

"It means Jorge lost his job."

"What?"

"He worked as a street cleaner. He hadn't been paid for eight months, but before that he made three minimum salaries. The new government has fired everyone, and they're going to hire new people and pay them only one minimum salary."

"Oh, no." I wondered how this would affect Jorge's entire family.

"Rita also lost her job."

"Why Rita?"

"Ask her. I'd say it's because she's too powerful. She might say something else." Fernando paused again. "But, she'll need money. Being your research assistant is fun. And at least we know you'll pay us."

"I see."

"I'm going." Fernando held out his hand to help my to my feet. "So, this Friday, we'll play each other in the capoeira roda, OK? To connect us until we meet again."

I looked into Fernando's face and felt a warmth of affection that moved through my blood and bones. "Yes," I said. "Until I see you happy and in love again."

Fernando slowly drew his finger along the edge of my cheekbone. He didn't smile. "You're getting more Brazilian by the day," he said. "It's going to be hard for you. Going back."

Having Rita as my research assistant was very different from working with Fernando. Fernando concentrated on written texts. Rita knew, or had connections to, every capoeira angola mestre in the city. At first, I conducted the interviews, but after the first few, I realized that when Rita asked the questions, people opened up immediately, whereas with me, they were reserved. Also, often a mestre would refer to some happening in Salvador history or some religious ritual, usually connected to Candomblé, about which I knew nothing. Rita was already well-versed in such references and could draw the person out about that topic, revealing interesting information that I would have never understood enough to even approach. So, our style changed. I generally just sat quietly and asked a few questions at the end about topics we hadn't covered or something in which I had particular interest.

One afternoon, after a day of interviews, I asked Rita why she had lost her job.

"After the elections, the city government did an upheaval, changing everyone. In my department, I'm the only black person except my boss." She poured me some beer from the bottle we were sharing as we sat together at an open-air street bar. "Do you know what I mean by black?"

"African descent." I thought about my conversation with Fernando, but said nothing. I wanted to hear what Rita had to say.

"Yes and no. I am dark and from the shantytown—my accent still gives me away on that, and I don't hide my neighborhood anyway. My boss, who is almost as dark as me, was brought up in a lower middle-class neighborhood. That his background is more middle-class than mine makes him whiter in the way people think here. At the time we both went to school, in the sixties and seventies, the school system worked somewhat better than it does now. If you were dedicated, a good student, you could get into public grammar schools that actually gave you a decent education. That's why either of us had any chance of going to university, but particularly me. These grammar schools don't exist anymore. They disappeared during the worst of the dictatorship." She took a sip of her beer. "My politics are known. I'm black. My boss was threatened by me. So he fired me."

"But how can that be racism—if he's black, I would think he'd stick up for you."

Rita laughed. "Oh, no. Here in Brazil, the blacks who were poor and then become middle-class are the greatest oppressors of their race and of the poor."

"Why?"

"They don't want to be reminded of their past, I suppose. They want the status quo. They want what the middle class has—more, they want to be the middle class, just pretend they're white and push away those connected to the misery they knew before. That's why we don't have an effective Black Power Movement here as you have in the States. There the blacks have to stay in their black neighborhoods, don't they?"

I nodded. "There is strong residential separatism in the States."

"Here not nearly so much, as I understand. And overt racism is illegal, written into our Constitution. So no one can openly call me a 'nigger.'"

"But they can fire you."

Rita bought a paper cone of peanuts from a small boy who came by our table. She opened the cone, laid out the peanuts for us both and ate a few before she answered. "They're not supposed to. I might even be able to file a legal suit in this case."

"Can you do that?"

"Yes. At least I can try." She nibbled more peanuts. "The legal system works to protect the Constitution and the laborers—if you can afford a good lawyer. Which of course most poor people cannot."

"Like Gato or Jorge."

"Like Gato or Jorge. In the countryside it's even worse. But Gato and Jorge at least have middle-class friends. So do I. Most people don't. The difficulty is that poor black people can, if they're lucky, get jobs like Jorge or Gato have. Or had … they lost them, didn't they?"

I nodded.

Rita snapped a peanut in half. "That's so screwed." She paused. "The bigger problem is that they can't get the education for better jobs, and their blackness keeps them apart. You look at the color gradation at any company, a bank, anything. The security guards are very dark, the tellers lighter, and so it goes to the top, where all managers are white. That's how racism works here. And blacks do not help each other; they do the opposite."

"You don't."

"I'm strange."

"An idealist, perhaps?"

"No. I was brought up too rough for idealism. Remember I grew up during the dictatorship, protesting, running, watching my friends get tortured and disappear. And now I see my friends and neighbors die of drugs and disease. Not an idealist. I'm a realist. And as a realist, I see that nothing will change unless we do it ourselves."

"But what about the aid agencies, those working for development? All those programs for street kids?"

"Right." The bitterness in Rita's voice startled me. It was a tone I had never heard in her voice before. "So-called aid agencies teach the street kids they can become waiters, maybe, or show them how to draw. The churches sometimes give starving people food—on Easter. But that doesn't change anything. The middle class doesn't really want to change anything; they just want difficulties that hamper their lives, like being robbed or mugged, to go away. So, they set up their little 'charitable' organizations, telling the poor what is best for them, never asking for suggestions. God forbid they would ever actually ask someone from a shantytown to advise them! And the poor people detest them and steal whatever they can. The overseas ones are even worse. They mostly bring in foreigners who have no idea what's going on and often cause more harm than good."

"But surely local people start their own groups, don't they?"

"Some." Rita refilled our glasses. "In case you haven't noticed, Brazilians aren't a particularly philanthropic people. Nearly all the grassroots groups are started and run by women in the shantytowns. But they don't know anything about accounts or legal contracts or that kind of thing. And the middle class isn't going to give them any support, let alone money. And if they get any money, someone who works for them generally steals it. So they start with good ideas and then collapse."

I swirled the beer in my glass and wondered if my next comment was smart considering I was now completely dependent upon Rita for her connections and insights with my research. I said it anyway. "So, Rita, since you seem so clear-eyed on this, why don't you start your own nonprofit? Work directly for social change?"

"I already do it with my photography, and with the stuff I do in the neighborhood. But..." She stopped speaking and watched a couple walking by, the girl about twelve, the man in his forties. "The prostitution here gets worse by the day," she said. "Her mother's probably at home waiting for that girl's money." She sat silent again. "I suppose," she finally said, "that even with all my education, I really don't know how to do that myself. I would have to have someone with me, a group perhaps, but one that wasn't middle-class, but knew the legalities. A group that maintained a power with the people being served, the people in my neighborhood, but with a structure that protected the group's interests." She laughed. "So, now I am being idealist. You were right, I'm an idealist. You'd think I'd learn by now."

"Not an idealist, Rita. A realist." I leaned forward in my metal folding chair. "You know, Rita, you're a determined person. I think if you really wanted to put together a group just as you describe, with all your knowledge and connections, you could do it."

Rita looked at me a moment and waved her arm at Nelson, the waiter, who stood behind the bar chatting with a friend. "So I'm an idealist and you're an optimist. A great pair. Another bottle, a final one for going home, shall we?"

I laughed and drained my glass.

One day, not many days later, I found my orixá.

No, Agnaldo helped me recognize my orixá.

He invited me to the small windowless room of the old Fort where he welded beautiful statues of the orixás and the symbols important to them. I didn't know about his artistry until that day. He'd never mentioned it.

"Here, this should be for you," he said, handing me a sculpture. "It's your orixá."

"Mine?" I said. "I don't have an orixá."

"Yes, you do. You have ever since you came to the Candomblé gathering that night."

"Which one is it?"

"I can't tell you." His voice sounded irritated. "You know. Just think about it." He put his welding glasses around his neck and turned away. "Those beads you always wear," he said. "Where did you get them? Why did you choose that color?"

"Actually someone gave them to me."

"Here?"

"Yes."

"Then they knew too." The beads were turquoise, a color I love. "And what about the picture you have hanging on your wall? Who is that? Who gave you that?"

"A woman in Cachoeira, where I went on a research trip with Rita, gave it to me."

"Didn't charge you, did she?"

"No. She said it would protect me..." I felt a cold touch in my chest. "Irmanjá," I said. "She's standing by the sea. I grew up near the sea. I worked as a commercial fisherman. I've spent a lot of time on the sea. My family in the States comes from near the sea."

Agnaldo snapped on his welding glasses. "You're very slow some-times," he said. He handed me the sculpture. "Here, take the statue. Burn a candle for her. Make her an offering." He paused. "Didn't you know who almost took you the night of the gathering?"

"How did you notice that?"

I couldn't see Agnaldo's expression through the dark of his glasses.

"Take the statue," he said. "It will be a connection between us. She's my orixá, too."

marginals

Languages are said to reflect the cultures that create them: Polynesian is said to have more words for love, English an extensive vocabulary in technology. Brazilian Portuguese has words that made me rethink my perceptions of my encounter with life. One was *saudade*. Saudade is that feeling of missing someone or a place, a longing. It is also nostalgia, remembering the sweet smell of autumn leaves, the honk of a ferryboat on a foggy day. There is no English word for saudade, but it's a sentiment we non-Brazilians know, one that's just difficult for us to express.

As I became fluent in Portuguese, I grew to love the language. Particularly the Portuguese that I learned, a Portuguese of the streets, full of slang, swear words, the tensions of survival, violence, religion, and love. And through learning the language, I began to understand more about how people I knew in Salvador viewed their world.

Brazilians also had a term they used for certain people, which, literally translated, meant "marginals." These people were neither inside nor outside society, but lived on the edge. Amazonian Indians were outside society, a white university student inside. But other people, the poor and nonwhite, who were they?

I never met a Brazilian, no matter how poor or living in what circumstances, who called himself a marginal, yet everyone felt they had encountered others who were. The only sure thing about marginals was that somebody else considered them worthless to society; a child begging on the street knew that he or she could be killed by tomorrow's dawn and society would not blink once.

I often visited Jorge's family for Sunday lunch, but one week, a few days before one of my visits, the police had chased a young man around their neighborhood and then shot him in front of Jorge's family's house. When he moved, not quite dead, the policeman turned. "You miserable marginal," he said, and shot him again. Twice.

Jorge's mother Zezé believed in law and order. She believed in the police. But when she heard the shooting, her first reaction was fear, not from the threat of the dead man, but from the police. She feared they had shot someone in her family. She knew her children weren't marginals, but police had a different perspective. So did the middle class.

The first time I went to visit Jorge's family alone I asked advice about the buses from the woman who lived next door to my apartment. She warned me against going at all. "It's very dangerous there," she said. "Most of the people living there are marginals."

Yet I arrived to a street full of people walking, laughing, and playing ball. In the midst of this poverty, people hated and died, but they also lived. Jorge's family had constructed their house bit by bit over the years and were now building two rooms in half of what had been a double garage. They planned to rent out these rooms for about fifty dollars each a month. Everyone in the family contributed, and by working together for years, they now had a comfortable house, a television, and, recently, a car. Lula, Jorge's father, was the only one who drove it.

After thirty years of marriage, Jorge's parents still adored each other. "I ran around a lot when I was young," said Lula, "but now I need no one but her."

The room project was clearly Zezé's brainchild and, on the day of my first visit, she brought Lula beers periodically (drinking half herself first) while he worked muddling the walls.

"My builder," she explained.

"*Our* builder," the youngest son, Duda, said, snatching the beer from her hand and taking a swig himself.

We hung out in the street. João, Jorge's brother in law, showed up with Mauro, his two-year-old son. Mauro had rubella, but this did not stop him from running, laughing, and trying to play soccer. He could already stop the ball with his foot and kick it where he wanted it to go, which was about as much as I could do.

João and a female cousin began telling stories. I quickly realized where Jorge had acquired his talent for storytelling. It was a street art, polished and perfected. I watched, fascinated, as they built their characters, mimicking movement and voice, choreographing a scene that surrounded us all.

Then they all paused. They were looking at me. My stomach clenched as I realized they expected me to tell a story now. I stumbled and began a tale about a funny happening with the child of a friend. I flushed with gratitude when they didn't walk away in boredom and even politely laughed at the end.

Jorge and I walked back to the house together. "How's things going with your girlfriend?" I asked. Jorge's girlfriend, whom he had known for years, was trying to pressure him into marriage.

"I don't know, Danger. She keeps saying she's pregnant and then she isn't. She screams at me all the time."

"Why?"

"She wants me to be home, not to play capoeira, to get a job here. But I love capoeira."

"And you're good at it, Jorge. You and Gato, of all the group, could be teachers. You half hold the group together already."

"You think I'm that good?"

"You know you are. And you have a calm that helps everyone else."

Jorge laughed. "That's because I have a good family," he said.

Later, over lunch, we talked about issues of racial oppression in Brazil. Lula and Zezé loved to talk about politics.

"One big difference between the United States and Brazil," Lula said, "is that the U.S. had a Civil War where the north fought for abolition—isn't that right? Thirty years later we got abolition here in Brazil, but no one fought for it. You know why we got abolition? Because the planters didn't need slaves any more. Economically they were better off without slaves. So we got abolition. In the United States, abolition was something dramatic, a challenge to the social system. Here abolition never touched the status quo."

"They say there's no racism here," Zezé said, "but if a white man and a black man apply for the same job, the white man gets it." She put more beans on my plate. "You aren't eating enough. Don't you like it?"

"I love the food," I said, "but I can't eat any more. I'm full."

"You hardly ate anything," Lula said. He rubbed his round belly proudly. "My wife is an excellent cook."

"Shush!" Zezé said and pretended to frown.

I concentrated on my plate and tried to stuff in a few more bites.

One evening soon after, Luzia and I got a telephone call from Dona Cida, Gato's mother. Gato spent half his time in Salvador and half with his mother in the small country village of his birth about two hours outside Salvador. "He's in prison," Dona Cida said.

Two police officers, out of uniform, had entered their house at midnight, one with a shotgun, the other with a submachine gun. "Give us the Rasta," they said.

Gato, who had recently begun to grow dreadlocks when our teacher finally expressed an interest in doing so himself, had offended the sheriff because Gato, a person from a poor black family, was teaching capoeira to young local boys who were also poor and black.

Pedro, a lawyer friend of Luzia's, and I arrived at dawn. We found Gato and one of his local students in open cages, naked, in the pouring rain. The jailer had ordered other prisoners to beat the fifteen-year-old student, and he was now a mess of bruised and broken skin. They had been afraid to touch Gato without a gun; skilled capoeiristas in such small towns were attributed almost mythical strength.

Pedro went into the office to speak with the sheriff while I waited outside. Several people came to look at me until finally, Dona Cida, who sat waiting beside me on the curb, invited me to go into a small bar next door. We ordered cold drinks and continued to wait. Dona Cida took out a small religious book and began to read.

"You can read," I said. Dona Cida smiled.

"I taught myself many years ago. Gato and I are here now, but you understand that we live over an hour's walk along the paths, in a smaller village?" I nodded. In Salvador, at the bar after practice one night, Gato had told me about his home.

"Well," she continued, "girls have babies very young there and many do not know what to do. And we have no doctor. People cannot come there. The girls cannot pay for a doctor. So, I decided to learn this. And I wanted to read about God. So, I asked an old man who knew a bit of reading. He taught me what he knew, and then I learned on my own. And I studied about medicine. I learned what the old people in the area knew. I help the girls before they give birth, help deliver the children, and I help them afterward." She smiled. "I think we have fewer babies die now. And mothers too." I wondered to myself if anyone had recorded this local natural medicine knowledge.

"I am glad you are there," I said. "Do you get medicine from the countryside?"

"Oh, yes," she said. "We have no money for medicine from the doctors. And much of the medicine from the forest is better anyway." She glanced up nervously, and I saw Pedro approach. He looked hot and frustrated, his temper barely controlled. He slammed himself into the folding chair beside Dona Cida.

"These country idiots!" he said. "He isn't following the law at all. He acts as though he doesn't even care! By law, he cannot hold a person for more than twenty-four hours without charging him. He must, by law, release Gato now. And that kid. He cannot have the kid beaten. I can prosecute him for that!"

Dona Cida laid her hand on Pedro's arm. It was small and dark upon his wide, light forearm. He was white, middle-class, and had lived in Rio much of his life.

"Please, do not offend Sheriff Teixeira," she said. "He makes his own law here."

"No, he doesn't," Pedro said. "This is part of national law and Bahia state law, just the same as everywhere else. He knows the regulations."

"Yes, he does." Dona Cida looked around to see that no one stood nearby. "We are poor and in the country. Let me tell you how the law works here. Sheriff Texeira was appointed from Salvador because he's a cousin to the governor. He hates this posting and thinks he should have something better. He does not live here, but comes out for his work. He arrests people who cross or offend him, or who do not pay him the bribes he wants. He only lets them go when he's satisfied they understand his control and when they have borrowed everything he thinks he can possibly get out of them. If people offend him too greatly, they are found beaten to death along the roadside."

Pedro reared out of his chair. "That is impossible! He can be called to pay for this, put in jail himself. Are you sure the people killed have anything to do with him?"

"I have lived here my entire life," Dona Cida said.

For a moment they stared into each other's eyes. Dona Cida was a tiny woman of perhaps four and a half feet, her face deeply creased from working in the sun, her eyes brilliant with worry and intelligence. Pedro, who had come out to see about this case only because he adored Luzia, was a big, fleshy man, his dark eyes reflecting confusion and doubt.

"And remember that whatever you do here," Dona Cida said, "after you leave, my children and I will be left behind. And Sheriff Teixeira will punish us forever if you publicly humiliate him."

At that moment, the jailhouse door opened and Sheriff Teixeira himself emerged. He was black by United States standards, but in Bahia he was considered, particularly with his middle-class connections, white, despite his light brown color and African features. He surveyed the three of us.

"So, this is why you have this fancy lawyer," he said to Dona Cida. He jerked his head in my direction. "Your boy hanging out with this white rich gringa now, is he? Thinks he's got too big for his place." He looked at me and leered. "You like young, strong black boys, do you?"

I looked back at him and, with every ounce of self-control I could summon, I smiled.

"I sorry, senhor," I said. "I not speak Portuguese so well. I visit my friend"—I gestured toward Pedro—"and he invite me come on his day work here. So I can see countryside. Your town beautiful." I smiled again and flipped my blond hair over one shoulder.

Sheriff Teixeira relaxed visibly and returned my smile. "Your friend's a bit innocent, isn't she?" he said to Pedro.

"She's a foreigner visiting my family," Pedro said. "The son of a cousin of mine plays capoeira with Gato in Salvador."

The sheriff nodded. Foreigners clearly could not be expected to understand anything.

"I have released the boy," he said. "My deputies have escorted him back to his family. As for your son," he said to Dona Cida, "after your lawyer friend here gets the papers we need, then you and I can discuss his release."

Dona Cida lowered her eyes. "Certainly," she said. "Thank you very much, senhor." Sheriff Teixeira nodded and walked away toward his lunch. Pedro stood up.

"Well, at least we're getting somewhere now. I'll go and get these papers he wants from Salvador. Is there a post office or somewhere here that has a fax machine?"

"Yes," said Dona Cida. "There's one just around the corner."

Dona Cida and I sat in silence after he left. The heat had become overpowering. Flies buzzed around us and the street emptied as people retired inside for lunch and to escape the sun.

"Please don't take this the wrong way," I said, "but in your negotiations with Sheriff Teixeira, would this help?" I quickly displayed under that table the equivalent of fifty dollars I had just removed from my bag. Dona Cida looked at the money and then looked at me.

"That's more than a month's salary," she said.

"I know." I paused, wondering how I could express, after what I had seen so far in Bahia, how much it would mean for me to actually be able to offer some assistance and have that assistance accepted. I didn't have the right kind of power or knowledge, but I did have a little bit of money. But I also knew that money gifts can undermine a person's self respect. They could be humiliating and reinforce the economic and social chasm between us. "Your son is a good teacher to me—and to the other students in our group. He takes the classes half the time now. This is from all of us." I laughed. "We want him back in class."

Dona Cida smiled. "He is very good at capoeira, isn't he? He could be a real mestre."

"Yes," I said. "He has grace and an intuition that's quite incredible. The mestres say he has a special talent and could be one of the great players in Salvador some day."

Dona Cida slid her hand under the table and took the money. "For my son," she said. "I am sure Sheriff Teixeira will be satisfied with this offering for his services."

Just then a young girl in a school uniform ran up to us. Dona Cida embraced her. "This is my daughter, Renata," she said. "She is going to school."

Renata carefully laid a notebook and a school book on the table. "I have a Portuguese exam tomorrow. When is lunch?"

Dona Cida laughed. "We all get to eat together at Aunt Marcia's today. Come," she said to me. "You will join us. I will send my nephew to invite Seu Pedro."

Renata waited until we had left the open street before she asked, "How is Gato? Did they beat him?"

"No." Dona Cida put her arm around her daughter's shoulders. "Because of that nice lawyer I think they will not beat him. And I will talk with the sheriff tonight and we shall see what happens."

That night, Renata and I sat on the curb beside her aunt's house and waited while Dona Cida went to negotiate with the sheriff. Pedro had ordered his papers and returned to Salvador. I said I'd return to Salvador by bus the next day. Dona Cida told Pedro that her home was always open to him.

"A beautiful, simple place," he said to me in English. "The bugs are too much, and I can't understand where they sleep, but the countryside is beautiful. Dona Cida is an intelligent woman, isn't she?"

Renata was studying her Portuguese by the street light as we waited. I watched the moon. Renata carefully began to erase a page of her notebook.

"What are you doing?" I asked.

"I have to write an assignment preparing for this exam tomorrow. This is last week's lesson, so I don't need it any more."

"But why are you erasing it?"

"So I can use the page again."

"Oh," I said, "of course." I paused. "Do you like school?" Immediately I realized the irrelevance of my question.

"I am going to finish high school and go to university." I wondered at the quality of this country school where Dona Cida must struggle to pay Renata's expenses, to which Renata walked over an hour each way. And I wondered at Renata's determination that she studied even while her brother sat in jail.

"Will they kill my brother?" she asked.

I thought about how to respond. Renata deserved more than platitudes. Besides, I knew they wouldn't comfort her. "I don't think so," I said. "I think your mother is very clever, and she will negotiate well."

"She will do her best," Renata said, and turned back to her Portuguese.

Several hours later, Dona Cida returned. She looked defeated. "They will release him tomorrow," she said. She walked to the back of the house without another word and began washing beans. Renata shut her Portuguese book. I lay down on the mat Dona Cida had prepared for me near the door. Bugs crawled over my legs, so I tucked the sheet tight around my body to stop them. I heard the soft slap of water as Dona Cida washed the next day's beans. Around us, like an immense dome, rose a silence defined by the cant of a thousand cicadas.

eight | sex and friendship

"They let Gato out of jail, finally," I said to Luzia. I was sitting at our table in the single room that served as living room, dining room, and kitchen. I was trying to type notes into my new laptop with minor success. Luzia sat across from me, combing out her long hair after having put some kind of special conditioner on it.

"He doesn't have anywhere to stay," she said.

"What happened to the room he was sharing?"

"He lost it. He's sleeping at the Fort now, in our capoeira room."

"But there are rats there!"

"I know."

I tried to write some more notes. Someone knocked on the door. Luzia looked up.

"You expecting anyone?" I shook my head. She rose and opened the door. Andrea walked in.

"Hi," she said. Andrea came sometimes to visit us, but not often. It was a long way by bus, and she seldom had bus fare. She flopped onto the sofa and stared at the floor.

I glanced at Luzia and shut my computer. "What's up, Andrea? You want some coffee?"

Andrea shook her head without lifting it and said nothing. I sat beside her and put my arm around her. "What's up, sweetie? You OK?"

Andrea threw her arms around me and burst into tears. Luzia looked over Andrea's head at me, then came and cuddled her from the other side. We waited for her sobs to subside.

"My father," Andrea said. "He beat me—again!" She held up her bruised arms for us to see.

"Oh dear." Luzia sat back on the sofa.

"What about your mother?" I asked.

"She can't do anything against him, or he'll just beat her too! I don't want to even tell her—she'll just get mad at me. He hit me with his strap!" She pulled up her shirt and I saw dark welts on her skin. Luzia went to the bathroom and returned with some ointment. "Ouch, that hurts!" Andrea said. But she let Luzia rub the medicine onto her wounds. "I'm not going home," she said. "Can I stay here?"

I cast Luzia an inquiring glance. She shrugged. "Does your mother know you're here?"

"Yes. She said it was fine."

We sat with Andrea for a couple of hours, until she said she was tired. She curled up on my bed and within seconds was sound asleep.

Luzia and I sat in the front room and talked about what we might make for a light supper. "Do you think her mother really knows she's here?" Luzia asked.

"You think Andrea would lie?"

"She's a teenager, Margaret. She probably just ran out of the house." We sat for a few minutes. "They do have a phone, don't they?"

"Yeah. So they can receive calls from Amsterdam."

"Why don't you call them. What's her mother's name?"

"Tatiana. All right." I sighed heavily. "I can't do it here though. I feel like a traitor."

"Put yourself in Tatiana's place." I nodded and went outside in search of a functioning public phone.

Tatiana picked up after the first ring. "Margaret, is that you? Is Andrea with you?" Her voice cracked with fear.

"Yes," I said. "Yes, she came here this afternoon."

"Why didn't you ring me? Why didn't you ring immediately? She ran away. I didn't know. I didn't know where she was. Someone could have kidnapped her. Why didn't you call me?"

My stomach clenched into a ball. "Someone beat her, Tatiana."

"Her father. Because she always wants to be out on the street now. She won't go to school. But you should have called me."

"Yes, I should have. I'm sorry Tatiana. It's just—she's all beat up."

"You know their father, Margaret. He's terrible."

"Can she stay with us tonight? If I tell her to go, she'll just stay on the street; you know that."

Tatiana sighed. "Yes, yes. I'll come and get her tomorrow." There was a pause in which I could feel her embarrassment. "Ah Margaret, when I come, could you pay for our bus fare back? I'm not sure I have the money right now."

"Of course, Tatiana." I wiped tears from my cheeks and put down the phone.

When I got back to the apartment, Luzia had begun preparing dinner. I told her about the conversation I'd just had.

"Oh God," Luzia said. "This is too much." She poured water over the rice and onions she was frying. Then she looked at me with the arched eyebrow I had come to know. "What we need, Margaret, is some sex. When things get too stressful, too chaotic, that's what can calm things down, some good sex!"

I laughed. "Oh Luzia," I said. "You're impossible." I shook my head. "And wonderful."

Luzia was an actress on stage and off, flamboyant, clever with words, expressive of face, and very sure of herself. She was tall and slender with olive skin, high cheek bones, and straight, long, chestnut-colored hair. In the United States, she would be considered incredibly beautiful. In Salvador, although her figure was too boyish to be considered traditionally attractive, she had some other quality, perhaps her complete assurance in knowing exactly what she wanted, that made her completely seductive. I always felt large and ungainly next to Luzia, and I knew my figure was considered even less perfect. Brazilian men, particularly in Bahia, appreciated large, rounded bottoms and small breasts. I had a flat bottom and fairly large breasts. Bahia women, who were always blunt about these kinds of things, often told me that I was OK in appearance, except my body, which was "unfortunate." Two women had suggested that I could be improved greatly by having a breast reduction and by injecting silicone into my buttocks.

Luzia and I had constant discussions about everything from philosophy to bodies to sex. In talking about sex, Luzia was always relaxed and completely forthright. In the discussions I fared well, but in attracting men, she won hands down. At some point I had learned that the two slang words commonly used in Bahia for sexual intercourse were "to give," which meant the act of being penetrated, and "to eat," which was to penetrate someone else. Most women, when speaking of having sex, said they "gave." (This always seemed counterintuitive to me.) Not Luzia. Whenever she felt the need for sex, she wandered around the apartment complaining.

"I want to eat. I need to eat!"

I once asked her why she used that term. "Because that's how I feel," she said. "I don't want to give. I want to eat!"

One day, Luzia and I arrived at our capoeira class to find that a man we both considered stunning had just joined the group. Both Luzia and I had a policy that we would not become sexually involved with men in the group because it just caused problems—but here was a possible exception.

"Since we are both attracted to him," Luzia suggested, "why don't we have a contest and see who can get him in bed." I was dubious, but agreed to give it a try.

We wandered over to him. He flashed us his white and perfect smile, and we began to chat. Within minutes, he was entirely smitten with Luzia. I didn't have a chance. Neither did he, for that matter, but he did not seem at all displeased by his entrapment. That night, Luzia suggested I entertain myself somewhere other than our one-bedroom apartment. Sullenly, I agreed, but told her I would be coming home by midnight and that she had to make me breakfast – for a week.

Interactions between men and women were markedly different in Brazil from what I had experienced in the United States and Europe. Flirtation in Brazil was an art form that often had little to do with a progression to actual sex, although sex was generally a possibility weighed equally by men and women. When I first arrived in Brazil, I was uncomfortable with the intense stares of men on the street and their continual sexualized comments. This interaction I found oppressive because of my experience in the States, where male street commentary always seemed to be accompanied by an underlying threat of sexual aggression. "Hey chick!" construction workers or others on the street in the States would shout. When I ignored them, which seemed the only reasonable reaction, they would shout afterward, "Well, fuck you then!" Such interactions seemed to stem from male frustration at not being able to connect with women in a way they would like, as well as a strange mistrust and almost dislike men and women often seemed to have for each other.

Under Luzia's tutelage, I began to learn how to react to male street commentary in Brazil. I took notes out of anthropological habit, but I also tried to adopt her suggestions. I noticed that my notes about general Bahian life had decreased to almost nothing. I mostly took notes on incidents related specifically to issues of race and gender or about capoeira. People around me had moved from being anthropological "subjects" to friends. Luzia's insights, however, were so perceptive that I often wrote them down afterward, just so I wouldn't forget.

A Brazilian man's commentary, Luzia told me, was an appreciation of the woman he saw, as well as a comment on his dominance in a public space. Luzia taught me how to ignore the comments and yet show acknowledgment. When men standing along the street stared at Luzia in apparent uncontrollable passion, murmuring such comments as, "Delicious" and "Beautiful," Luzia appeared to ignore them. But with the toss of her head or the swing of her hips, she indicated that she had heard, and implied that, "Yes, I know I'm sexy. But I'm not available to you."

It was yet another game of flirtation. Gradually, I came to find such male appreciation added to my sense of well-being. I began to dress carefully each time I went out because I knew people would be watching. Because others overtly expressed appreciation for my appearance daily, I began to feel that I was more attractive. I found it interesting that every Brazilian woman I knew, whether plump or slim, tall or short, dark or light, considered herself beautiful. Most U.S. women I knew thought they were fat and not particularly attractive.

I was not, however, sure I would ever learn to negotiate the Brazilian labyrinth of dating and *namoro* (which could best be translated in English as "courtship"). I met Mauro, a friend of a friend of Luzia's, when we all went to the mountains for the June São João festival. The trip was wonderful, with bonfires, dancing, and good food, but Luzia's friends—I wasn't sure. They all meditated before meals—that was fine—but, their idea of meditation seemed to involve connecting with invisible lightning that periodically zapped their chakras. I felt no zapping. It appeared to me that nearly all Brazilians were spiritual at the same time they were secular, so if Candomblé or Catholicism didn't work for them, they went for Pentecostal or New Age. These friends of Luzia were New Age. They all wore crystals.

Mauro was one of these friends. He was tall and Italian-looking, with a sculpted jawbone. Luzia told him of my interest in Celtic literature and history, so he began chatting with me, asking me about druids and stone circles. We took long walks at sunset. He was a great dancer.

A few days after our return to Salvador, Mauro asked me to lunch at his family's middle-class apartment. Their maid served us an ample meal. All was going swimmingly until his mother began talking about the twelve-year-old boys from the nearby *favela* who kept stealing food and toys from her shop.

"I complained to the police," she said, "and Grace of God, the boys aren't coming anymore. The police went into the favela and shot them." She raised her hands in thanks. "Grace of God," she said.

I declined dessert.

Later Mauro and I retired to his bedroom, the only private place in the apartment where we could sit and talk. He showed me the books he was reading on Egyptian history, Celtic druids, and the powers of pyramids. At some point in the conversation, Mauro leaned over and began kissing me. This proceeded for a time until he stood up, extended his hand to me, and said, "This won't work. I feel strange with my mother around." Then he said something I didn't understand, but decided to ignore, thinking I could ask Luzia about it later.

We left the apartment together and got into Mauro's car. He drove to a place nearby that was surrounded by a high wall. A gate opened as his car approached, and he drove up to a glass window. He and a man behind the window spoke for a time and then we drove inside. I could not see the man inside the kiosk, and it seemed that the window was designed so he could not see me either.

The door closed behind us, and we drove to a garage, where the door again automatically opened as we approached and closed behind us. I was growing increasingly confused. In the garage was a narrow stairway, which we ascended. Mauro opened the door, smiled, and stood aside for me to enter.

I walked into a gilt room. It boasted a mirrored ceiling, a round bed, a small fridge, large sink, and an open bathroom where I could see the edge of a large beautifully tiled shower.

"What's this?" I asked.

"It's a Love Motel. That's what I suggested at the house, and I thought you agreed. We couldn't make love there, not with my mother around."

"Right," I said. I sat down on the edge of the bed. "You used a different word. I didn't understand what you meant, Mauro."

"Really?" Mauro sat beside me. "Do you want to make love?"

"Um, no. Not now. I'm sorry, Mauro. You probably had to pay for this, didn't you?"

To Mauro's great credit, he stood up immediately and extended his hand once more.

"Yes, but that's fine. We can just leave quickly. I never realized you didn't understand me." He flushed. I studied details of the carpet. Then he opened a second door I hadn't noticed that led into a small hallway, rang a bell, and a man appeared. Mauro paid him some money and we left.

"Is this common that people go to these Love Motels?" I asked him as we drove out. "Are there many of them in Salvador?"

"Oh, yes," he said, apparently relieved to be talking about anything. "And some of them are very fancy, with ceilings that open, fetish rooms, swimming pools, whatever you want, depending upon what you can pay. It's what everybody does here. If you live with your parents until you get married, what are you going to do? You have to go somewhere. And if you want to have an affair, it's a safe place to do it. Once you drive your car in, it's in a garage, hidden, and no one knows where you are. You could be having an affair in one room and your wife in the next and neither of you would know the difference."

I nodded. "Interesting." I touched his hand that was on the wheel. "Thank you for being so polite," I said.

He glanced at me and gave me an irritated look. "Of course," he said. "What would you expect?"

Later, I made the mistake of telling Luzia about all this. She broadcasted my story to her theater friends at the Bastidor. Bastidor, meaning "backstage," was a bar close to our apartment that was frequented by theater and film people. It also attracted a wide variety of genders, colors, and identities. The owners were a flamboyantly gay middle-aged man and a transgendered person who made loud rude jokes with everyone while she waited tables.

None of them would let me forget my *faux pas*. They would think up the most outlandish slang or euphemism for Love Motel and invite me. Luzia loudly encouraged me to go out with a man commonly known as Mala (*mala* means "suitcase" in Portuguese).

"Why is he called *mala*?" I asked.

"Because he packs a large suitcase!" Luzia replied amid loud guffaws from the entire bar. *Mala,* I had just discovered, was also a slang word for "penis."

Just when I thought my Portuguese was great, something would happen, and I'd realize how little I knew. As a part of my research, I had developed a relationship with the Anthropology Department of a major local university. My second grant was running out. I wanted to stay, so I had begun discussing with the department the possibility of becoming a visiting professor and teaching some seminars for them. They liked the idea and invited me to give a paper on my research at the university, in Portuguese, of course. I spent weeks on it. Because my written Portuguese was not nearly as good as my spoken Portuguese, I wrote the paper in English, knowing I could loosely translate as I gave the talk.

The day of the lecture arrived, and I was presented to an audience that included faculty, other academics, and graduate students. I began to speak. Gradually, I noticed that within the polite silence, I heard periodic titters. I wasn't sure I had heard correctly until the titters became giggles. Then came periodic outbreaks of loud laughter, followed by people nearly falling off their chairs in an uproar. It was as though I were a very successful comedienne. I bit back distress and tried not to let my humiliation show. What was I doing wrong?

Finally, an Italian colleague came up to the podium and intervened. "At least it is clear that she works in the favelas she writes about," he said. Resounding laughter.

After the paper, people asked me questions, even wanted to go out for a beer, but I only forced a smile, shook my head, and ran for the bus home. I arrived at the apartment in tears. Luzia made me a cup of tea and sat me down. I told her what happened.

She stroked my hair. "Oh, Margaret," she said. "It wasn't your paper or your ideas. It's your Portuguese." I burst into tears again. "No, no," she said gently. "It's not bad. The Portuguese is fluent. It's just that, well, it's not middle-class. Your accent, the way you use your verbs, the slang you use—it's all lower-class. And Margaret, you use terrible swear words." She smiled. "Things no middle-class woman would ever say. I don't think you know it." She giggled. "But your ideas and your vocabulary are sophisticated, very educated, academic. The combination is very strange. I can just imagine, in an academic paper. The only favela people your audience would know are their maids. Your paper, in your speech, must have turned their world upside down. Like their maid expounding intellectual, complex theories while throwing in vulgarities to spice things up." She laughed and shook her head. "Oh, I wish I'd been there. I'd have loved it."

I bought a grammar text and decided to practice middle-class Portuguese. The only middle-class person I knew, however—except Luzia's theater friends, who delighted in inventing their own outrageous swearing vocabulary—was Mauro. He had continued to visit. He seemed to feel that the Love Motel debacle was his fault. I felt shy and probably talked too much. I started telling him about my capoeira friends, my adventures in the favelas, and about Penambuas. One night he took me to an expensive Chinese restaurant. After we'd ordered, he produced a packet of dried leaves.

"I want you to wash yourself with these," he said.

"What's this?"

He looked down at his plate. "They're very cleansing. I think they would protect you."

I turned the packet over. "Is it Candomblé?" I asked.

"No. Well, not really."

"New Age?"

He looked up suddenly. "I don't think it's safe. These people you hang out with. You don't understand about Brazil. You like too much the simple people."

"How exactly do you define 'simple people'?" I asked, setting down my wineglass. The term *os simples* in Bahia was generally used by middle-class people when referring, in a fairly condescending way, to poorer people with no formal education, suggesting they did not possess equal intelligence.

"Those people you consider friends. You could get in trouble with them. The police could arrest them for marijuana smoking or something."

"You should talk," I said. "More middle-class people here smoke marijuana than the poor, as far as I can see. You really mean that I shouldn't associate with poor, darker people who live in the favelas, don't you?"

Mauro blew out air in frustration. "There you go again! You North Americans think you know everything. These people are more like beasts than they are like us. They live among the rats and the cockroaches!"

"Beasts."

"You mistranslate."

"Beast is a fairly basic Portuguese word."

"But you don't understand. You are using your First World brain here. You don't understand Bahia. I mean they're like the beasts in a good sense; they are closer to the earth than we are. They understand certain things we don't. They are people who live closer to nature."

"They do live closer to nature. Many have dirt floors and their sewage runs in front of their huts. We're not talking about Indians of the forest here, Mauro. We're talking about people who live in the same city you do, who want basically the same things you do, but who seldom have enough to eat and no chance of any decent education to give them a different life. How many times have you even entered one of the hundreds of favelas that surround this city, Mauro?"

"Don't be stupid."

"That means never, presumably."

"It does mean never. They're not good places, not for me, and certainly not for a woman like you. If you want to do research with these people, you should hire someone to interview them. You can get everything you need that way. You're deluded to call any one of these people 'friend.' They're only using you. They could get you involved with bad things and get you arrested."

I put down my napkin. "I am a foreigner here, and I don't pretend my country is any better," I said, "and there are many things I do not understand. Particularly about how the middle class here can live with so much misery surrounding them each day. How people like your mother can be delighted at the murder of malnourished, brutalized little boys..." I paused. "But I do know one thing." I stood up. "I don't think I can have dinner with you." I held out my hand. "Goodbye, Mauro."

Mauro looked at my hand. "What? You can't just go like that."

"And what about Luzia? She's middle-class. She associates with the 'simple' people."

"She shouldn't either. Luzia is an actress. No one can control her."

"I see. Thank you for inviting me to dinner, Mauro." I headed toward the door of the restaurant. Mauro followed me and stood in the doorway.

"You can't leave like this! How will you get home?"

"I'll take a bus. Like most the people who live here."

I walked to the curb and caught the first bus that came by. I had no idea where it was going, but it had to be better than where I was. I sat on the bus, and the woman sitting beside me touched my arm. "You're crying," she said.

"Yeah," I said, "yeah, I guess I am." I turned to the window and stared at my distorted reflection on the dark glass.

nine | rain

A month or so later, I was walking along a quiet road in central Salvador, looking for a certain shop. Two large men fell in step behind me. They began muttering insults. "Whore! Daughter of a big bitch. How about I fuck you, whore?"

After a time, I grew so annoyed that I turned around. "Don't you dare say such insults to me!" I shouted at them. "Just because I'm a foreigner and you think I don't understand doesn't give you any right. You wouldn't say that to a Brazilian woman. Give me the same respect!" Then I stomped into my shop.

When I came out, the men were still there. I crossed the street to avoid them, but they crossed as well. They rushed upon me. One of them grabbed my arm. They began to drag me into an alleyway. My response was so swift it surprised even me. I dropped to the ground and rolled onto my hands, a capoeira angola move that they were certainly not expecting, one that came to me without conscious thought. With one leg, I kicked one of the men in the groin as hard as I could. Then, with the other leg, I kicked upward and smashed the other's collarbone. I felt it snap. Then I sprang to my feet and ran away. Fast. The entire incident lasted less then ten seconds.

As I ran, expanding the distance between us, I felt an overpowering sense of exhilaration, joy, and exuberance that made me almost bound as I fled. It was adrenaline and power, sheer unadulterated power. I tried to tell myself that this was bad, that I should be feeling some compassion for those guys, that any violence was wrong, but even as I scolded myself, I giggled and pranced.

Afterward, I tried to analyze this exhilaration, to excuse it in some way, but I really couldn't. The pride continued as a bubbling undercurrent, and at practice I had to crow about the incident to our teacher and some fellow players. The other players joked and teased that they would have to be careful of me now.

"That's good," said the teacher. But he didn't smile, and he didn't really even look pleased. He did, however, begin to include me in the group of players he took to the other rodas in the city.

I became aware that, because of the strength of my daily practice and the lethal potential of capoeira, if I were in a conflict with someone, unless they had a weapon or knew capoeira themselves, I would likely win. I learned that this was not the kind of confidence people expected in a woman, and that if one had it, it gave one a great advantage. For example, I was walking down the street one day when a man leapt in front of me, prancing toward me in an aggressive manner. I was carrying my berimbau, something most tourists who visit Salvador buy. "Capoeirista!" he mocked while slapping his hands toward my face.

I continued to walk directly toward him. When we came level, I placed one foot on the side of his knee and sharply pushed. Not hard enough to break his leg, but enough to hurt. Then I smiled at him.

"Fuck!" he said and backed away.

What I did not understand was how to balance this newfound power with caution. This confidence protected me but also led me into spaces where I had no business being. One night, late, I was walking home along a dark street. It was a Sunday, the most deserted night of the week, and I was moving through the area known as Baixa dos Sapateiros, traditionally a shoemakers' street, but now a busy general shopping area during the day. On Sundays and during the nights, however, when it was deserted, it always felt dangerous. I generally avoided it during those times, but that particular night, the only bus I could get back into the center of town dropped me there.

In front of me, I saw a group of five men. One of them held a sixth man up by the scruff of his neck, a man who, from appearances, was a street person. The other men spat at the street man and laughed. "We can kill you," one said with a slightly drunken slur to his voice. "No one will care." The other four echoed his laughter.

I felt a surge of anger so fierce it surprised me. How dare these five healthy men threaten this half-starving fellow who had likely been sleeping on the sidewalk when they accosted him?

I walked up to the group and stared at them. I said nothing but my thoughts were so strong I think they reflected in my eyes. "Don't you dare touch him. You will not harm him as long as I'm here. I am his witness." I could almost hear my thoughts they were so loud. Fear or anxiety never entered my head. Nor did I think how strange it must have been for all six in the group to see a white, obvious foreigner, walking alone in the middle of the night on one of Salvador's dangerous streets, confronting them with such anger.

The man holding the street man dropped him. "Fuck!" he said. The street man made some small joke and ran. I walked straight through the group, down the block, and turned the corner up a side street. I did not look back.

Only after I had reached the relative safety of the more populated hilltop, did I begin to shake. The insanity of my actions crept through my fingertips and spread out from my shoulders. I stumbled twice on the ten flight climb to our floor and could hardly get the key in the lock.

"Are you drunk?" Luzia asked when I got inside. I shook my head, lay on my bed in the room we shared, and stared into the dark. It was a hot tropical night, but the sweat on my arms was icy.

Even after the research funding ran out and I was teaching at the university and doing various consulting jobs, I kept Rita on part-time as a research assistant. She knew every favela in the region and knew every capoeira mestre. Her knowledge of local history and her analytical abilities continued to stun me. She also clearly loved interviewing, spending long hours discussing theoretical issues related to race, class, and gender. I could hardly have had a better teacher.

One day we decided to interview the famous capoeira mestre, Paulo dos Anjos, Paul of the Angels, at his home in Malvinas, at the time considered the most dangerous and violent favela of the city. When we met at Salvador's central bus station, Rita looked me over.

"No watch?" she said. "No earrings? Good. You should probably give all your money to me to carry since you'll more likely be robbed than me."

I handed over my wallet. "You inspire such confidence, Rita. How badly do we need this interview? I mean, if even you're this nervous."

"Here's our bus!" We ran for the bus, paid our fare, and settled in for the long ride. "You can't write about capoeira without interviewing Paulo dos Anjos. And he's agreed to meet with us. He doesn't often do that."

"For you, he's agreed."

"I'll take that as a compliment."

"And so it was intended."

We sat and watched the mixture of high-rise buildings and vast tracts of shacks that was Salvador pass; then we turned onto the central highway that led out of the city. After about an hour, the bus turned off the highway onto a dirt track. Then it stopped. Everyone got off.

"Doesn't the bus go into Malvinas?" Rita asked the fare collector.

"Only this far," he said. "We've been held up too many times. When you want to leave, you can pick up the bus here."

"I see."

We descended from the bus and followed the other passengers along the dirt track away from the highway. The shacks were further apart here than closer to town, and each one was attached to a small piece of land. Space for a garden, I thought.

"This actually looks pretty, Rita. Not so crowded. I like it."

"Yeah. It looks that way." Rita's voice clearly revealed her opinion to the contrary. She stopped a young boy standing beside the path watching us. "Where does Mestre Paulo dos Anjos live?"

"The Mestre knows you're coming?" the boy asked.

"Yes."

The boy thought a moment. "I'll walk you there," he said.

We followed him perhaps a half mile to a central square, a dusty dirt area where several tracks met. We continued past a shack bar that looked abandoned, another bar-like structure that appeared to be a store with nothing to sell, and a group of boys playing soccer. Everyone stared at us as we passed.

"Wait here," the boy said. "I'll tell the Mestre you're here."

We stood in the shade of the tin awning that hung above the outside counter to the shop. "We're here to see Mestre Paulo dos Anjos," Rita said as a way of explaining our—or my—presence.

A woman next to us nodded. "The Mestre."

Soon the boy returned with a frail-looking man.

"Mestre," Rita said.

"I've seen you play before," Paulo dos Anjos said. "And you play the berimbau. You should come to our roda sometime."

"I'd love to," Rita said. "This is my friend, Danger."

Paulo dos Anjos nodded to me and turned back to Rita. "We have a girl in our group now," he said. "You should play with her."

We walked along the path, Rita and Paulo dos Anjos in front, me behind. He took us to the building where he taught capoeira. "Do you mind if we record our conversation?" Rita asked.

Paulo dos Anjos looked at me. "As long as no one makes any money from it, I don't mind," he said.

"She's at a university. I work with her."

Paulo dos Anjos nodded. "That's all right. What do you want to know from an old man like me? I don't know so much."

Rita laughed. "Mestre. Every capoeira angola group in the city has your sayings printed on their walls."

Paulo dos Anjos smiled. He knew this to be true. "I have played a few years. Capoeira, she has taught me some things of life. And of death too."

As they began to talk, Paulo dos Anjos spoke of his life in capoeira, of his many students—now well-known teachers themselves—of his spiritual ideas, of stories he knew of capoeira history, of early fights and escapes from police. Then, gradually, he began to speak of his children, the ones he knew he had, then more about his students.

"We're having an event soon. You should come." He nodded to me, extending the invitation to me as well. I nodded, gratified at being included. "Let me show you what we're doing." We walked to the back of the building. Some students had arrived for a class, boys in ragged shorts, bare feet, only a few in white. "I teach anyone. I live for capoeira, not from it." Suddenly we heard rain on the tin roof. It got louder and louder as the tropical torrent increased. We looked out the door. The dirt paths had turned to muddy streams. "You'd better wait," Paulo dos Anjos said. We waited over an hour. It was well past dark by then.

"What time's the last bus?" Rita asked.

"Yes," Paulo dos Angos said. "That is a problem. You don't want to miss that. You'd better go now." He looked into the dark outside. "But you shouldn't go alone. It isn't safe, you know." He slipped on his sandals.

"No, no, Mestre," Rita said. "You'll get wet." But her voice carried little conviction and Paulo dos Anjos did not even bother to answer her. So we sloshed through the streams, the three of us, through the dark of Malvinas, two women, one clearly a foreigner, and an old man. But I felt completely safe, knowing that this man's reputation, built over a half century, protected us. We reached the place where the bus had stopped.

"*Oi*, Mestre!" a young boy shouted. "You aren't going to catch a bus, are you? They've gone! They don't come off the highway after dark anymore!" We stood in silence a moment.

"We'll go out to the highway," Rita said. "We should be able to get a bus there."

Paulo dos Anjos slowly nodded his head. "Yes, that is the best. Two girls like yourselves. Any bus will stop."

We bade goodbye and walked toward the highway. The rain came so thick we could hardly see. Malvinas had no street lights. We walked along the highway until we found a bus stop. We waited, our hair and clothes soaked. After a half an hour Rita saw a bus in the distance. She began to wave, but it didn't even slow. It rushed by, spraying us with mud and water.

"I was afraid of this," Rita said. "Buses won't stop on this part of the highway at night. Not even for women. Here." She pushed me forward. "Maybe they'll stop if they see you first, a white woman."

"They're going to think it's strange," I said.

"True," Rita said, "but perhaps they'll stop."

In the next half hour, two buses passed, both at full speed, not slowing an iota when they saw me. The rain continued unabated.

"How much money do you have with you?" Rita finally asked.

"About ten *reais* in my wallet that I gave you and another twenty in my bra."

"Good." Rita smiled. "I don't think any bus is going to stop for us here. They probably think there's some robber hiding in the dark behind us ready to hijack the bus if they stop. We'll take a taxi to my house. It's much closer than yours. You can go home in the morning." Rita waved at the first taxi she saw. It slowed, then stopped. We climbed in and Rita quickly negotiated the price.

"Pretty dangerous place for you to be standing," the driver said once the price had been agreed upon. "I wouldn't want my sister out there."

"No," Rita said. "The buses weren't stopping."

"They never stop here after dark."

"What happens if you want to go somewhere in the evening?" I asked.

"You don't," the driver said. "Or you come back the next day."

"I was surprised you stopped," I said. "If a bus wouldn't stop, why did you?"

The driver laughed. "I'm only responsible for me. And if I see someone coming out of the bushes, I can just pull away fast. People are also less likely to rob me than a bus—the robbers here know that we taxi drivers can generally defend ourselves."

I didn't ask how.

We arrived at Rita's neighborhood, and the driver dropped us off as close as he could get to Rita's house.

"Be careful of the stairs," Rita said as she unlocked the iron gate. "I haven't finished them yet." I remembered the stairway and trod carefully in the dark. Rita went first and unlocked the house door. I walked in, and she switched on a light.

As the room illuminated, I stepped into another world. Rita had transformed her house. The living and dining rooms were now one airy, open space. White tile covered the floors, and the walls were trimmed in beautiful Amazon dark wood. The windows were covered with skillfully crafted shutters of the same rich wood. The kitchen was open, separated from the dining room by a half wall topped with wood and tile. The living room contained two sofas, a stereo, and a table. In the dining room stood a lovely wooden table and matching chairs. The dark and white of the decor was offset by varied rich greens of the tropical plants in pots around the rooms and hanging from the ceiling.

"What happened, Rita? This is incredible!"

Rita laughed in delight as she handed me some dry clothes and a towel to dry my hair. She set about making tea. "Didn't I tell you? I won my suit."

"The one about you getting fired?"

"Yeah. They paid me an entire year's wages and then some. So I finished my house with it. Except the top verandah. And the stairs. I ran out of money for those."

"That's incredible. So the system does work, you can sue against wrongs of racial discrimination."

"Well, sometimes. The law is written in favor of the plaintiff, but the reality is that most plaintiffs would not, and cannot, get a lawyer."

"But you did."

"I am the exception." She handed me a cup of tea and sat on the sofa across from me. I had changed into the shorts and shirt she gave me and was sitting with my feet curled up beneath me. Rita's home had become an oasis hidden in the midst of this favela.

"You're the only Brazilian I know who has designed her kitchen so that it's part of the dining room. This looks much more like a European home than a Brazilian one."

"I designed it the way I thought I'd like my house to be, light and airy. The main difference, Margaret, is that I have designed it to never have a maid. Nearly all Brazilian homes, including the apartments, have a maid's room. The kitchen is closed off because that's where the maid is. You don't want to have to encounter her cooking and washing in front of your guests. I'll never have a maid, so I'll be doing the cooking. And I want to talk with my friends while I cook."

"A political choice, I gather."

"Yes, of course. The only way the patronage system of Brazil is going to change is for the middle class to start taking care of themselves and cleaning after themselves—in more ways than one." Rita laughed again and took a sip of her tea. "This is easy for me to say, of course. I love to cook."

ten
burnt knives

Local research assistants have always formed the backbone of anthropological research. I was very lucky to have worked with first Fernando, and then Rita. My anthropologist friend Don also had a brilliant research assistant, Keila. Keila was a transvestite prostitute, mannish, squat, medium dark skinned with frizzy hair that she dyed blond. She was also highly intelligent. She had an analytical mind and explained to Don the meanings of colloquial words. She helped him transcribe and interpret interviews. She also read Brazilian research articles about transvestites and offered her opinions of them to Don. On top of all this, Keila was a wonderful cook and had several times prepared special meals for Don and myself, examples of her own particular Bahia recipes.

She often regaled us with stories of her previous night's encounters. She had plenty of business. Men with particularly large members often got sex for free. Keila would graphically describe their huge dimensions. I had no idea if her stories bore any relationship to reality or if, in the manner of a good fish story, size depended upon the audience.

Among anthropologists, there are some who conduct their field-work at a distance, remaining in comfortable living situations and visiting their field site each day—the kind of anthropologist Mauro wished I were. Then there are those, and my friend Don was one of these, who live cheek by jowl with the people with whom they do research. In keeping with his (and my) idea of "good" fieldwork, Don rented himself a room in the tenement where the transvestites lived. This tenement was located on a street that my friends who have lived in the favelas all their lives were nervous to walk during the day, let alone at night. The building was late eighteenth-century and had not been repaired for more than fifty years. The planked floors were rotted, the walls dripped mold. The building housed perhaps fifty people who shared a single toilet at the back. Rats hid beneath the meager furniture and bolted across the room if someone sat on a sofa too hard. Behind the toilet was a large open area a floor below the level of the main building floor. Everyone threw their garbage there.

This garbage was never removed, and with the coming of dusk, the entire pile would become a swarming, seething mass of huge rats. One could lean over the concrete railing on the main floor at dusk and watch them.

Beside the toilet was a dark stairway that led below. There, beneath the stairs, lived those who could not afford the rent of the rooms above. They still paid rent, however. These basement dwellers included a few families who survived by selling *cafezinhos*–small shots of coffee–or popsicles on the street, but most were prostitutes, often single young mothers, who had few possessions and preferred to spend their money on clothes and perfume than rent. "Especially," Don commented, "since they might skip town at any moment."

Don's room was near the front on the upper floor. In an attempt to cheer the place up, he'd painted the entire room pink. He bought a narrow bed and a small writing table. Despite his beautification endeavor, he found he was unable to sleep because cockroaches kept falling on his head, so he hung a brightly colored cloth across the ceiling. I visited him a few days afterward.

"The ceiling cloth has a strange sag," I said. Don took one look at the ceiling and put down his pen. The sag, of course, was an accumulation of cockroaches waiting to cascade down in one huge mass. We walked out of the room.

Don and I had actually met each other some ten years before while we were both doing fieldwork for our doctoral dissertations in Papua New Guinea. There is a bond anthropologists gain in the field that is like no other friendship I know. We tend to learn obscure languages and have deep experiences that, when related to outsiders, sound like long travel monologues—or like bragging about all the exotic places we've known. But, with each other, we can relax and find unembarrassed joy in speaking together languages only heard in remote jungles—or relishing colorful slang only used on the streets of Salvador. Don first came to Salvador to visit me, and because he was looking for a new field site, I showed him the best time I could; I wanted him to return. I knew that with him I could giggle, or grow over experiences no one else would understand. Don, with his pert nose and gentle smile (belying his often acerbic commentary on the world), was the only person I had ever met, Brazilian or otherwise, who, within a day of arriving in Salvador, and after I had dragged him to a capoeira roda—which completely bored him—decided to walk back to my apartment alone at night. I let him go because I knew that he, unlike most other people, would survive the walk.

Like me, Don became fascinated with Salvador, received a grant for research, and had then returned. He is an annoyingly good linguist and he learned Portuguese quickly. His plan was to stay about a year, then write a book on the sex and gender complexities of the transvestite prostitutes. Unlike me, he followed his plan. He also somehow managed to keep his relationship with his boyfriend intact. When, after about a year, he told me he was leaving, going back to Sweden and his boyfriend, I nodded and wished him luck. But I felt bereft. With whom now could I talk about the elements of Salvador that almost drove me mad with anger? Who would I tell about the horrors of the poverty, the complacency of the middle class, of the parts I had come to detest?

I hadn't seen Agnaldo at capoeira for some months. When I asked our teacher about him, he just shrugged. "He'll show up when he wants to," he said.

Finally, he did, but something seemed wrong. Agnaldo had always been slender, but now his high cheekbones jutted too far above hollows where his cheeks had once been. His eyes darted around in a disturbing way, and his concentration when he played, always brilliant before, was erratic. I didn't want to say anything to others in the group, but I wondered if something had happened, if he was depressed and drinking more, or if, perhaps, he had some degenerative illness. When Agnaldo invited me to his home to discuss the history of Candomblé in Salvador, I was pleased, more for the chance to talk with him privately than anything else.

The following Sunday I went to Pelourinho to find him. The local government had recognized the tourist potential of Pelourinho and was investing millions in its restoration. Tattered old buildings were being gutted and rebuilt. The façades were being restored with remarkable skill, transformed from derelict structures into stunning mint condition edifices, complete with traditional detail and craft work. The former residents had been paid a stipend and forcibly evicted to neighborhoods out by the airport. Our old capoeira space, from which we had been evicted the year before, was now a ballet school. The old bars were unrecognizable as swanky jazz clubs. The change was swift. Pelourinho was becoming tourist central. I heard it now referred to as "The Historic District."

But when I walked through the tunnel to the hillside near Agnaldo's home, nothing had changed, except, I thought, it looked a bit shabbier with some particularly ratty looking new shacks near the entrance of the tunnel. The other shacks and trees still stood as they had when I first arrived. People stared at me as I walked down the path alone. The wind blew warm, and I could hear birds in the trees.

As I neared Agnaldo's home, a sense of disorientation crept over me. The small front porch area—dirt shaded by a tin roof—was filthy. Rubbish and debris were everywhere. Chickens ate the refuse, and I could smell excrement nearby. The single door and window both stood open.

Suddenly, a woman burst from the door.

"Get to work, you fucking bitch!" a man shouted from inside. It did not sound like Agnaldo. The woman started as she saw me, but quickly reverted to disinterest, her skin and eyes slack. She wore too much makeup and high heels. The makeup did not hide the bruises that covered her face and shoulders.

"Are you all right?" I asked. She didn't even bother to answer. She trudged up the hill toward the street, toward tourists, and, presumably, paying clients.

I paused before the house, then decided to leave before anyone else emerged. But I hesitated too long. A skinny, short man with a tattered shirt came out. He stared at me.

"What are you doing here?"

"I was supposed to meet Agnaldo," I said.

"Oh. Yeah. Well." And he stepped inside to the dark. A few seconds later Agnaldo emerged. He seemed completely drunk, hardly able to stand; his eyes seemed sunken into his face too far. He stared at me for a moment, almost without recognition.

"I'll come back another time," I said.

"Oh. Danger. Were you coming today? I wasn't thinking you were coming."

"That's OK. I'll come back another day. We can talk later."

Agnaldo took me by the arm. "No, no. You should come in. We

can talk. I didn't remember the day."

"No," I said, trying to disentangle my arm. "Really, I can come back."

"No, no," said Agnaldo. "Come in. You have to meet my girl-friend. She's sleeping in the back. She's pregnant, you know." He dragged me inside.

It took a moment for my eyes to adjust to the darkness after the bright of the sun outside. When they did, I saw people everywhere. Bits and pieces of rubbish littered the dirt floor. The stove and radio were gone and only a few scattered boxes remained as furniture. Two women lay sprawled against one wall. Another woman sat on the floor holding a pot full of beans. A small boy, about two, stood in front of her. The woman slapped the beans ineffectively with a spoon, her arm seeming to have no strength or coordination. The boy leaned over and picked out single beans, eating them. Then he stumbled and fell, face first, into the beans. He tried to pull himself out and began to scream. The woman hit him with the spoon, with no power behind the hit, and told him to shut up. He wandered away, wiping beans from his face with his hand and eating them.

Agnaldo pulled me into the windowless back room. I could hardly see. I discerned a mat on the floor covered with some material, perhaps sheets, perhaps clothes. A woman lay there and a man sat against the wall. Agnaldo sat next to the woman on the mat. "Get up! Get up! We have a friend here. I want you to meet her. It's my capoeira friend."

The woman opened her eyes languidly and Agnaldo propped her to a sitting position. She was perhaps six months pregnant. She held out her hand in greeting. I took it and, unsure what to do, sat on the mat beside her.

"Do you want some coffee?" Agnaldo asked.

"No, thank you," I said. There was clearly no coffee nor any way to make coffee in the house.

"Well, we can share this then," and Agnaldo took from his shorts a packet that he unrolled to reveal white powder. He laid out little piles of the powder on a cloth covering a board. He pulled out a straw.

"Is that crack?" I asked, using the word derived from the English.

Agnaldo looked at me blankly, then used a slang term I didn't know. "It's good. You'll like it."

Many people I knew in Salvador used marijuana, and cocaine also seemed popular. People on the streets sniffed glue to dull hunger pains and to give themselves a brain-killing high. Prescription drugs were also readily available and, I knew, used widely by street workers of all kinds. But crack was new. From my observations, it had come into Salvador in a one-month period in January 1996 on a well-organized distribution plan. I never learned who was behind this organized move—I considered direct questions on this topic dangerous enough to be foolhardy, and besides, the people I knew clearly only knew how they bought it, not the larger infrastructure.

From street conversations, I heard only vague rumors, but the change had been dramatic. Because of his close association with the transvestite prostitutes, Don saw the effects of crack more quickly than I did. One month, no one had it; the next, every prostitute had it for sale or knew someone who did. People sold it cheap and, Don was told, cut it with talc or speed (or whatever cheap white powder substance they could find).

Agnaldo's girlfriend rose to a kneeling position and snorted some of the white powder, then the man nearby. Agnaldo then offered the straw to me.

"No, thank you," I said. "I have a capoeira roda later."

"But it will be good for our talk," Agnaldo said.

"That's fine."

Agnaldo snorted a pile of the white substance and quickly slumped against the wall.

I sat confused as I watched the three of them zone out. This was too strong. Could it be some heroin-crack mix? As I stood, I realized I was shaking.

"I'll see you later, Agnaldo," I said. He stared at me, his eyes vacant. I stumbled to the outer room, and one of the women grabbed my hand. "Are you Dutch?" she asked.

"No," I said, trying to disengage my hand.

"I am going to Holland," she said. "I can dance. They like dancers there, I hear. I am going there, and I can make a lot of money there. Are you Dutch? You look Dutch."

"No," I said, "no, I am not Dutch." I heard my voice break.

I ran from the house and stumbled up the path. The man with the tattered shirt sat under a nearby tree. As I passed, he fell in step behind me. "I'll walk with you," he said. "It isn't safe here to walk alone."

"I'm fine."

"No," he said. "I'll walk with you."

I was almost running now. The man stayed close behind. I rushed to the tunnel, seeing Agnaldo's ravaged face in the shadows, racing across the damp cobblestone.

Suddenly the man shoved me hard from behind. I stumbled and hit the side of the tunnel. He pushed me against it, my back to the wall. I felt the drip of slimy water seeping from the ancient building above. He shoved his face close to mine, and I felt his foul breath.

"You're beautiful," he said. "I want to kiss you."

"Fuck off," I said.

"Then I'll rape you."

I smashed him in the groin with my knee. Then I picked him up under the armpits and tossed him against the far side of the tunnel. He slammed against the wall and hit his head. He began to slide down the wall, seemingly unconscious.

I ran from the tunnel. "Fuck," I said, "Fuck. Fuck."

I tried to breathe, but my lungs had shut down. Blinding sunlight hit me. I tripped on a stone and fell into the street. A car honked, and nearly hit me. I knocked into two tourists looking at a basket for sale.

"*Oi* gringa, you want something?" the vendor asked. I ignored him and fled up the street toward the main praça.

"Hey, capoeira friend!" someone shouted to me across the street.

I looked up to see Marcos, the fellow who'd been beaten by the policeman years before. He still defiantly wore bright loose Africanist clothes and dreadlocks to his waist. He gave me a wide smile and waved his crutch. Since leaving the hospital, one leg had shriveled to a long hanging flap that he dragged along. He propelled himself with his other leg and his crutches. He had stopped drinking, and he now painted bright pictures that he sold to tourists in this Historic District. He lived with a girlfriend. From all reports, he was doing well.

With a pretense of normality, I waved back and indicated that I had to hurry, but would catch him next time. At the top of the hill, at the main praça, I slowed, steadfastly ignoring the many vendors who shouted at me. "Amiga! You speak French? You speak German? You speak Italian? You are beautiful, gringa. You want to buy?"

At that moment, I knew I would always be a stranger in Salvador. I wanted to go home. I just wasn't sure where that was.

A few nights later, I wandered down a central city street, a soft wind touching my hair and a full moon over the bay. I listened to the litany of the men I passed: "Sexy, you look delicious. Amiga. Gringa. Beautiful, beautiful, come with me." Because of my physical appearance, everyone knew I was a foreigner. Even if I lived in Salvador twenty more years, this would not change.

I had been speaking that afternoon with a man of German ancestry whose family had lived in Bahia for three generations. He laughed when I told him of my feelings of alienation in Bahia, of always being the outsider. "I am *baiano*," he said, "I was born here. But in the popular concept, I am too white to be *baiano*. People always take me for a foreigner. And this is in my homeland."

Rita, who was quite dark, walked with street confidence, a classic *baiana*. But, walking with me caused her periodic identity crises because through visible association with me, people often included her in their foreigner-directed commentaries or demands for money. One time she stopped dead in the middle of the street and began shouting to the vendors and anyone else who cared to listen. "I am not a foreigner! I am *baiana*! Leave me alone!"

I suggested that she walk apart, disclaiming acquaintanceship with me. She growled that she didn't believe in such discrimination. "You just have to become more black," she said.

My concern was not robbery, violence, or any other disaster, but how ethnicity, nationality, and economics affected relationships between me and the people I had grown to love. How much of what Mauro said was true? Rita, Luzia, Jorge and his family, Gato, Agnaldo—what was the reality of their expressed affection, of their repeated endearments, calling me their *nêga* (black one), telling me that although my skin was white my soul was *baiana*? These assurances of acceptance fractured like light on the broken stones of the mosaic sidewalk. I was like a piece of chalk left outside, waiting for the first rain. Such a rain would melt me.

Insecurity, the vagabond's bane. When I went from being a traveler to resident, I became involved. I was now unsure which, if any, locale I considered "home." I had also lived in Europe and Australia, but they were not "home." I slid between communities, change itself being my most solid constant. I realized that it was friendship that made my life possible.

As I toyed with the idea of returning to the States, a place I had not lived for years, I wondered what connections I would make with old friends there. Or how I could leave these friends in Salvador behind. The ones in Salvador I would place in a memory box, petrified in time and space until I saw them again. The friendships in the States could, by now, for all I knew, be destroyed through neglect and perspectives that were literally a world apart.

I considered the difference between the vitality of an immediate friendship and the memory of a friend, how the memory increasingly becomes a personal invention bearing less and less connection to a real person. How much disjuncture would I find between my memories and the memories my friends had each created of me?

I tried to walk relaxed, but confusion, and the knowledge of loneliness, gnawed at me like the rats I feared. Then, on one corner, I saw an old woman, a peanut vendor I had seen many times before. She was stooped from years of hard labor and osteoporosis, her hair bound beneath a bright red scarf that accentuated the gauntness of her jaw. She roasted peanuts over a charcoal fire and served them warm in paper cones. Over the years, when I bought her peanuts, we'd pause and chat about local politics, a subject about which she had strong and informed opinions. I learned a great deal from her.

She looked at me intently and then gave me a huge smile.

"Don't be sad," she said. "My peanuts, they keep the heart warm."

eleven
a stranger

Luzia moved south for an acting gig, and we gave up the apartment. While I was trying to figure out what to do next, Rita kindly invited me to stay with her. I was sleeping in her living room. One day, I returned to the apartment after visiting a friend, lay down on the mat she'd prepared for me, and felt the symptoms of dengue fever. I had caught it before, so I recognized the signs immediately.

Dengue fever is transmitted by a mosquito. It was limited to Asia for some time but had recently spread to South America. In the city of Salvador, it was an epidemic. Its symptoms include violent headache, high fever, change of pressure behind the eyeballs that makes them feel as though they're being wrenched from your skull, an intense aching of the bones that turns into unendurable internal itching, and the inability to get up or eat anything. Rita was away visiting her father and not expected to return for a week and a half.

From a nearby bar, a band blasted out samba music, the singer continually flat. At midnight, a fundamentalist Protestant church began a service, and the preacher screamed in competition with the samba. Soon, it started to pour. This did not dampen the spirits of the noisemakers, but a waterfall erupted from under the wooden shutters and began to cascade down the living room wall. I hurriedly gathered my things and moved them across the room. By the time I got to the mat, it too was soaked. I found rags that clearly had been used for this purpose before and piled them along the bottom of the window frame. I started to mop the floor, but could feel the dengue gaining in strength. I stumbled to Rita's bed and collapsed.

I passed out. When I regained consciousness, I realized I could no longer move. This attack was worse than my previous two. My bones had ached intensely before, but now they felt as though they were shattering, breaking into a thousand pieces and then breaking again. I tried again to move, to prop myself up on a single elbow but my body refused to cooperate. Interesting, I thought, only vaguely concerned, I cannot reach even those pools of water beneath the window, let alone the kitchen sink. Thirst could kill me before Rita returned.

You should survive, I thought. Look at your friends. Survival is like an undulating litany to them. Survive, at all costs. Survive, and those who don't, watch them pass with more determination to survive yourself.

Some survive better than others, I thought. Gato—would he survive? He'd left the capoeira room one night after rats had eaten his clothes. He'd stayed with Luzia and me for a week or so and was now sleeping in a back closet of a friend's bar, helping out in exchange, acting as a night security guard. He told me that a female European visitor had come for a few weeks and developed a passion for him. She wanted to pay his way to Europe so he could live with her there. After much self-doubt about whether this was prostitution or if he was allowing himself to be enticed into some kind of sexual slavery, he had decided to go.

"What other chance do I have?" he asked. "I think she's a good person."

What would I do in his situation? I thought. "Be careful," I said. "Try to figure a way to teach capoeira, to make your own money, as fast as possible."

"Yeah," he said. "That's my only independence, isn't it?"

I asked about his family. He said that his sister, Renata, who was now sixteen, was still going to school. I smiled and shook my head. Gato didn't smile and pretended that his sister's continuance at school was of no interest to him at all.

Of all my friends in Brazil who were not from middle-class families, only Rita had continued school beyond grade six. The capoeira teacher managed first grade. Jorge, by going to night school, was, at age twenty-five, in grade six. Gato said he had finished grade five. According to official statistics, the majority of African-Brazilians in the northeast of Brazil were illiterate. Children began very young to contribute to a family's survival, and even if parents sacrificed the children's potential income, bus fare and school materials were luxuries that families who often did not have enough money for food could seldom afford.

This year, Gato said, Renata would finish all the schooling available to her in their small town. On all the visits I had made to Gato's family since his run-in with the sheriff, Renata was always studying: Reading after she'd fetched the water from the well, writing after she'd laid the washing in the sun to dry, doing her math in a tattered notebook as she sat beside the dusty track in front of their home. She used each notebook again and again, doing her assignments, and then carefully erasing them.

She always said she wanted to go to university, and each year I expected to hear that she had given up, that a boyfriend had convinced her to get married or that she had gone to work as a maid in some middle-class household. But so far, this had not happened. Over the five years I had known this family, Renata's will had continued, a flame that refused to be extinguished.

I asked Gato what she planned to do.

"She's going to Feira de Santana," Gato said. The nearest high school of reasonable quality was in Ferra Santana, a city about two hours away.

"How can you pay for that? Where will she stay?"

"She'll stay with an aunt. No, we don't have money." He laughed. "She says she's going anyway."

In the midst of this—or some other—rumination, I thought I heard Rita's door open. Perhaps it's a robber, I thought. They could kill me and save me the torture of dying of thirst.

Then, through blurred vision, I thought I saw Rita's face. It disappeared just as quickly. Oh well, I thought, as consciousness slipped away again. Hallucinations.

Some time later I awoke to feel someone tugging on my arm. Pain shot through me. I yelled and opened my eyes. Cecilia, Edilson, and Rita stood around me.

"Come on," Cecilia said. "Let me help you up."

"I'm sorry to call you so late," Rita said. "You were the only people I could think of who had a car."

"Of course you should have called," Edilson said. "I've already called the hospital and told them to expect us."

I tried to turn my head to look at Rita as she supported me with her arms around my waist. "Why are you here?" I struggled to shape the words. "You're supposed to be gone."

"Don't try to talk," Rita snapped. Then she spoke in a softer voice. "I had a feeling something was wrong, so I caught a late bus back this evening."

I said nothing. I hung like a corpse between Rita and Edilson. Among the confusing shadows, I kept thinking about the strange eddies that make up survival.

"Where's your key, Rita?" Cecilia asked. She opened the door for us. "I'll lock up behind you. And make sure she doesn't trip on the steps."

At the hospital, a doctor injected me with something. Cecilia passed them my credit card. I fell asleep and woke up again at Rita's. I still couldn't get up, but I could eat if Rita helped me. She said I could only eat certain foods, and she made me drink disgusting tea. She said it was medicinal. My eyes throbbed, and I lay for days with a cloth over them. Rita dosed me with very strong Tylenol, the only thing that apparently works to lower the fever. After about a week, the "healing" itching began, and I writhed on my mat on the floor in irritated agony.

"You are a terrible patient," Rita told me, forcing yet more tea down my throat. After about two weeks, I was reasonably recovered enough to make my debut back on the street. Nobody seemed to notice much.

I decided to leave Brazil at the end of my visiting teaching contract at the university. I couldn't face looking for another apartment, and poor Rita had endured far more than could be expected of any friend. I was originally from the Pacific Northwest, where my biological family still lived, so I began to look for teaching positions near Seattle. Perhaps there, I thought, I would find solidity.

After I told Jorge of my plans, his family invited me to a good-bye lunch. I ran from the bus to their house through a tropical downpour, the streets running with mud, each one a small, silted torrent. I sprinted from shop to shop, leaping over the sewage and garbage that came sliding into the road with the mud. It was no surprise that entire communities slid away during Salvador's rainy seasons.

Jorge's family was their usual joyous collective. But then they brought in little Mauro. He looked very skinny. He leapt onto my lap; I touched his slender arm but said nothing. Zezé noticed my glance.

"Did you not know?" she said. "João got shot, two months ago. He and friends were coming home from watching Olodum at a music show. They were waiting by a bus stop at the center, and there was a man fighting with a woman. João, like everyone else, went over to look. Then the man turned around and shot him."

Mauro wrapped his arms around my neck. I remembered João with this boy on his shoulders, running down the street, pretending to be a horse, Mauro screaming with laughter, the neighbors egging him on. João told clever stories and terrible jokes. He was always proudest of the bad jokes.

"What did the police do?" I asked.

"Nothing. The killer—he was middle-class—said João assaulted him and he shot in self-defense. Many people came forward as witnesses, saying that João was only a passing spectator, that the murderer killed for no reason, but," Zezé began laying the table for lunch, "none of those giving evidence were middle-class, so the police ignored them."

"So they did nothing? The man never went to prison?"

Zezé smiled at me and ruffled Mauro's head. "And this is a pain," she said. "Since the death he just keeps getting thinner and thinner."

Jorge walked in with his new girlfriend. She looked about fifteen. After lunch, he and I drank a coffee together on their front verandah that overlooked the street.

"What's your girlfriend's name?" I asked.

"Lucinha. Pretty, isn't she?"

"Yeah. Pretty young."

"She's sixteen. But she's very smart, Margaret. She wants to finish high school, go to university and become a doctor."

"What grade's she in now?"

"Six. She works as a maid and goes to school at night. We only get to see each other on Sunday."

"What happens if she gets pregnant?"

Jorge looked at me with mock horror and laughed. "We're not having sex yet."

"Really?"

"Really. I want to support her, help her become a doctor. She can read really well, Margaret. Maybe I haven't done so well, but I think I can help her do what I haven't."

"You're pretty smart, Jorge. And what about capoeira? You aren't coming to practice anymore. What's up with that? You and Gato are the best, you know. You could be a teacher, make money that way."

"Yeah." Jorge fidgeted, pulling on his fingers. "I'm doing weight training now. I get so tired. I'm working as a porter at the school now. It pays eighty dollars a month, so I have to work during the day too. I help a mechanic down the road." We sat in silence a moment or two, sipping on our coffee. Steam rose off the dirt street as the heat dried the mud.

"I want to build a place of my own," Jorge said, "where Lucinha and I can live, so I can move out of my parents' house. When I'm not working or sleeping, I want to spend time with Lucinha. And capoeira costs money—for the bus. Our teacher doesn't pay me when I teach for him. And I have to pay for the bus both ways."

"Yeah. I can see that. That's hard."

Jorge got up and shouted at Mauro, who was now in the street playing. "Did you hear about Agnaldo?" he asked me.

"No."

"He died."

I sat still on the folding chair. Jorge put his arm around my shoulders. "I'm sorry. You didn't hear, did you?"

"No." An image flashed before me of Agnaldo's zoned-out face, then an earlier one of his smile as he played capoeira with me. "How did he die?"

"Beans."

"What?"

"Because of the heat. Beans are a heavy food. People eat them when it's too muggy, too humid, and they die of stomach heat. Their stomach gets too hot and they die."

"What do the doctors call this?"

Jorge shrugged. "I don't know. It happens all the time."

Agnaldo. Through the dust and afternoon heat, I began to hear his music. I saw his face, full of so much intelligence, so much promise, and so much joy. Destroyed by crushing, mind-numbing poverty. I hate this country, I thought. I hate it.

The day before my flight to Seattle, I met an Englishman at capoeira who was a student of one of my friends in England. I took him around the city for a half a day. He had English pink cheeks and looked about twenty. He and his girlfriend had come to Brazil with very little money, and he had already found a job teaching English for about ten dollars an hour—an excellent hourly wage. The job was four hours a week, and he and his girlfriend planned to live on his earnings.

"That's not much to live on," I said.

"People here live on sixty dollars a month," he said. "I want to live simply, like people here."

We went to their apartment, a small two-bedroom in a middle-class area. The air was thick with marijuana smoke despite an open window. On the small stereo they had clearly brought with them, Indian sitar music played.

I smiled and suddenly felt old.

"We plan to go camping," his girlfriend said. "Take our tent and live off the land somewhere north of here on the beach."

"That might be difficult," I said. I constructed in my head the scene: in a small beach-side town a group of locals watch in utter amazement as two foreigners, clearly loaded with valuables, put all their belongings into a flimsy cloth shelter and then blithely walk away, leaving everything behind.

"I'd give your tent five minutes before it disappears," I said.

A twilight moon shone through the window, and I wanted to be outside. The man got up to change the CD.

"The people here are so honest. Not like people in England," he said. The new music sounded like Eastern meditation chimes.

"Do either of you speak Portuguese?"

The woman crossed her legs under her on the couch. "We find goodness is the same the world over," she said. "We don't really need Portuguese to communicate. We see people, we smile, and we all understand each other. It's in the energy."

I realized that I must sound like a lecturing know-it-all. It was time to leave.

part two | treading water

twelve | encountering seattle

I was offered a temporary teaching position north of Seattle, for which I was grateful, but I knew I couldn't handle small-town America just yet. I wanted to be near the bigger city, but the city disoriented me. It was so encumbered with…stuff. I found it hard to shop in the large grocery stores; I became lost in the overwhelming selection of too many items. I decided to move to Vashon, an island near Seattle that was easily accessible to the city via a fifteen minute ferry ride. I thought I wanted tranquility, solitude, and quiet.

Soon after my arrival, I was standing with some newfound friends near Pioneer Square, a touristy downtown "historic area" (shades of Salvador). People packed the chilly autumn street, laughing, talking, and shouting to each other from sidewalk to sidewalk. A squadron of motorcycles zoomed by, then parked along the curb. My friends and I were waiting to be let into a crowded dance bar. We were not the first in line.

A man, drunk and dark-skinned with black hair, walked near the first couple in line. Under his arm he carried what appeared to be a bedroll and a jacket.

"It's a good night," he said, slurring his words.

The couple pretended they hadn't heard.

"It's a good night," he said more aggressively to the couple next in line. That couple shifted so the woman stood on the inside, protected by her companion.

"It's a fucking good night," the man said to me, standing close to my face.

"Yes, it is," I said, "it's a very good night." I looked at the Northern sky. "You won't get rained on tonight."

The man looked at me and smiled. "Thank you," he said and stumbled away.

Boundaries have always fascinated me, and now they seemed everywhere. We use boundaries to give our world definition—boundaries of space, of time, of dimension, of the inanimate and animate, of the living and the dead. Boundaries also influence the way we construct our identity; with them we mark private and public space. They allow the entire concept of possession to exist: our nation, our home, our family, our traditions, our ethnicity.

And what constitutes compassion? How does it relate to boundaries? Does compassion, as distinct from pity, mean crossing skin-defined borders to a space outside of one's body? Is compassion that ability to move out of the narrow perspective with which we generally contain our worlds and reverse it, actually place ourselves outside of our selves? How much is this possible? Perhaps the ultimate personal boundary is not life and death, but self and non-self.

A few days after the bar incident, I encountered what I think I recognized as true compassion in the sense I was exploring. I went for a walk along a residential street near Seattle's downtown. Beside the sidewalk, I saw two huge bins of vegetables, one of red peppers. Crowds of people milled around the bins. I strolled over.

"You have to go inside first," a man said.

"Oh." I headed to the warehouse beside us.

Inside the warehouse, I stood in line for a minute or so. "Here," a man said when I reached the counter. He pushed a sheet of paper toward me. "Just sign here."

"What's this for?" I asked. Then, I suddenly realized where I was. "Is this a food bank? I thought this was a market or something. I can pay for the food."

"It's OK," the man said. "You only have to sign this sheet."

"No, no," I said, my cheeks reddening. "Really, I didn't understand."

Behind me I felt a hand on my shoulder. I turned to see two men. They both gave me gentle smiles.

"It's all right," one said. "We all have to do it sometime."

I took long walks in the rain, watching the autumn colors change and fade. Everything around me felt too raw, unformed, and disconnected. I missed emotion, missed people touching me. I kept talking to strangers on the street. Few of them responded.

I realized I was depressed.

My years of living in London before I went to Brazil had influenced my attitudes about depression. In the United States, one is not supposed to get depressed. If depression approaches, one should immediately do something to get rid of it. Take drugs perhaps, go into trance. Our separate and individual responsibilities are to achieve and maintain constant states of happiness. Depression is antisocial and perhaps even deviant. The national emotional standard is set by drawings of smiling faces and a ritualized directive to "have a nice day."

In London, however, my friends regarded depression as a sign of emotional depth. According to them, given the current state of the world, a person who is continually happy must be ignorant, superficial, and entirely lacking in a social conscience. Even more damning, an incessantly happy person is boring.

My friend Andrew in London seldom left his house; he had a paranoid fear of the outer world. "My depression is like a comfortable cloak," he told me once. "Without depression, what would happen to art? Great world writers such as Lessing, Dostoevsky, Hemingway, Harding, Atwood and Cheever—can you imagine them happy all the time? The image of a happy Kafka sends shivers down my spine. What about our world thinkers, painters, musicians?"

"I don't like happiness," another English friend, Alex, said to me once when we had drunk a little too much wine. Alex was an aristocrat, good looking, had received his Ph.D. by the time he was twenty-four, started a business at twenty-five, sold it for several million when he was thirty-three, and was now on his way to becoming an acclaimed painter. "Happiness can too easily slip into smugness. One stops questioning." He adjusted his wire-framed glasses. "Let me think about that," he said. "Not all depressions: some depressions are creative, others are merely selfish. I am selective about which depressions I entertain anymore. But depression is important you know, for without depression, one can never experience joy."

I never managed to banish my depressions into U.S. mists, nor did I wear them as an English cloak. But over the years I had grown to recognize them, even to categorize them by type and color. My first Thanksgiving morning after coming to Seattle, I found myself enmeshed in Depression 24693J, otherwise known as "I Want to Be a Prom Queen." Its general theme was this: Everyone I know has been invited to exciting parties. I have been invited to none, and those to which I have been invited are not nearly as exciting as those to which I haven't been invited. What's wrong with me? (It should be noted that

Depression 24693J, like all depressions of inadequacy, has no relationship to fact; one could be exhausted running between invites from Aung San Suu Kyi, Noam Chomsky, and the Dalai Lama and still slide comfortably into Depression 24693J.)

Depression 24693J was interrupted by a call from my mother. I was to meet her and her husband in Pioneer Square for lunch before we all went to different Thanksgiving dinners.

I caught the ferry in the pouring rain. My mother, her husband, and I wandered rain-soaked Seattle streets looking for a restaurant. We finally settled on the only place open, a comfortable old bar. I looked at the other patrons also there on this national holiday. A young couple sat holding hands over neglected mashed potatoes and turkey. An older man across the room shared his table with a large stuffed teddy bear. The bear sat in his own chair and wore an overcoat. On the back of the bear's chair hung his umbrella.

On the ferry trip back to the island, I wondered whether Depression 24693J—which, as was his habit, departed without saying goodbye—was not loneliness in disguise. And what is loneliness? A friend described it as a lack of purpose. Another person suggested it comes when we feel disconnected. It certainly has nothing to do with being solitary: I thought of the excruciating loneliness that comes only in the crowded room of a party, or the liberating completeness of sharing a windy beach with only the sky and annoyed-looking cormorants. What about the loneliness I felt while I lay in bed in Salvador, listening to the night bar music and never finding sleep?

Arriving home a few nights later, after another one of my walks, I recognized the greeting handshake of Depression 81572P, better known as "I Could Have Been President." Its theme: everything I try takes an incredible amount of time, and the results are mediocre. Everyone else seems able to do things much faster, and their results—which I could have thought up just as well—are acclaimed as brilliant. What's wrong with me?

"You know something?" I said to Depression 81572P when I entered my house and saw him darkening a corner of my couch. "I don't like your style. You are a selfish, low-grade depression. And besides that, you're boring." And I sat on him.

Beside the couch on a small table stood the statue Agnaldo had given me. Above it hung the painting of Iemanjá. I took from my neck the turquoise beads I wore and curled them around the base of the statue. I lit a candle.

Then I sat down, picked up the telephone, and called Rita. She had recently acquired a cell phone, much cheaper to set up in Salvador than a land line. It didn't work most of the time, but to my amazement, the connection went through this time and she answered.

"You know that idea of a nonprofit," I said. "How we talked about an infrastructure, a group that would really work?"

"Yeah."

"Let's do it."

Rita laughed. "Is that what you called me for? I knew you'd call once you tried to live in the States again. Probably part of the reason I got the cell phone."

"I see." I tried to sound annoyed and couldn't quite manage it.

"This won't be easy, Margaret. Once we start, we can't back out."

"I know."

"You teaching? You get off for a few weeks for Christmas?"

"Yeah."

"Well, then I suppose the best thing is for you to come back down here, and we can begin to talk about what we should do."

I put down the telephone. I passed a slightly squashed Depression 81572P on my way to put water on the stove for tea. He had slid to the other side of the couch and seemed to be trying to transform himself into what looked suspiciously like a small Pacific atoll in the process of being strip-mined.

"Nice try," I said. "It's a start."

I realized I had started to hum a little samba tune.

thirteen | ideas

I arrived in Brazil two months later. A taxi driver friend of Cecilia's picked me up from the airport, and we immediately began chatting. My God, it felt good to speak Portuguese, to relax into conversation with no preamble or formality. We passed under a stand of high bamboo that arched over the road a short distance from the airport, and I breathed a sigh of contentment. I knew this feeling wouldn't last, that the inequality would soon begin to grate on my nerves, but for now I was content just to be back.

Rita and I met at our customary bar for our customary beer. Nelson always seemed to be running the place, regardless of the hour. His bar had metal tables painted with beer advertisements, and it was separated from the busy central Salvador street, in part, by a high fence constructed of metal bars. I felt as though I were a caged zoo animal in this barred bar, although anyone who wanted (except for the wandering crazies whose brains had dissolved through sniffing glue) freely moved in and out.

"Where do we start?" I asked.

"I would start by asking people here what they think is important. We could go to my neighborhood, and also Penambuas where you lived. Ask them what they think."

I looked into my beer. "But in a perfect world, what would *you* like to do?"

Rita laughed. "In a perfect world we wouldn't feel compelled to do something like this at all. But," she paused, "definitely something related to social justice. I don't really know much about the environment. Except that it's being damaged. Nor do you, right?"

I shook my head. "I grew up playing in old growth forests that no longer exist. My grandmother used to take us to dig camus root—a native plant there—at a place she called The Sacred Meadow. The Indians camped there in summer when she was a child. It's a shopping mall now. I loved these places, but I think that kind of loss doesn't have any power to people who never knew these places to begin with. And scientific stuff, I never got beyond beginning biology."

We sat silent for a minute.

"I'd like to do something with women," Rita said.

"I'd like to do something with men."

"No, no," Rita said, "with women's equality."

"Yeah, that sounds good. It's something we understand. Inequality, I mean."

"But we really need to ask people here." Rita flagged down Nelson and ordered another bottle of beer. "The idea has to come from the people in the favelas. If it doesn't, then they won't care. They'll just think it's some middle-class or government project, so the local people will steal whatever they can."

"Not cynical about your neighbors, are you?"

"Not cynical. I know them. They're my neighbors."

Nelson arrived. He popped the lid off the bottle and poured the beer into our cups. "My daughter's baby is getting baptized this Sunday," he said to Rita. "Can you take some photos?"

"Of course, Nelson," Rita said. "Is it the first Mass or the second?"

"Second. The entire family's coming."

"Do you charge him for all the photos you take?" I asked as Nelson walked away. "Or does he just pay for what he wants?"

"Only the ones he wants. I take a few for him and others for the record. I'm collecting all the photos I've taken, for maybe ten years now, to make a documentary history of my church, the Church of the Blacks. It's fought for black equality since before Abolition, you know, 1888. The priests there have always mixed Candomblé ritual within the Mass." Rita smiled. "The other Catholic churches don't like it much. Anyway, what do *you* want to do with the project? What interests you?"

I thought for a moment. "You know Rita, what really interests me is the infrastructure. There are tons of good projects and a lot of change needed, God knows, but I'm interested most in how it's put together, in the creation of the organization."

"Go on." Rita topped off my glass and refilled her own.

"Well, grassroots projects here have good ideas, but the middle class doesn't give them any money, the people involved lose heart and give up."

"Or," Rita said, "if they get any money, they steal it. You can't give money to someone who doesn't have enough to eat and not expect them to use it for themselves and their family first."

"And if they get any money, they just seem to end up fighting over power."

"Or when they are perceived as having money, one of their volunteers or staff sues them. The same kind of laws that protected me protect them. And contract systems are very complicated. If a worker or volunteer sues, they almost always win." She laughed rather nastily. "So, the worker wins and takes everything the nonprofit owns. Even the fridge or whatever. And the whole project collapses."

"Nice," I said. "Pleasant country, this."

Rita saluted me with her glass.

"But on the other side," I continued, "and you've said this yourself: I see middle-class or foreign 'aid' groups coming in telling people in the favelas what they are sure is best, and most of the time not understanding the reality at all. These groups get funds for, say, computer projects in favelas where food and electricity is a problem. These groups make lots of money themselves, and in the end little or no change happens at all."

"Which is why we have to ask people what they want. Otherwise we're doing the same thing."

"True."

"Another problem is that when you get the middle class involved, you run into the patronage system," Rita said.

"Special favors for those who give you their 'charity.'"

"Exactly. My sister needs help, or my uncle wants to start a new business, or the computers you buy have to come from my wife's company. They'll control the whole thing in no time, and in the end the entire project will be assisting them and their families more than anyone else."

"Of course the foreigners will likely do the same thing."

"Which is why the power—the center—has to remain with favela people."

"The power and the idea have to be grassroots, but must have an infrastructure designed with international accountability."

"Is that what you're saying interests you? To take the best of both, mesh them, and see if we can make it work?"

"Yeah, I guess so ..."

"Well, you have the international understanding to do it."

"Maybe." Nelson brought another beer. "You order that?" I asked. Rita nodded. "Yeah. This is hard work."

"So, I'm thinking of this infrastructure as more of a circle than a top-down hierarchy," I said.

"Yeah? That would be different. But how would you make it actually work?" Rita filled our glasses.

"So, this is just an idea, right?" Rita nodded. "OK. I'm thinking we visualize the structure of the project, whatever that is, with the people here at the center, and all other people involved in a circle around it."

"You're still a bit abstract," Rita said.

"All right." I began making marks on the table with my finger. "Instead of one Board of Directors in the States, say we have one here and one there. The program becomes a legal nonprofit here in Brazil, independent."

"With you and me on the board?"

"No, no. Not me. You and people who are somehow involved with the project. I form my own board in the States, a U.S. nonprofit, completely independent as well. That way the group overseas has no legal control over the project here."

Rita nodded slowly. "Keeping the funders overseas would help keep their noses out of the daily working of the project."

"Maybe. Actually, as I think of it, I might be able to set up a nonprofit in England, too. They would, again, be completely separate. Then the project here would not be dependent on any single group. It would have its autonomy. The project would really be the center of the organization, even though the organization would be international."

"Sounds good," Rita said. "So you do that part. It excites you, doesn't it?"

I laughed and looked into my empty glass. "It's ideas. I like the creativity of it. But you'd have to set up the nonprofit here."

"With your help," Rita said. "I don't want to be alone on this."

"You know, Rita," I said slowly. "As much as I would like to, I really *can't* be the person doing the project here. I'm white, middle-class, foreign–First World even. If I do the project, it won't change anything. It will just reinforce the usual patronage system we know: whites holding power, whites teaching browns. I can think I'm different, I can make links, have understanding that others don't, but I can't change who I am. I can assist with on-the-ground change, but if I actually do it, then it's not really change. Not at a deep level."

We sat silent for some time. Then Rita sighed. "You *are* different, which is exactly why you understand this."

"So you have to be the director," I said.

Rita shoved her warm beer aside. "But I don't know how to do that. You know better that kind of thing than I do."

"Maybe." I poured her warm beer into the gutter and refilled it. Across the street, two men walking together started to laugh. One tugged at the other's backpack, an action that for some reason made them only laugh harder. They stopped walking, and still giggling, they wiped the tears of laughter from their eyes. "You know how to make it work," I said, still watching the men. "How to get people's support here."

"You know how to write grants."

"I hate writing grants."

"And I hate administration. I have no idea about budgets. Do we really want to do this?"

"Every project has its boring bits."

"Yeah, but it means you'll have to stay in the States. You'll have to find the money." I looked into my beer. A fly had drowned in it. Rita took the beer and poured it out for me.

"I can try living in the States," I said. "I think I can handle it if I know I have a reason for leaving on a regular basis, if I have strong connections outside. My friends in London have good connections for money. I could ask them to get involved too. Then I'd have to visit Britain regularly as well as Brazil!"

Rita shook her head. "Start a nonprofit so you can continue to be a vagabond."

"Sort of." I leaned back in the metal folding chair; it was cool along the top of my back. A solitary man now sat on the curb where the men before had stood laughing. "So, what do we do?" I asked. "Just start talking with people and see what they say?"

"Sounds like a plan to me. And then see what happens." Rita poured the dregs of the bottle into our cups and signaled to Nelson that we were ready to pay the bill. "And think about your infrastructure. I'll probably have to keep my cell phone, won't I?"

I laughed. We stood and pulled grubby notes from our pockets. Rita gathered the money together and waved it at Nelson. "Nelson!" she shouted. "Here. See you tomorrow!" Nelson nodded and came over to take the bills.

Rita and I walked along the narrow sidewalk that still emanated warmth from the heat of the day. We joined the crowd at the nearest bus stop and, together with the others, hugged the building as the buses came close to the curb. We all watched for the names at the front of the buses, waiting for the one that would take us home.

Rita and I talked with group after group of people. Everyone was in a festive mood getting ready for the Christmas holidays. They all said they wanted education. Everyone thought that if they could have even one year of good education they would get good jobs, leave their favela, and find everlasting happiness. They kept saying they wanted "good" education, not just an elementary schooling or learning how to read well enough to become a waiter. They wanted education that would lead them to professional jobs. Was that possible? Did they understand the huge undertaking they were requesting? Not only on a sheer academic level, learning first how to read and write, then learning math, then geography, literature, geometry, pre-med, but also culturally. These people didn't really understand the purpose of a library. Most had never been in a restaurant or cinema. Many had never even been to the center of this city. But still they saw their way out as "good" education and professional jobs.

And everyone was telling us to focus on women. This delighted both Rita and me, the feminists we are. "The boys at least can sell drugs," one man said. Everyone laughed. Rita didn't. Neither did I. "Why can't women sell drugs?" I thought to myself. But they didn't, or very few did. I knew that. Instead, they sold themselves, either as maids or prostitutes. Either way, they gave up their souls. Mothers sent their eleven-year-old daughters out to the streets to sell whatever they could and then beat them if they didn't return with cash. After all these years of living in these favelas, of seeing desperation and disintegration of the human spirit, this still haunted me. What was happening in the mind and soul of a mother who would do this?

"You educate a boy, and when he is a man, he'll just walk away," a woman told us.

"Yeah," another woman added. "He'll get himself some good job, a middle-class, white girlfriend, and walk away from his children and the mother of those children. And we won't see him here in the favela ever again."

"It's true," a man said, laughing. "It's true. That's what I'd do." He looked at the group of us talking. "So, if you want to make things better here, you should look to the women. If anyone's going to do anything, it's them."

I told Zezé and Lula about this conversation. Lula had been trying to get his pension since he had reached retirement age. He had worked as a bus driver for thirty-five years, but the company was trying to deny it to him. They said he really hadn't worked long enough, that he took several years off in the middle, and that his starting date was five years later than it actually was. But Lula had kept thirty-five years of pay stubs and had hired a lawyer.

"Lula will win," Zezé said as she laid out plates for Sunday lunch. "He knew this kind of thing would happen when they first told him about the pension when he was twenty-five. I just feel sorry for all those people who aren't as clever and prepared as he is."

Zezé and Lula had bought a small piece of land near the beach about an hour out of Salvador. This was where they planned to retire.

"It's too violent here," Lula said. "We want to be able to walk, see the sky, listen to the birds as we did when we were young."

But when the developer realized to whom he had sold the land—Lula had used a lighter-skinned, more middle-class friend to complete the transaction—he suddenly decided that the land he had sold them, near the entrance of the development, was a mistake. He couldn't really sell that piece, he said. It had already been promised to someone else. And despite the fact that the entire area was up for development, he had no others to sell either.

"He's a racist," Lula said as he spooned himself some beans. "But all the papers are signed. I think he's stuck with us."

"So, should the project be to educate girls?" I asked Zeze, Lula, and Jorge after lunch. "What about you, Jorge? You're working as a security guard. Wouldn't you resent that?"

"My girlfriend," Jorge said, pouring me a beer, "she will do much more than me. She's smart. She wants to be a doctor. Educate girls like her."

"Girls are stronger," Lula said. "Boys are stupid, they get shot. Women hold society together." He glanced at Zezé. "Men just try to please them, that's really all we men think about."

Zezé laughed. "Listen to what Rita says, Margaret. She knows. And you do too. You listen. That's a good thing about you; you sit and listen to what people here have to say. You respect our knowledge, words, and ideas. You've lived here in the favela a long time. Outsiders don't do that. That's why you and Rita make a good team. You're smart." She paused. "And you're women."

Lula and Jorge laughed. "Watch out," Jorge said. "I see Danger coming."

fourteen | life change

I picked up the phone shortly after my arrival back to Seattle to hear the voice of an old friend. "I have some hard news about Jill, Margaret. She has ovarian cancer. But she caught it early. The doctors at first told her there was nothing wrong, that she only had a stomachache, but she knew. So she went from doctor to doctor until finally the fourth one did the right tests. And she knew. She's at the university hospital. They're giving her a hysterectomy."

I sat down. I had known Jill from before I ever went to London, let alone Brazil. I had a flashback of us skiing together only a few months before, of her incredibly smooth telemark turns. She was a dancer on any slope. An image came of Jill belaying me on a rock face, her smile and laughing eyes peeping over the cliff edge, urging my aching limbs and burning fingers to climb on. Jill, the English teacher, as a guest just this year in my Introduction to Anthropology class, laying out in clear and simple terms how my students really could write a term paper, and making them laugh while she did it. Jill, the artist, making her quilts, infusing in the patterns and vibrant color her own understanding of the intuitive confusion and joy that is life. Why Jill?

I sat in the darkening living room a long time. Then I remembered a conversation with Jill from perhaps twenty years earlier. We had been sitting at a bar together after a hike, drinking something mixed.

"My mother died of cancer," Jill had said. "Ovarian cancer. I wonder, should I have a hysterectomy?"

I remembered, even twenty years later, the color of the wood in the room, the bar lamp light. I hadn't looked at her. I knew little of cancer. My grandparents had died of cancer, but they had been old—at least from my perspective then. "I don't know," I said.

We spent a long minute looking into our drinks.

"My mother was also mad," Jill said.

"You mean crazy?" I asked.

Jill's silence answered my question.

Here I felt on firmer ground. My own companionship with depression and insecurity I knew, even then, came partly from genetic makeup and partly from an upbringing in a family that was less than stable.

I looked at Jill and put my arm around her shoulders. "You're not crazy," I said. "You are one of the sanest people I know. We all learn from you."

Jill leaned into my hug and smiled. We raised our glasses to a toast. "To sanity," I said.

"Except in love," Jill replied, and we laughed.

As I began work on the nonprofit, I kept thinking of Jill. I visited her at the hospital. She was her delightful, laughing self. Brave beyond my understanding. I didn't really know what to do, how I could be of help. Her husband was there. I didn't know how much to come or stay away, what was intrusive, what was supportive. I saw the pain in her eyes even while she laughed.

In the meantime, I enrolled in a tax class. I planned to learn how to file nonprofit papers with the federal government to get IRS tax-exempt status. It was impossibly complicated. I listened to the teacher go over everything step-by-step, then followed her instructions. She said I could give her completed forms before I sent them in, and she would make comments. Yes. Definitely a good plan.

I then had to ask people to be on a board; this was a legal require-ment for incorporation. I asked Pat, an ex-union organizer who was a bus driver on the island, to join the board.

"I'd be honored," he said, revealing confidence in an idea even I found dubious.

I asked Meps, a business consultant who could also do web design, who I had met in a salsa dance class.

"Will we have boring meetings?" she asked.

"No, no. We'll have fun, exciting meetings. In a bar."

"Then sure."

I asked Eduardo, an African-Brazilian musician who lived in Seattle. He had worked in education in Salvador. "You have started a project for my people, in my city," he said. "How can I say no?"

"Rita and I are starting it," I said. "Together."

"Well, I know you. I'd love to do it."

And finally, Mark and his wife. Mark was a retired marine ship designer whose mother started a school for orphaned girls many years ago in the eastern United States, so he already had a commitment to the idea of girls' education.

We had our first meeting at a pizza joint. I explained the project as Rita and I had put it together so far. We would start with one girl, send her to a top quality private school, and give her tutoring as needed. If all went well, we would expand to a few more girls. We would pay all their expenses for the school and hire a tutor. I then explained my concept of an infrastructure. The group didn't seem all that interested in my exciting infrastructure. They nodded pleasantly and grew distracted.

They were more excited by the project itself.

"Together we can do this," Meps said. "We'll each put in fifty dollars and think how we go next."

"To change with my people," Eduardo said. One by one, they each laid their hands on the table, one on top of the other, unified.

I looked at their faces and hands and curbed my impulse toward tears. These people didn't know Rita, and had never, except for Eduardo, even been to Brazil. They only knew me, and not very well at that. I realized that I was the cornerstone for the U.S. group. I had focused on Brazil, the responsibilities we were building there. But, I realized, I was also cementing a contract here in Seattle, one that was being constructed entirely upon my words and people's trust of those words.

I was scared. It was a strange feeling for me. I didn't fear the project in Brazil. That part was exciting—and I was doing that with Rita. I was not alone. But Seattle was different. I was expected to figure it out all by myself. Would I be able to do what was expected of me?

But then, what right did I have to be scared? Jill faced lurking, leering Death every time she sat up. With humor and grace, she made even her doctors laugh, cracking puns, making her pain easier for all of us to bear. Where did she find this courage? This love? My fears had no place in the face of such strength. I just wished Jill were well again, and that she could have been part of this project. We could have laughed over foibles. She would love Rita.

Eduardo thought of a name for the organization, which I broached to Rita: Bahia Street. She liked it. So did I. It contained the name Bahia, where we intended to work, and which represented the African culture and influence in Brazil. Much of life in Salvador took place in the street, so "street," an English word we thought most Brazilians would understand, was for the action, the activity, the life of the group. And we were hopeful Americans wouldn't get too confused by one foreign word.

During summer break, I returned to Brazil. When Rita asked how I could afford these transcontinental trips, I laughed ruefully. "I can't," I said. But I managed. I had lived a life for so many years in Bahia that required very little beyond subsistence and beer that I had lost the habit of spending much. My salary seemed huge. It was easy to save for flights; I just didn't save much beyond that.

A few days after I arrived in Salvador, Rita and I visited some prospective girls for the program.

"You know, Rita," I said as we walked up a shantytown hill after one visit. "I don't really like children that much. I mean, some are OK, but generic children, just the mere fact of them being children—it's never grabbed me."

Rita stretched her back and gazed at me over the tops of her recently acquired glasses. "I've never had children either, but I think I'm definitely more maternal than you."

We caught the bus to our next interview. Juliana was an orphan being raised by her older sister. She seemed older than her eleven years and was very bright. And she could read.

"Shall we start with her?" Rita asked as we boarded another bus toward her house. "She has the best chance of entering directly into a private school, her sister is supportive, and Juliana is an impressively dedicated student. When we get more funds, we could tutor a couple of other girls—maybe four?—until they can read and do math well enough to get into a private school themselves. Juliana could study with them after school, to give her extra help as she needs it."

I nodded. It all seemed rather haphazard, but I saw no different way to proceed.

"We only have money for Juliana right now, but, yeah, when we get the money we could include a couple of others."

The four other girls we chose included Christina, a tiny, beautiful eight-year-old who was a neighbor of Lula and Zezé. Everyone in the neighborhood said she had always wanted to learn to read. I went to interview her alone. When she saw me, she burst into tears. Apparently her mother had always told her that if she didn't behave, the "big bad gringa" would take her away. Great. So, big white me arrived, asking if she would like to go to school with me. She screamed and ran away. It took hours for her mother and friends to calm her. Next time, I thought, Rita goes to visit her.

Another girl was Rita's eleven-year-old neighbor, Claudia. She, her mother, and five siblings all lived in one suffocating room with a caved-in tin roof. Neighbors told me that the year before, Claudia's mother's ex-boyfriend had raped Claudia. The neighbors heard her screaming and chased him out of the neighborhood, shouting that they'd kill him if he came back. So, he hadn't. Claudia said she wanted to study, probably because of Rita's influence, and to get a high school degree. Her mother said she supported the idea of Claudia going to school, but kept asking if she herself would make anything out of this.

The third girl was Lidia, the very bright daughter of a capoeira teacher I knew. And finally, Patricia, who lived in Alagados, a favela built on rickety piers over a bay that, after years of having no toilet facilities, had become a cesspool. I'd been there once before to consult a Candomblé Pai de Santo. That time, I'd walked barefoot on the broken filthy walkways, feeling for secure footholds. This time, I was relieved to see, we did not have to walk along the piers. An Italian nonprofit had paid for the hillside above the bay to be plowed up. Huge amounts of sand were being poured into the bay, and one - and two-room brick houses were being built on the sand. I considered the environmental havoc of this plan, but presumably the area was so polluted that nobody cared. The idea was to get the houses off the water and to put in some kind of sewage drainage system—which would still go straight into the bay, but not so close to people's living spaces.

A sociologist friend of Rita's who was working with the Italian project had told us about Patricia; over the year and a half she'd worked with the project, she'd taken Patricia under her wing and was trying to teach her to read. She told us she thought Patricia was one of the brightest girls she'd ever met. Patricia's family, or extended family—it was unclear how many of the numerous children and young people working and hanging around the one-room brick house they were building with the Italians' help were family—all seemed to have some kind of interest in the house. Patricia's father looked very old and frail.

I was told he had tuberculosis. He kept shouting at the people working on the house and asking us what money he'd make if his daughter went to school. Rita and I glanced at each other and then ignored him. It was the politest response we could muster. Patricia was even smaller than Christina despite being three years older. Malnutrition, Rita told me. Patricia told us she wanted to be a banker.

Rita and I next selected a school for Juliana. The contrast was unnerving, even for us: airy, stucco rooms; paved, tree-shaded walkways; happy, well-fed, light-skinned children who tossed their books carelessly on the ground while they played. We—or I should say I, since he ignored Rita—talked with the director, who spoke reasonable English. By weird coincidence, he had gone to university in Washington state some forty years before. He loved Washington, so he was inclined to give our idea—clearly farfetched from his perspective—a chance.

Eduardo was also in Salvador, visiting his family. He took on the task of tutor recruitment and had advertised through the Bahia Teacher's Association. It turned out that his aunt was director of the Association, so she also offered us the use of a lovely, large room on the top floor of their centrally located building. Of the forty-five applicants, Eduardo interviewed six. Of these, he recommended one, Madalena, a woman he'd known when he was a principal in Bahia before he immigrated to the States. He thought she'd be good because she'd worked with special education children, the idea being that maybe this experience would give her an advantage in helping these favela girls learn the discipline needed to study. Since Rita and I had previously discussed whether the teacher should be African-Brazilian, I asked Rita about Madalena. By my U.S. definition, she was definitely "black," but by Brazilian standards, or more precisely, by Bahia standards, I wasn't sure.

"She's brown," Rita said, "but I would call her white or at least 'earth-white:' someone who's white but has African blood." She shrugged. "But, I don't know. Eduardo seems to understand a lot more about this education system than I do. If he thinks she's good, then I'm fine with it."

I nodded. I, of course, hadn't a clue. We thought we should get approval from the board in the States, but since Eduardo and I were both members and none of the rest of them knew anything about Brazil, we decided to just go with Eduardo's selection.

"So, when she starts the tutoring, she works with you and you let me know how it's going, right?"

"And I ask you what you think I should do next."

"Right, Rita. And what do I tell you then?"

"Maybe I could teach the girls photography. Then we wouldn't have to hire a tutor. I'd love to teach photography."

"And you always say that it's your photography that got you through school, right?"

"Yeah. But no one we asked said they thought photography was going to change the future of Salvador, did they?"

"No. Maybe someday when we have all these girls and some kind of good program going, we could offer photography as well as whatever else we're doing."

"Yeah, right."

"You don't believe me," I said.

"Photography would take an entire expensive photography lab."

"Well, Rita, I think we have to dream in this project of things *we* would also really like to do. So, no harm in dreaming about photography. After all, aren't we asking more than that of these little girls?"

Rita laughed. "All right. So, I'll dream about my photography lab. What are you going to dream about?"

"I don't know, making the thing actually work on an international level?"

Rita shook her head. "Nope. Not enough. You have to think of something better than that."

I avoided the question and suggested we go out for a beer. I was completely out of my depth; I had no clue how to swim in these turbulent waters. Why was I doing this? Because I couldn't handle being in the States with no connection with Brazil? Because university life was too confining for me? No matter what other people had begun to say, it certainly wasn't altruism nor was it just thinking it would be fun to try this. Even more disturbing, I thought, how in the world was it actually going to work?

To Bahia Street Mailing List of 15: January 10, 1998

Dear Founding Donors,

Well, we have paid the admission fee for Juliana! So, here we go. She will start in February. Our next payment, made in a few weeks, will cover books and uniforms for the year, a month's worth of bus tokens, and a $50 payment to her family. The board made the vote last week to go for it because of the support from all of you. I cannot express how much your support for Juliana and for Bahia Street means. You are the people who believe in us from the beginning, our founding donors. When we are a big organization with a secure endowment, numerous girls in school, in tutoring programs, and have numerous other programs in place—you are the ones I personally will remember most strongly for your support now.

We have about $1000 from the meetings on Vashon and in Seattle and currently have $225 a month committed for Juliana. We are sending out grant applications to cover the tutoring program for four other girls and to cover administration costs. Eduardo's (our Vice President) band Show Brazil has also donated their time for a benefit concert at the Tractor Tavern.

With all this activity, I have total confidence that we shall find the support for Juliana. Regardless, we have committed to her and in no circumstances will we let her down. In a worst-case scenario (which I don't think will happen) I have committed to pay whatever shortfall we may have in her expenses.

Let me tell you about Juliana herself. Her mother died about six years ago (there has never been a father mentioned), and she and a younger brother are being brought up by an older sister. They live in a shantytown about an hour from the center of town and about an hour from the school she is attending. However, the bus service to her new school is excellent—one of the reasons we chose it—so she can get a single bus direct from her house to a half a block from the school. Juliana was able to be admitted to the school because, through a redevelopment project, she received a scholarship to a private school in her area for the first four years of schooling. This was a much lower standard school, but Juliana is bright and this earlier opportunity allowed her enough school-ing to make the present opportunity possible for her.

So, onward. I would be delighted to speak before any group you think might be interested in Bahia Street. If any of you know of anyone you think would like to donate or volunteer for Bahia Street, please let me know. We need people to help with the benefit and many other bits and pieces. We are particularly looking for a volunteer lawyer and accountant. I shall be teaching Tuesday through Thursday, so expect me to return your calls on Mondays and Fridays.

And again, I want to express how much your support of Bahia Street means.

um abraço (a hug),
Margaret

fifteen
letting the outer skin be social

I was in my office after teaching an evening class at my new job at a university in Portland, three hours south of Seattle. I had just started. My plan was to commute, spending four days a week in Portland, and the rest in Seattle working on Bahia Street. I set down my pen and stared at the wall. I sat immobile for a long time.

What am I doing here? I thought. Why do I think this job is so important I had to come anyway? I should be in Seattle.

I had already canceled my first two classes of the term. Jill was going in for yet another operation. I went to the hospital, and her husband let me sit with her for a while. Jill opened her eyes and smiled at me. "Oh, Margaret," she said, "I'm glad you're here." Then she closed her eyes again.

And that was the moment I realized that she was dying. Somehow I never expected this to happen. All the way, I kept expecting she would come through. I knew few people as strong as Jill, with such spirit, such strength and courage. Somehow I never faced the fact that she could actually die.

I got up from her bedside, wiping from my chin tears I could not control. Her husband took my place. He wasn't crying. How could he not? I realized it was because he had already known for some time. His pain was beyond tears. He knew he had limited time in which to give his love to her. He could cry later.

We stood in the hospital hallway as they rolled Jill to her operation. She opened her eyes again and took my hand. "Thank you for being here, Margaret," she said. "I love you."

How could a person be so selfless? So strong? She was expending her last energy giving to others.

Then I told Jill's other friends and her husband I couldn't stay, that I had already missed the first classes, that I couldn't miss the third as well, that I had to leave and go to work. How important is work? I thought afterward. Would these students have really cared if I canceled class again?

I had a small buzzing in my head, a background noise that continued all day. And then, in the evening, just before class, it stopped. I knew Jill was dead. I rang the hospital. A nurse answered. Her hesitation confirmed what I already knew. "Let me get one for her friends for you," she said.

One of Jill's closest friends, Debbie, came to the phone. "She just died," she said. Debbie sounded peaceful. Twenty of Jill's friends had sat in the hospital room with her, holding hands, touching Jill with their thoughts. Jill had come out of her quasi-coma once. "Am I dying?" she asked her husband.

"Yes," he said.

Jill had closed her eyes for a minute. "Then," she said, "when you're finished being sad, have a party."

I arrived at the first Bahia Street fundraiser a few days later, feeling depressed. I kept thinking of how I could have done more for Jill. A green-colored Depression, 214M, sidled up to me as I entered the door. I called him "This Project Was Stupid And Who Am I To Think I Could Do It?" He was accompanied by his red-eyed close companion "I Don't Really Like These People Anyway." When I saw all the enthused, expectant faces, I felt even worse. How was I going to make animated conversation or even be civil?

I had worn a short white dress, and brushed my hair long. I had debated wearing the dress: a cute, sexy outfit could make me feel good about myself, give me confidence. But if I were already feeling low and inadequate, I sometimes couldn't live up to the outfit and would stand, feeling like a dork, acutely aware of every imperfection. These times, it was much better to wear slacks and a neutral shirt. Then my self and my appearance were at least in balance. I had worn the dress and now regretted it. I shook my head, trying to shake myself free.

"Look," Kyra, one of the volunteers, said, "we've begun a presentation table, put up some of your photos. What do you think? And Pat's taking the door."

I looked at the beautiful display. Beside Kyra—a very bright student of mine from the year before—stood Karey and Aaron. All were in their early twenties and all looked at me expectantly. When I didn't say anything, I saw their smiles tremble and begin to fade. My internal struggles with clawing, varicolored Depressions leapt out toward them as disapproval.

"Don't you like it?" Karey asked. She was a Latin American Studies major who wanted to become a professional social activist when she graduated. I saw worry and hurt creep into her eyes.

"No, no," I said, "it's great!"

I examined the photos pasted to a black poster board with colorful writing above. A bright tablecloth covered a table decorated with Brazilian trinkets and hats. I had no idea who had brought the materials. "Did you put this together?" I looked at the volunteers. They nodded. "It looks fantastic!"

I watched the doubt disappear from their eyes and the smiles re-emerge. "This is wonderful," I said. "I'll be right back."

I ran to the bathroom and kicked a roll of toilet paper across the room. "Fuck you," I said to the demons crouched inside. "Fuck you all."

I stood before the mirror and put on lipstick (armor). Finally, I understood: how I personally felt was irrelevant. I was on stage. I had to be a persona. All feelings of inadequacy or depression could be polished and indulged in solitude, but for now, they had no place.

I had never thought about how doing this project would affect relationships. People expected me to be inspiring now, not to tell them how lousy I felt. I realized further, with some shock, that since I had already involved all my friends in Seattle with Bahia Street, I could talk with no one about depression or grief. If I were going to spearhead this project, my doubts, my fears, my insecurities had to remain my own. I could not tell anyone involved with Bahia Street when I was overwhelmed, depressed, or just plain tired. My feelings would pass on to them, and they would lose their own enthusiasm. I saw a narrow, but very deep, crevasse open between myself and others involved, or potentially involved, with the organization. It's strange, I thought: in starting a community I have ensured a certain kind of personal isolation.

I felt a bone-wrenching wave of loneliness and then crushed it. I thought of the almost unbelievable strength Jill had shown. I could at least honor her by being strong now.

"What cage have I built for myself?" I asked, still looking into the mirror. I smiled, practiced a laugh. I remembered Andrea getting me to dance all those years ago at my first Carnival. "Dance," I said. "Dance. It is the only choice."

On the way out, I picked up the roll of toilet paper and placed it on the shelf. No demons now, just a boring toilet paper roll. I walked onto the dance floor.

"And it's ……….. Margaret!"

I looked up to see Adam, one of the drummers in Eduardo's band, laughing. He began a percussive beat. The other musicians took his lead, all laughing. "The Margaret Willson Funk!" Adam shouted into the mike.

I laughed, grateful tears pulsing at the corners of my eyes. I leapt on to the stage and grabbed the mike.

"OK, guys!" I shouted to the crowd. "Let's dance!"

After Jill's death in January, I went for a night ski. I grew up skiing, but had neglected it for years going only a few times the year before—with Jill, in fact. The knowledge came back swiftly. I thought of this ski as an homage to Jill, for all the times we had skied together. I wore a hat she had knitted for me, thinking that in so doing her spirit could somehow be out there in the snow with me. I skied ahead of my companions, seeking solitude, sliding swift, feeling the rhythm of my body, the snow, silence, a night frosted with blue. I skied to a ridge, and below me lay the valley, beyond it the crests of distant peaks, glaciers, and a deep stream. I began the descent, gaining speed, no fear. On the wind came images of my childhood: the smell of summer grass as we lay looking at the stars, the hard current of a river sliding across my belly the first time I tried to swim across, the excitement of exploring an unknown wood. Here, in the exhilaration of this night, lay super-imposed my past. Transcendence comes with experience, knowing comes with joy.

I raised my ski poles above my head and shouted into the night. I felt Jill with me. I dove; the trees rose around me, and my shoulders knew the moon.

Some months later, I was invited to London to give a paper for a conference on film and gender, something with which I had been deeply involved before I went to Brazil. I stayed with my friend Alex, the one who had given me such good insights about the nature of depression. I told him about Bahia Street.

"It's just beginning," I said. "We enrolled one girl. I'm not sure when we can enroll the next one or what our next move will be."

Alex leaned back on his sofa. "I'll give you two thousand pounds," he said.

"What?"

"Sure." He adjusted his glasses. "Sounds like a decent idea."

"But, Alex, I wasn't asking you for money. I didn't mean to imply that. I was just telling you about it."

"I know that."

"And you don't really even know much about it yet."

"But I know you, Margaret." He smiled and took a sip of his gin and tonic.

"I'm not sure what to say. That's a lot of money." I fidgeted with my own drink, poked the lime wedge deep into the ice.

"You say, 'thank you,'" Alex said and smiled over the rim of his glass.

"You're enjoying this, aren't you?"

"Yes—for two thousand pounds I'm allowed to." Alex paused and set down his glass. "Look, Margaret, if you're going to do this project, you have to become comfortable with asking people for money. You have to believe in your own project enough to believe it is a worthwhile investment for others. If you don't believe this, then how can you possibly expect others to do so?"

I looked at the lime, now encased in ice cubes. "That's true, I suppose, but I still don't feel very good about it."

"Margaret, I have lots of money. You know that. Each year I put aside a certain percentage of my investment interest to give to charity. My trust lawyer tells me how much I have to give, and I decide where I want it to go. I generally give it to big groups that have a good reputation, like Oxfam. But your project, because I know you, I know that nearly all of the money I give you will go toward the project itself. You know the people and the area where you're working, and you have integrity. For me, that's a good choice and a good investment." He smiled. "And your project is so small I know that what I give you will make a big difference. Giving the same amount to Oxfam is only a drop in their very large budget."

"This means we can add a second girl right now, you realize that?"

"Use it as you think best. In a year, let's see where you are. I could make this an annual thing."

I stiffened my lips to keep them from trembling. After a few moments I spoke.

"You know, Alex, this money—you're right, it will make a huge difference, and I very much appreciate it." I looked at him and looked away. "But what that money represents—your support, the confidence you're showing for this daunting idea—that perhaps means more than the actual funds."

"I know that." Alex gave me a small, smug smile. "But the money's good too."

"You are also a very annoying human being."

"Thank you."

A few days later, Alex and his wife, Susie, invited me to a party in a small town outside London. At the party, a very attractive man, with whom I thought I had been flirting, asked me about Bahia Street. I went into some detail.

He looked at me, in my black outfit, which I thought looked rather slinky, and said, "Oh, so you must be a nun, then?"

I walked away and quickly drank two scotches. What was happening to my identity? I was a vagabond, the antithesis of a nun. I walked around the party, stared into the large outside bonfire. Why was I doing this? To be my own boss, to have people look up to me? To push away those demons of hopelessness that visited with the news each morning?

I wandered into the house and saw another cute guy. I asked him to dance. He told me he lived in Italy. We began to dance, and I forgot all about Bahia Street. At least he could flirt. And he clearly didn't mistake me for a nun.

To a Mailing List of 25: March 25, 1998

Dear Donors,

It is strange how opening my mailbox has taken on new meaning. I find I am excited to get mail for Bahia Street. Does this sound corny? Even the bills, the letters from the IRS, the city telling us they require a business license (costing $75!)—all of this somehow reaffirms the legitimacy of Bahia Street. We are an organization and we are growing.

So, here are some highlights of what has happened in the last two months: Donations: People have given or pledged $6,875 new donations since January, coming from people as far afield (to Seattle, not far afield to themselves of course) as London and Amsterdam. The generosity of these people, together with those of you who have given previously, means that we can fund the schooling for a second girl, Patricia. Thank you.

I am commuting each week to a teaching job in Portland, so if I take several days to respond to phone calls, please do not take this personally. I shall be finished in early May and will then be able to devote all my energy to Bahia Street for the summer.

In closing I wish to tell you about the telephone conversation I had last night with Rita (who, like me, is currently volunteering her time). She said that when the first month's vouchers for books, uniforms, and transportation arrived, Patricia and her aunt both burst into tears. Until then they never really believed this opportunity was real.

Patricia has a very difficult year ahead of her: the studies will be much more difficult than she is used to, and she will have to make a dramatic adjustment from living in a shantytown to going each day to a middle-class school. This is a lot for any eleven-year-old to handle. But Patricia understands that she has an almost unheard of opportunity and the responsibility that goes with it. She also understands that she has the support of a number of people in a country far from her own.

Patricia's chance is a very small step in terms of world inequality, but it is a move toward change nonetheless. I realize when I hear from Rita that if we are proud of nothing else we have done in these weeks, we can be proud that we are part of this change.

Do get in touch with any ideas or thoughts.

All the best,

Margaret

sixteen | of race and remembering

I was asked to give a talk in Seattle sponsored by the World Affairs Council as well as to write a paper for a conference in San Francisco. This time I decided to talk about Bahia Street. This meant I had to justify the organization, not in terms of what the people in the favelas told Rita and me, but in terms of statistical and academic writings. In order to be "credible," the local situation had to be couched in the knowledge and phrases of outsiders.

Cecilia had once shown me an article from *Veja*, a Brazilian newsmagazine, published in 1988, the same year the new Brazilian Constitution prohibited racial discrimination. The article claimed that slaves in Brazil had been better off than African-Brazilians were then, in the late eighties. As I started to read about racial inequality, I found that the raw and impersonal statistics put in blunt terms what I had seen on the streets.

At the time I wrote these papers, the late 1990s, the mortality rate among African-Brazilians was 30 percent higher than whites. Their illiteracy rate was double. African-Brazilians stayed in school an average of two and a half years. Only 13.6 percent finished elementary school and only; 2.1 percent completed high school. No wonder, even learning Portuguese on the streets as I had, my friends in the favelas had long ago begun asking me to read things to them. I was white, so it was assumed that I could read, regardless the language. In addition, African-Brazilians earned less than half (44.1 percent) of what whites earned.

And Brazilians claimed they had no racism.

Rita told me about an experience she and a black *baiana* friend had had in a middle-class area in Rio. Every restaurant they entered was closing—for them in particular, it seemed. This was prejudice against them for being from the Northeast as well as for their color. And Rita often said that she thought prejudice among poorer people was worse than among the middle class.

I remembered a conversation my friend Herns and I had had a few years before. Herns was a black Haitian anthropologist. He went to the

Sorbonne for his first degree and won an incredible scholarship that funded him to do a Ph.D. at any university he desired in the world. With great idealism, he chose the Federal University of Rio de Janeiro. I met him through Cecilia when he was doing his thesis research on "the black family in Bahia."

"I thought I would escape racism by coming to Brazil," he told me. "I believed all those things I'd read about Brazil being a divine center for racial harmony and hope." We were sitting at a roadside café in Salvador after an intense night of dancing *pagode*, a form of samba that was infectious and took exhausting muscle control.

"So, what do you think now?" I asked him.

Herns mused in silence for a few moments. "When I first moved to Rio—I have a good scholarship, you know—I rented an apartment in an upper middle-class neighborhood."

"At least they let you rent it."

"Well, actually a white friend set it up, so I don't know that. But the place had a swimming pool. Rio was hot, so a few days after my arrival, I decided to take a swim. When I got to the pool, it was fairly crowded with swimmers—all white. I got in and immediately they all got out."

"What! They all left, like that?"

"Yeah. Like I contaminated the pool water or something. So, after a bit, I got out and started back to my apartment."

We sat in silence. I considered the humiliation I would feel in that situation.

"But," Herns finally said, "as I was walking up the stairway, I thought to myself, 'I am an anthropologist. It certainly appears as though the swimmers left on my account, but it could have been coincidental. As a scientist, I need further experimentation.'"

"Herns, what did you do?"

"Well, I returned to my apartment, collected a book and an air mattress I had, and headed back to the pool. Put the mattress in the pool, climbed on, laid back and began to read."

"And?"

"All the swimmers left."

I laughed. "Bloody hell, Herns."

"So, I had the pool all to myself." He took a sip of his mineral water, a pleased smile now on his face. "After about fifteen minutes, a woman slipped into the pool, a very attractive blond woman actually, and she slowly swam past me. As she got close, she asked, 'Are you French?' The book I was reading was in French— I'd forgotten about that, that they might notice the French. I knew if I said anything she'd hear my French accent, so I said nothing, just kept reading. 'You're French, aren't you?' she asked again. Still I said nothing.

"So, after a few minutes, she climbed out of the pool and returned to her friends. 'He's a foreigner,' I heard her say. 'He doesn't speak Portuguese. I think he's French.'

"After that, one by one, the swimmers returned to the pool, and as they passed, they smiled at me. I ignored them."

"So, you only contaminate the pool—you are only 'black' black— if you are Brazilian black, not French black."

Herns shook his head. "You tell me. I don't know. I can only tell you what happened. You interpret it as you like."

"So, a black European—or American, presumably—foreigner is 'whiter' than a black Brazilian. Rita's talked about this. But what about somebody from Africa? You could have been from Senêgal. Or Haiti for that matter—a nationality that clearly didn't suggest itself. Would that make you 'blacker'?"

Herns laughed. "Gets a bit complicated, doesn't it? It's amazing what we internalize and come to believe. We aren't even aware sometimes how we know what we know."

Alex called me early one Saturday morning.

"My trust lawyer says you have to register as a charity in Britain for me to give you any more money."

"How do I do that?"

"I don't know. There are people here who do, though. When can you come over to set it up?"

"Well, finals are next week, so I suppose I could come after I get my grades in."

I set down the phone with a sigh. This was what Rita and I had planned from the beginning, but now it just sounded like work. I now understood how complicated the legalities were. I didn't know how to set up nonprofit status in Britain, but it was sure to be much worse than the States. I felt defeated and alone.

It was more than just administrative bureaucracy. As an academic, I was also supposed to be publishing. Between teaching and Bahia Street, I had absolutely no time left for research. I had planned to get some writing done over the summer, but this plan was fading fast.

I also had a worry that I could admit to no one. I was not sure Bahia Street was working. The director of Juliana's school had said he supported the idea of a favela student, but the teachers clearly didn't agree. Juliana's math teacher told her repeatedly that children from the favelas always fail. And because her fellow middle-class students didn't see the need to study much, Juliana wanted to follow their example. She wanted expensive tennis shoes, she wanted the new style pink backpack.

Rita had also sounded depressed when we had finally been able to talk on the phone. I tried to perk her up, but even to my ears my cheery words rang false. Because phone calls were expensive and the connections so difficult to maintain we were, in reality, working in separate and parallel paths. The school director may have been very open to me—the white foreigner—but Rita told me that he was uninterested in speaking with her. "Wait until Dr. Willson comes," he said to her. "Then we can resolve things." Madalena also didn't want to discuss Juliana's grades with Rita; rather, she wanted to send them to Eduardo or me.

"They won't treat me as director," Rita said. "I'm black, with a favela accent. They want you."

"But Eduardo's black."

"Not here. You know that. He's middle-class, lived in São Paulo for many years, and now lives in the United States."

"So, I somehow have to disappear, and you have to act fiercer to those middle-class people, really be the director."

"Margaret, what are we doing? Working hard to create little black mimics of middle-class values who will later happily oppress their former neighbors?"

I had no answer for her.

We both realized that we had to rethink this. If we were providing African-Brazilians—and by the mere fact that they were in the favelas to begin with was almost complete assurance in Salvador that they would be African-Brazilian—with the tools to enter the middle-class, why did this mean they would challenge the status quo and effect change themselves other than providing for their families? Indeed, every indication pointed to quite the opposite.

The black Brazilian writer and activist Thereza Santos wrote that in São Paulo during the military dictatorship, when she and other mothers confronted the Rota 66, which was assassinating their sons, they couldn't count on the participation of the black movement in any confrontation because its members, many of whom had favela roots themselves, wanted to be seen as middle-class.

Likewise, Rita had told me about numerous incidents where the worst racial discrimination in job situations she and other African-Brazilians faced came from African-Brazilians who themselves had been poor and who had, usually through some very lucky chance, entered the middle class. This was particularly undermining when one considered the tiny percentage of African-Brazilians who were able to make this transition.

One African-Brazilian friend of Rita's, originally poor, argued with his white, middle-class wife that they should not pay their maid more because it would make it more difficult for other middle-class people to hire them so cheaply. This man's mother had been a maid herself.

Example after example in Salvador showed that middle-class African-Brazilians did not tend to support their birth communities. Indeed, they shunned them, associating mostly with whites and up-holding a status quo that kept the vast majority of African-Brazilians impoverished and powerless.

It was becoming clear that education alone would only produce African-Brazilian middle-class upholders of a middle-class status quo.

I shelved these concerns and went to England anyway.

I had never understood how much class affected bureaucracy in London, how it determined how affairs were done. It was not an area of that society I had ever entered before.

Upon arriving in London, I visited the aptly named Charities Commission. Contrary to my preconceived ideas, Britain was much more organized than the United States; the Charities Commission had a brochure listing all the forms we needed and even a template of the answers to their questions.

Alex and Susie helped me through the entire registration process. Alex rang John, a lawyer friend who specialized in nonprofit formation and law, and invited him over for dinner and an excellent bottle of wine. Susie was co-director of the largest wine importer in Britain, so excellent wine was expected and available. John was very pleased with the wine, and we had a great chat. He told me exactly what to do, what to say on the forms, and what pitfalls to avoid. This type of knowledge took me months to acquire in the United States. In London, it took me less than a week.

The second night, Alex and Susie invited their friend Rob over for more excellent wine. Rob was a consultant specializing in nonprofit incorporation and networking. He arrived with a folder which listed, from his incredible database, all the nonprofit organizations in Britain that had anything to do with Brazil. He just handed this to me, free of charge, as a favor to his friends Alex and Susie.

We gathered a group of trustees, which included Alex, Susie, the accountant from Susie's company who had worked with several nonprofits before, and Tom, a friend of mine who had been at the London School of Economics with me. Tom was at that time Economic Advisor for Europe for a major economics think tank.

I turned in all the paperwork to the Charities Commission, had it officially stamped, and we had our first trustees meeting.

"It will be fine," the accountant said, leaning back into Alex and Susie's sofa, sipping a wine he clearly appreciated. "They will want to meet with some of the trustees to determine if we are the 'right' sort of people to be trusted."

"How can they tell?" I asked.

The accountant swirled the wine in his glass for a moment. "I am sure they will think this group is fine. We can invite them down for lunch at my house in the country—they always love that kind of thing—and I doubt there will be a problem."

Alex laughed. "That's what this is all about really, isn't it? Getting your nice lunches, going to the proper society 'dos.'"

The accountant smiled in acknowledgment.

"So, do you want an overview of the program?" I asked.

"A brief one," Alex said. "We are helping poor little girls get an education in Brazil. That's enough for me."

"But there is a political infrastructure. The way it's put together makes the organization particularly effective in promoting lasting hierarchical change in the social structure."

Alex yawned. "Yeah. Well, I'm not interested in all that. That's your part, you worry about that."

"We need to put together a database," Tom said. "I'll donate a decent computer."

"We have enough money now to hire an administrator," Susie said. "I think we should put aside a bit for that from the beginning."

"Yes," Alex said, "and take what money we have now and divide it by twelve so we know how much we'll be giving for the entire year. Then next year we may have the money to give or not, but we can determine that then."

"Is that how you're doing it in the States?" Susie asked.

"No, I'm scrabbling the money together in any way possible. We don't know from month to month if we have enough money for the entire month."

"That's not good," Alex said. "We will commit to a certain amount each month for a year and then see if we can commit again the following year or not." The others nodded in agreement.

Alex leaned back into the sofa and chuckled. "Now I'll force Nick to write me a fat check to pay him back for the rather largish check he forced out of me at his little gathering for that charity project he's all involved in now."

"And there's Paul," Susie said. "He's Alex's trust lawyer, a lovely fellow. You'll like him. We must include him."

"We can send out letters to a select group of our friends," Tom said. "Not too forceful, just telling them about Bahia Street."

"And only once a year," Alex said. "And we can have a party, invite someone fashionable to draw people here, then get the checks out of them."

"And I have several clients who are football stars—soccer stars, Margaret, you understand." I nodded. "They might be interested."

I shook my head and followed the accountant's example of sinking into the sofa and sipping my wine. It was indeed a wonderful wine. This branch of Bahia Street, I could see already, was going to be a completely different animal than our rough and ready one in Seattle. I wondered what Rita would say when I told her about this. I just hoped the project would live up to their confidence.

Letter to Mailing List of 60: October 11, 1998

Dear Donors and Volunteers,

I feel it has been so long since I last wrote, in part because so much has happened.

The largest piece of news is that Bahia Street is to be registered as a charity in Britain. I shall keep you posted on that as it develops.

Eduardo went to Salvador for two weeks and visited the girls. Juliana is doing well at school. She ranked just below average for her first term. This was considered quite satisfactory by all her teachers, who say she is very bright. She is well-liked so far and is clearly going through what her teachers call an adaptation phase. Juliana herself loves the school.

Of the four other girls who will hopefully be entering the tutoring program, Lidia and Patricia are both attending the fifth grade in public school. Patricia's father (who has thirty-nine children) has contracted tuberculosis for the third time, so he is not expected to live much longer. Her fourteen-year-old brother has recently joined a local gang. When told that this means that the police will likely kill him, he said he didn't care. "I'll die anyway," he said. We also learned that a man came by Patricia's family's home selling books. When Patricia heard the family had sent him away, she was very upset and somehow managed to find the money so that when he came back, she bought a book for herself. Both Patricia and Lidia are excited about the tutoring program and want to start as soon as possible.

Claudia thought Bahia Street had disappeared from her life, even though Rita told her about the tutoring program. Her living situation is particularly bad now that the rainy season has started. Their shack has no windows and a collapsed tin roof; in the rainy season it becomes a suffocating steam room.

I don't know what will happen with Christina, sadly enough. Her mother had tuberculosis and was told not to work for six months. She has, of course, not been able to do that. She has now started working as a domestic servant for a family (they do not know she is recovering from tuberculosis.) Because this doesn't make enough money for her to survive and feed her children, she has started working as a prostitute at night. Christina is now home alone except when she is able to stay with neighbors. I will be telephoning friends of the family this weekend to see if they think she can handle the tutoring program in this situation. She is not going to school, so the worry is that she may be too far behind to be able to catch up. Christina is very bright, but without our help she will soon have to start working (probably selling things in the street or as a young domestic servant). We also have to consider that her mother (who is now twenty-six) will very likely contract tuberculosis or AIDS from the intensity and type of work she is doing. Since neighbors want to help, we will probably give Christina a chance (how can we really do otherwise?) at the tutoring program and hope against hope that she can somehow manage to succeed. One idea we are exploring is dividing the family stipend money between her mother and a neighbor who would help look after Christina and make sure she has enough food.

People in Salvador are becoming excited about Bahia Street. Eduardo spoke before a group of about a hundred teachers who expressed their interest in helping. Rita is also exploring what processes we need to do to become legally recognized in Brazil.

I have to say that I am startled by the strength of this response in Salvador. One of the problems I see with many so-called "development projects" is that they often consist of people in a more powerful country telling financially impoverished people in a less powerful country what they should do. Sometimes these projects are useful, and sometimes they are a disaster; it is generally true, however, that they are seldom controlled by the financially impoverished people. Bahia Street is a link of cooperation between people in Brazil and people in other parts of the world to curb cycles of poverty and to learn about each other. Bahia Street is a unique organization in that it is neither a "grassroots" project nor a "top-down" NGO. It is developing with the cooperation and ideas of people in the shantytowns of Salvador who understand the problems of poverty, oppression, and opportunity very well. Its success is dependent upon all of us— including the girls who are at its center.

I will be going to Salvador during the Christmas break to give support to Rita and Madalena. Eduardo, Rita, and I are realizing that several short trips work much better than fewer long trips. Those in Salvador who are on the front line, dealing with the daily problems and issues that arise, need our support. The major problem is the cost of flights to Brazil. We desperately need an airline or company to donate flights. We will go stand-by or via Calcutta (did I actually say that?); we just need some way to visit Salvador frequently. Anyone with ideas or contacts with airlines or travel agencies, please, please let us know.

We also wish to thank Aaron for the two terms he worked as an intern for us and to congratulate him on the scholarship he won to the University of Washington and for an educational trip to South Africa winter term. Our new intern this year is Karey, who has been a valued volunteer since we began. And welcome to Joyce, a professional grant writer who is donating invaluable advice and assistance.

As a part of this, I am making a plea again: we need an office. Some people on Vashon very generously offered office space, but we really need an office in Seattle. I, myself, will be moving to Seattle soon.

I close with a quick thanks to SENDEX, the Brazilian store in Seattle, for their continual support. And to Pat, our Vashon treasurer, who celebrated his sixtieth birthday by trying to slice off his index finger while cleaning salmon and required sixty stitches (to equal his sixty years— I didn't realize a hand could take sixty stitches...)—HAPPY BIRTHDAY. And to everyone else, I wish you well in this season of pungent smells, of fallen leaves, husks of chestnuts, green walnuts, overripe apples being pressed for cider, and the scattering of new rain.

Um abraço,
Margaret

more sides of bahia

I was staying at a small Italian-owned hotel in Salvador because Rita said she didn't want me to stay with her right then. She said it was fine to come and visit, but that her neighborhood was just too violent at the moment, that she would feel concerned about me coming home alone at night. Everyone now seemed to have guns, Rita said. She heard gunfire daily.

I had been at the hotel only a few days when, at breakfast, I met some Americans. They told me they were bird specialists. They had been tracking certain birds, trying to determine why the birds were disappearing.

"We stand on a sand spit in the sun all day, watching, counting birds," one of the scientists said with a laugh. "We wear big hats."

"So why are the birds disappearing?"

"Could be pollution. We want to know exactly their diet. These birds are rare. We want to get the Bahian government to protect them."

"So, why don't you ask some local people? They might know."

The scientist didn't manage to conceal the disdain that touched the corners of her lips. "We do have scientists here with whom we have discussed this."

"No, I mean local fishermen. They might know something."

"Well, I don't speak Portuguese, but I'm not sure we could trust anything they might say anyway. The poor in this city are like peasants, anything they'd tell you would just be folklore anyway."

After breakfast, they all left for their boat, science equipment and food hampers in hand. Doing research by spending all day in boats and on the beach sounded fun. Perhaps I should have been a bird specialist instead of an anthropologist, I thought.

I had lunch with Rita that afternoon at her house, and while walking through the remnants of her neighborhood market, which was still surviving I noticed, I asked her about the birds. I didn't know their name in English or Portuguese, so I described them as the scientist had described them to me.

"Oh, yes," Rita said, and she gave me a name I didn't know.

"There used to be thousands when I was a child. You don't see them much anymore."

"Why not? I mean why are they disappearing?"

Rita shrugged. "There aren't as many kinds of fish here anymore either. They probably don't have enough food. But we can ask João. He'll know."

We walked up to the old fish seller. He nodded an acknowledgment to me as Rita inspected his fish. "So why are these birds disappearing?" she asked him.

"Nothing to eat," he said. He poked one of the plump tuna that lay on a newspaper on a board in front of him. "Caught him this morning. This kind of tuna is still common. But that bird, she only eats one special type of tuna; it's very small. And once they put in that factory north of here, that tuna pretty well disappeared. Then the birds, they started to go, too."

"So, they won't eat any other tuna?" I asked him. "I mean, tuna all look pretty similar."

"To you maybe," he said. Rita nodded at his plump tuna, and he began wrapping it for her. "But I've been here some seventy years, most of it fishing, and I've never known those birds to catch or eat any other tuna but that one."

That evening, coming back from Rita's, I saw the scientists again. They had just come off their boat, and they looked hot and tired. Maybe bird biologist wasn't the best profession after all.

I hurried to the scientist I had met earlier, pulling out of my pocket the scrap of paper where I had asked Rita to write the name of the disappearing tuna. "Hello!" I said. "I may have a clue in your search."

The scientist looked at me.

"Here." I handed her the paper. "This is what those birds eat. And probably the pollution from one, or several, of the factories around here is killing it. So the birds are starving."

She looked at the paper scrap. "I don't know this word."

"It's a kind of tuna."

"We have a list of the fish here and this isn't one."

"Well, it's mostly gone now."

"Yes. Well." She shoved the paper into her bag where it clearly would be lost by the time she reached her hotel room. "I must head in."

I continued on my way. Time and time again, I was reminded how credibility has less to do with knowledge or information given, but instead with the class and power of the person making the statement. Too bad for those little birds.

One day, I visited the tenement where Don had lived when he was in Salvador. He'd published his book on transvestites in Salvador and had asked me to take a copy to Mabel, the transvestite whose bright and smiling face appeared on the cover. Along the way, I looked for the transvestite prostitutes who had protected me during my nightly walks through these neighborhoods. They were gone. Instead, designated tourist police who wore special tourist uniforms now stood at almost every street corner of the "new" Pelourinho. Its central streets had been cleaned and repaired, its buildings restored with remarkable skill and painted bright pink, orange, and vermilion. The narrow lanes, now cloaked in a sheen of apparent safety and prosperity, were crowded with foreign tourists and middle-class Brazilians buying handicrafts and stopping at the freshly painted cafes and expensive restaurants. But, when I reached the top of the street of Don's old residence, I saw that the transformation had not as yet touched it. The contrast was so stark that I laughed. A tourist policeman standing at the street's entrance tried to bar my way.

"You shouldn't go on that street," he said with a condescending smile. "It's not safe."

"I'll be all right," I said.

"No, really," he said, standing directly in front of me. "I really can't let you go down there."

"It's OK," I said and smiled back at him with equal condescension. "I have friends down there." He looked at me, his face hardened, and he stepped aside.

I found Mabel on a bed in one of the rooms of the tenement. Her eyes were sunken, her skin stretched across her cheekbones, her lips almost invisible, the ravages of AIDS etched in every crease in her once smooth face. Her arm on the sheet was so thin I could see its separate bones. I was afraid if I touched her I'd break something. I tried to keep the dismay from my eyes, but I'm not sure I succeeded. Other transvestites must have been paying her rent because she clearly couldn't work any more.

I showed her the book, holding it close to her eyes so she could see. "Look, Mabel," I said. "It's you."

She smiled. "I'm famous," she whispered. She ran one frail finger lightly along the contours of the photo of her smiling face. "I was so beautiful then."

I sat at the little table in my hotel room trying to write, making notes of what I had learned that day. I had spent the day visiting with Jorge and his family, then the evening out at our usual bar with Rita. The hotel room was insufferably hot. I opened the wooden shutters wider and splashed my face with water. Rita had been talking about her time at university. She said that nearly all her close friends—who were, like her, African-Brazilians—were from the rural interior of Bahia, not the city. She thought this was because the infrastructure in the small towns and countryside was much better than in the city. Families in the city, she said, lived in bairros that had no central community. The children got lost in the streets while parents worked to survive.

"And you, Rita, why are you an exception?" I asked. "Why does one child make it and millions don't."

Rita had laughed. "Don't make me so exceptional," she said. "Although I grew up in the city, both my parents are from the interior. And remember, Nordeste was like a small village when I was a child, nothing like it is today."

We talked about how these neighborhoods were always changing. Bonocô, the neighborhood where both Jorge and Christina lived, was better at present in terms of street violence and gang activity.

"It's because they killed them all."

"Who's 'they'?"

Rita shrugged.

I tapped my beer glass in frustration. Jorge had told me exactly the same thing—and had been just as vague on the identity of "they." Jorge seemed to think the killings were fine as long as "they" kept to the more violent offenders who, in Jorge's opinion, were trying to take over the neighborhood.

Rita smiled ruefully when she saw my exasperation. "Bonocô may be getting better," she said, "but Nordeste Ameralinha is getting worse. Three or more young men are killed a weekend." She paused.

"That makes about 180 a year in Nordeste alone."

"Who's killing them?" I asked, yet again.

Rita filled up our glasses and looked over her shoulder. "Gang activity, police, death squads. My street is particularly dangerous right now because the young man next door, Pedrinho—remember, you met him last time you were there—he's become an assassin lately and accidentally shot the wrong person in a gang fight. Now, the opposing gang is taking pot shots at his house hoping to kill him. I can't go out on my verandah anymore. I might get shot."

I said nothing, and Rita waved to Nelson to bring us another beer. "And make it really cold!" she shouted. Nelson laughed and gave her the thumbs up.

"I read today that there used to be more men than women in Salvador," Rita continued, "but now the ratio is 800 men to every 1000 women. And that deaths are almost all in neighborhoods like mine."

The beer Nelson poured from the frosty bottle was so cold that it came out in a slush of ice. Rita looked at it suspiciously. "Doesn't look very cold to me. Warm, just like always." She flashed her eyes at him, and Nelson laughed as he walked away. Rita sipped her beer with a satisfied smile.

"Everyone has guns for sale," she said. "The police, kids… ten-year-old kids are selling them to each other. It increases the boys' professional options—they now have a choice between the time-honored drug seller or the up-and-coming paid assassin. Good money, with a life going at about twenty reais each." I glanced at her. "Do I sound jaded or cynical?" she asked. "Last weekend, two young men were shot on the next street to me; I've known them since they were born. Then, the police came and shot a third young man. I knew him, too. I start to feel battered after awhile, all this waste of young lives. How can we have a community when we all have to build mental walls around ourselves to keep from going insane?"

Rita drained her beer in silence and, after a moment, I refilled it.

I sighed. "Jorge told me some news of Gato," I said. "He's still in Europe, but things aren't going well. His sister, Renata quit school and has a boyfriend." I shook my head. "That was supposed to be a cheering change of topic, but it didn't work, did it?"

"Well, my neighbor's husband's *amante*—his mistress—rang my neighbor in some kind of competition to say she was pregnant. So, my neighbor, instead of throwing the jerk out, also got pregnant." Rita shook her head. "I don't know why she stays with him, she's just afraid to leave. And I don't think he even really likes women."

"Well, I guess that's just his loss, isn't it?"

We both giggled. Nelson walked by, glanced at us and shook his head.

"As long as we can laugh," Rita said, "we have courage."

First Year Letter: To a Mailing List of 80: February 15, 1999

Dear Donors and Volunteers,

Winds of middle winter slip along the window panes. Outside, pouring rain makes mush of fallen leaves while I, snug inside, sit warmed by the tones of Gal Costa, one of my favorite Brazilian singers. This is a letter with meaning: it is one year since Bahia Street began operations.

Madalena has turned out to be a wonderful tutor; she is involved, knowledgeable of good teaching methods, and very caring (whenever Rita and I tried to be hard-nosed about which girls should continue, Madalena fiercely fought to keep them all). We are very lucky to have such dedicated people working with us in Salvador. Rita is spending much time working with the families, the school, and with the girls themselves, not to mention banks and the financial administration. For this, we are currently paying her $100 a month, which goes about twice as far as $100 here in the States. Paying for Internet access and a living, part-time wage to Rita is a priority.

Here is an update on the girls:

Juliana: She has been studying at the tutoring class in the morning and Dois de Julho in the afternoons. To do this, she leaves home at 7:30 AM and returns at about 8:00 each night. She still wants to be a doctor. Her older sister (both her parents are dead) supports Juliana and her sixteen-year-old brother by baking pizza, which she sells on the street.

Dois de Julho has been giving Juliana some problems. Some of the teachers are stating explicitly that they do not think children from the shantytowns could possibly succeed at their school. It is no surprise then that Juliana, despite doing extremely well at the tutoring, studying continually, and being very bright, is being given nothing but below average marks. She is becoming very frustrated (the rest of us are angry).

Because of these difficulties, we have decided to change schools and tell the new school nothing about the project. We will have the girls take the entrance exam and succeed on their own merits. We think this will give them a better chance at equality. Juliana is very happy with this plan. The new school we chose is São Bento, a Catholic school (most private schools are religious) that has an excellent academic reputation, is only two blocks from where the girls are being tutored, and is affiliated with a natural medicine school.

Lidia: Because of problems with her public school, she only started the tutoring in August. She came to the program semiliterate despite being in the fifth grade. Despite Lidia's dedication, to jump from semiliteracy to actual sixth-grade literacy in three and a half months is almost impossible, and she may not pass São Bento's language entrance exam (she will pass in public school with no problem).

Interestingly enough, she will have no problem with math as she is showing a startling aptitude and will soon be above average for her grade level. When I asked her last year what she wanted to do as a profession, she said she wanted to be a doctor. This year when I asked her the same question, she replied that she was no longer sure, she was only positive that she loved math. "Are there professions where I can use math?" she asked me. "Because that is what I want to do." We are keeping our fingers crossed for her. Her father has liberated her from household activities until the test to leave her plenty of time for study.

Claudia: Here we have a sad story. If it were easy to change poverty and lack of education, the world would presumably be further along than it is. Claudia is very bright, and her public school was somewhat better than the others, so she will likely have little difficulty passing the private school entrance exam. However, her mother has a nineteen-year-old boyfriend, who is spending most of his time at the house and not doing much else. He and all of Claudia's family continue to live in one room. Claudia, understandably, has become distracted from her studies, and her mother is not encouraging her toward study at all. In fact, her mother steals her bus money. Because of Claudia and Patricia's families, we have added some rules: families are paid their stipend at the end of the month, and if the girl misses more than three days (unless she is sick), they do not receive the stipend for that month. If a girl misses more than three days for three months, she is expelled from the program. Madalena is also now in charge of all the bus tokens, and as each girl arrives for tutoring, she is given her bus tokens only for the next day. We are allowing Claudia to take the entrance exam; the rest is up to her and her mother.

Patricia: Her story is the saddest of all. First of all, we found out that Patricia's father does not have thirty-nine children—he has forty-nine. His wife, Patricia's mother, Maria, got herself sterilized after twelve children;

this was apparently such an affront to the father's masculinity that he has now impregnated another woman (why this woman had sex with a seventy-seven year old man with tuberculosis is beyond me). Patricia is very bright and likes to study, but her mother often keeps her at home to look after the other children. Some time before Patricia entered the program, she began skipping school. Since she started the tutoring, she dropped out altogether, although she continued with the tutoring and studies enthusiastically. Rita told her that she would not be able to continue with the program if she did not pass the fifth grade, but she would not go back. She says she hates the public school but will not tell us why. She is the only one of the five girls who will not be taking the entrance exam. Patricia is confused and upset, and we fear she is suffering under conditions she will not discuss. The tutoring is clearly her only stability right now and is a lifeline. Because we do not want to abandon her, we have told her that she can continue to attend the tutoring, but that we shall cut the stipend for her family. Rita has also ensured that she can reenroll at her public school. Her mother was extremely angry at the loss of the stipend and threatened to press charges against us with the military police—the exact nature of these supposed charges was unclear—but it appears that her threat was a bluff. In reality, it is unlikely that she wished to draw her family to the attention of the military police. Although we need to stay clear of Patricia's family, we will not lose contact with Patricia and will offer her help when it can be effective.

Christina: She is the eight-(just-turned-nine) year-old who came to us illiterate and whom we seriously considered dropping because of family problems. Her mother is now working twelve hours a day, six days a week as a maid, and earns about $100 a month. She has recovered from tuberculosis and is not working any longer as a prostitute (I think we can thank the half-stipend we give her for that). Christina's mother sleeps on the floor of a friend's two-room shack and hires Rosa, a neighbor, to care for Christina and Christina's younger brother. For this she pays about $30 a month. She visits the children on Sundays.

Rosa lives with her husband, another foster child, Christina, and Christina's brother in a tiny two-room shack. All six of them sleep on the floor. Rosa's husband takes care of the other children every morning while Rosa goes with Christina to the tutoring, waits for her, and then takes *her home. We are now paying Rosa's bus fare as well as Christina's (about $1.50 per day) and giving her half the monthly stipend. Christina has not missed a day of the tutoring. She was illiterate in May and now Madalena thinks she can enter the second grade. Christina is extremely bright and Rosa takes great pride in the fact that soon Christina will be able to read better than she can.*

What we are doing for the girls is beginning to show. We do have a problem right now that we don't have much money. Not counting administrative costs, the program costs about $1,500 a month, and at present we only have enough to last one month. When Rita walks through the shantytowns, people know who she is. They have heard of Bahia Street, and they bring their daughters and neighbors to meet her, hoping that their daughter, relative, or friend might be a girl chosen for the program. They are telling her that this is the only time an aid project has actually touched their lives. We would love to add two new girls to the tutoring program this year. Bahia Street is small, but in a world where most money goes for materialist concerns, we are making a difference.

Karey from the University of Washington continued to work with us in Seattle this term, and a new volunteer, Mary, has gone to Salvador, where she will stay for a year and a half helping Rita with accounts and with the process of making Bahia Street a legal entity in Brazil.

Here in Seattle, the winter is sliding its rainy, muddy way forward, but just today I noticed crocuses showing their heads and buds fattening on the trees. There is a subtle scent of spring when one wakes in the morning. It may be dark and rainy outside, but we have homes, we have food, and we have a future.

Um abraço,
Margaret

eighteen | a view into the abyss

"I think you have to go to Brazil, Margareth."

"What? Eduardo, how can I go? And you just got back. What happened?"

Eduardo lowered his head and stared at his hands. He looked exhausted. We were sitting in the living room of the Seattle house I had recently bought. The housing market in the area was booming, so I had been able to sell the ramshackle cottage I had bought on Vashon only a year and a half earlier for double the price. With that money, I had managed to buy a 1905 fixer-upper in a neighborhood of Seattle known as the Central District. Nearly all my white friends in Seattle had told me that this was a bad idea. The Central District was mostly African-American and, for Seattle, inner city. Already, I'd noticed a drug and prostitution business being run out of one house across the street. The real estate ad had called my house a "farmhouse in the center of Seattle." Maybe, I thought, with a great stretch of the imagination. When I moved in, all of the windowpanes were painted black. And they were all covered with bars—the prison farmhouse look. The backyard sprouted old bathtubs and toilets instead of grass and flowers.

I had set up a desk and filing cabinet in one room for the Bahia Street office. Eduardo and I were sitting on a mattress on the living room floor. I hadn't acquired much furniture yet.

"I went to visit Claudia," Eduardo said. "It was so hot, Margareth, that I couldn't go inside. Most of it doesn't even have a roof. Did you know that?" I nodded. "Well, it was getting ready to rain, but the sun on the tin roof of the one room where they live, it was terrible. Where do they sleep? They all must just sleep together on the floor! I don't know how they do it."

"I know Eduardo," I said. "It's bad. But why do I have to go down?"

Eduardo continued as if he hadn't heard. "Claudia's mother told me that her grandmother died and left her pension to Claudia's brother. But he has decided to give it to her, so she can fix up the house."

"That's great."

"Yes, maybe. I hope she actually does that and doesn't spend it on her boyfriend or something."

"Yes, well, we can't do anything about that. How was your family, Eduardo?"

"Good. Everything is fine with my family." I waited. "Margareth... Claudia told me that she is 'dating with responsibility.'"

"Claudia is dating?"

"Well, her mother doesn't set the best example. I think her mother is encouraging her to date. Claudia also said that she 'knows everything about abortion.'"

"Great. Abortion is illegal in Brazil."

"Yes. I presumed that she meant she knows how to do it herself. I told her that the best thing would be to avoid getting pregnant in the first place so she wouldn't have to worry about it. I pointed out that an abortion was very dangerous for a girl her age. She said, 'I know that. My neighbor, she was thirteen. She gave herself an abortion and she died.'"

"Fantastic."

"Rita can't handle all this, Margareth. I was wrong to suggest Madalena. Madalena doesn't like Rita, I think. And Mary, that new volunteer, don't take me wrong, but she's too American. She's going to take over. I'm afraid Rita won't stand up to her; she'll just let her do it. But Mary can't do Bahia Street. It'll fall apart."

I stood up and walked around the room. The floor felt spongy under my feet. I hope this floor is solid, I thought. The last thing I could afford was rebuilding the foundation. "I wish I could call her," I said. "Give her some support."

"If she had a phone. She stopped her cell phone, you know. She needs you, Margareth." He watched me for a moment. "My wife's pregnant," he said.

"But you just got married, didn't you?"

He grinned. "Not long."

"Well...congratulations." I hoped my voice didn't reveal my true thoughts. How was Eduardo going to support a baby? He'd only been in the States about two years, and he was planning to make a living by being a musician. Most native-born Americans couldn't do that. Now he'd have a baby to support.

He got up. The exhaustion had ebbed from his face. "Yeah," he said. "It's wonderful. We're excited."

I laughed and gave him a hug. "Did you tell your parents?"

"Not yet. I think we'll wait a few months. Things can always happen... ."

"Of course. Congratulations again."

"Thanks." Eduardo picked up his jacket from the mattress. "You have to go, Margareth. Soon. I know I'm Brazilian, but I think Rita needs you. I don't know if even you can do it, but I do know that if you don't go, Rita's going to quit." He paused at the door. "And Margareth?"

"Yeah?"

"I won't be able to go so much after this, you know. When the baby comes."

"I know that."

"Oh, I almost forgot." He handed me a packet of letters. "The girls wrote these letters. You'll like them."

I shut the door behind him. I returned to the mattress in the living room and leafed through the lined sheets, each letter written in a careful cursive hand. I thought of Andrea's history paper. "CLAUDIA" was printed at the top of the first sheet.

"Thanks to Bahia Street for keeping Madalena teaching for a second year," Claudia had written. "Madalena is a wonderful teacher and I have never met a teacher like Madalena. I used to hate math, but now I love math because Bahia Street made me learn. I promise to miss no more days of the tutoring program and want to be like Juliana who never misses a day at school or tutoring."

I smoothed the sheet and laid it aside before picking up the next one. "JULIANA," I read.

"Bahia Street is better than last year. I feel you are all closer lately and we know more about Bahia Street. We would like to be included in meetings between parents, teachers, and Bahia Street directors because we want to talk too.

"We need more classes and tutoring. How about arts, music and dancing?

"São Bento is much better than Dois de Julho. They know our needs and I am happy the kids do not know I am from a charity project. This way everyone treats me the same way as they do the other kids.

"In my opinion, it is much better if Bahia Street gets girls who are attending the first grade because, in my experience, I think it is much better if we can attend a private school from the very beginning. I had a hard time starting a good private school in the fifth grade."

I pulled out the last letter. "PAULA." Beneath the name in someone else's hand, Madalena's I presumed—it wasn't Rita's—was written, "Lidia has decided to call herself Paula now that she is a teenager." I laughed and continued to read.

"Bahia Street is more organized. Thanks for giving us the space to talk about us. I love Madalena. She helps us in doing our homework and she explains to us about teenage life and helps us to understand things our parents do not explain to us.

"The room is great! Here we have a library, kitchen, refrigerator, and nobody bothers us and here it is as if we were in a home. Everyone respects us.

"Bahia Street is being a help to us in our personal life. It means— it helps us to avoid being on the street, getting pregnant early, and other bad things that can affect our lives. Bahia Street will make my dreams come true—to be a doctor. Bahia Street opens a big door to bring happiness to us.

"Bahia Street is my life now. It is my opportunity and I do not want to throw it away."

I put down the letters and leaned against the wall. A year ago these girls could hardly write. I got up and walked into the kitchen. It was carpeted in purple and brown paisley. I poured some water into the tea kettle, jiggled the burner to make it connect properly, and began to boil water for tea. The floor in the kitchen felt a bit spongy as well.

My mother wasn't going to be happy about me going down to Brazil over Christmas again.

I turned in my grades for the classes I was teaching that term, packed a bag, and caught a plane from Seattle to Los Angeles to São Paulo to Salvador. The trip lasted twenty hours total. I had been exhausted when I left; I was catatonic when I hit Salvador. I went straight to the borrowed room we used for the tutoring program and met Rita for lunch.

"Leave your bags here," Rita said. "It's safe."

We went to a *comida a quilo* or "eat by the kilo" place nearby. These buffet lunch restaurants had recently sprung up all over the city. You got a plate, piled on what you wanted and paid by the weight at the end. Prices varied depending upon how fancy the restaurant was. Rita had discovered a moderately priced one that specialized in salads and "natural" foods.

"You'll love this place," she said as she led me through the throngs of people that crowded Avenida Sete de Setembro, the main business street of Salvador. "It's in one of the old municipal buildings from the early eighteen hundreds. They haven't destroyed it." She turned into a narrow entrance, went up some stairs, and we were in a high marble-floored hallway. At the end of the hallway, a marble stairway curved to the cool dim spaces above. Through glass doors we entered the busy comida a quilo, still marble floors, but with casual Formica tables and plastic chairs, noisy, and full of life. A waiter shouted a greeting to Rita. She waved at him and laughed.

We got our food and sat in silence while we ate. Then Rita asked me about my flight. Finally, after the waiter had cleared our plates, I asked Rita what was going on.

"It's amazing how easily this whole project could fall apart," she said. "I can't do this alone."

"What's wrong, Rita?"

Rita stared at the wall. "About a month ago, Claudia came to tutoring very sick. She'd missed a few days, and when she returned she could hardly sit in her seat. Then she fainted." Rita sighed. "At first she wouldn't talk. Then I made her tell me what had happened. Thank God she came in. I don't know how she made it on the bus." I waited. "She got pregnant, Margaret."

"Oh, fuck." I put down the juice I'd been drinking.

"Then she gave herself an abortion by drinking an overdose of this medicine that's supposed to be used for treating ulcers. You can buy it over the counter."

"The same one her friend, the neighbor who died, used."

"Yeah. Eduardo told you? For some reason, all the kids are using it now. They don't know what else to do, and they hear it works. It kills them."

"What happened, Rita?"

"I ran out to an herbal store. I got something to ease the pain and to flush out her system."

"You're amazing, Rita."

"Not so amazing. I told her mother that we would pay for a gynecologist so Claudia could get treated. But her mother refused."

"Her mother what?"

"Refused. Because abortion is illegal, her mother is afraid that *she'll* get in trouble if someone finds out that Claudia gave herself an abortion."

"Her daughter was in danger of dying!"

"I know. I kept giving Claudia herbal medicines and finally the vomiting and bleeding stopped. She's still weak, but I think she'll be all right now."

"Your knowledge of herbal medicine is remarkable, Rita. How'd you learn?"

"My mother. And I was always interested. But I wasn't sure I would save her, Margaret. She could have died."

"What are we doing, Rita? This is so hard for you."

"There's more." I looked at her. "Let's go somewhere else for coffee and I'll tell you."

We wandered into a relatively quiet side street and sat at the counter of a small café that both Rita and I liked.

"You're back?" the waiter, Reinaldo, asked me as he wiped the counter in front of us. "Can you take me back with you in your suitcase?"

"I'd love to," I said. "But you'll have to shrink somehow."

"Your feet are too big," Rita said. "Now get us some coffees. Mediums. With milk."

"I know what you want," Reinaldo said, and he flicked his towel at Rita.

Rita picked up the sugar container and shook it aimlessly. "It's all falling apart, Margaret. Maybe we shouldn't have started this."

Reinaldo slid our coffees across the counter. He looked at our faces and politely left us alone. "Is it the girls' parents?" I asked.

"That, but no, it's more. It's Mary, that volunteer from the States. She knows how to run an organization much better than I do. Maybe she should just take over. I don't know how to do this."

"Rita, what are you talking about? She's supposed to be helping you. You're running it."

"Yeah, well. I feel I don't do stuff fast enough for her. She wants our registration done now. It's wonderful of her to help, don't get me wrong, but then she gets annoyed because an office is closed, or she comes back for some papers and no one has looked at them yet, or I haven't finished what she asked me to do the day before. She doesn't seem to realize I have another job, that I'm trying to do my photography as well."

"She probably doesn't realize that."

"She wants meetings; she gets upset when people don't show up on time; she wants things she calls 'time plans.'"

I laughed. "Welcome to the United States. She's North American, Rita. Poor Mary."

The corner of Rita's mouth curled up in spite of herself. "I don't think she understands that she's offending people. But she acts as though she understands Bahia better than I do!" She paused. "And I made a mistake, Margaret. You and I have to get email or talk on the phone more. I know it's expensive, but somehow we have to do it. I started talking with Mary about management issues—I needed someone—and then she just gradually began to think she should make most of the decisions herself. People will listen to her more easily than they will to me. She's the kind of person they expect to see as director of Bahia Street, not me. I can't do this, Margaret. We have to make a decision, either Mary becomes director and I quit, or you get Mary to leave."

"Me? How can I tell her to leave?" Rita stirred more sugar into what was left of her coffee. "But, Rita," I said, "I was like that too when I first arrived in Salvador. It's our Northerner attitude, our belief that 'efficiency,' as we define it, works not only for our own Northern lives and businesses, but also for people about whom we know nothing. When I first moved to Salvador, I also kept trying to 'get things done' in a timely fashion. It was hopeless. Obstacles seemed thrown in my way all the time. But then I relaxed, went with the rhythm of the place, and I met just the person I needed while out drinking a beer. That person knew someone else, and things happened. I arrived late for a meeting and everyone else was late as well, so we all arrived at the same time and the meeting went perfectly. Just give her time, she'll learn."

"No, Margaret. If she does, she needs to learn alone and not within

Bahia Street. It's not just me, but everyone.

"While Eduardo was here," she continued, "we all went for lunch together to talk about the selection of the girls for next year. At the end of the lunch, Mary protested when we started to pay, saying that Bahia Street should pay for all our lunches. I said no, that we had no money, and that we could not be using Bahia Street money for lunch. She turned to Madalena and told her that in the NGOs where she had worked before, this is how it was always done and she was sure Bahia Street had plenty of money to pay for these things. Eduardo said that this was not the case and that we were not some big group, that this was a project of all of us, not the States and us in a different group. But Madalena looked troubled. Mary intimated that Madalena was being cheated. Things with Madalena were bad before, but now they're worse."

"What's wrong with Madalena? I thought she was being fantastic with the girls."

"In many ways she is, but she won't work with me. She wants only to talk with you or Eduardo. She won't show me the class grades, says we should wait until you or Eduardo comes and she will share them with you, then you decide what I get to see. It's straight prejudice. Exactly what we're trying to change, we have in the middle of our own program."

Despair settled over me like a suffocating blanket. I realized I was angry—at myself, at Rita, at nothing, just angry. Nothing I could think to say sounded helpful. "Oh, Rita, it sounds awful," I finally murmured.

"I can blame everyone else and everything," Rita said, "but I have to learn too, I suppose, to be a director even when I feel intimidated by whites or arrogant middle-class foreigners." She shoved her cup aside. "And there's more."

"Please, no." I shook my head and waved to Reinaldo. "Reinaldo! Could you please get us two more coffees? I think we need them."

Reinaldo bustled in our direction. "Boyfriend trouble?"

"I wish. Boyfriend trouble would be better."

"No, the only thing worse than boyfriend trouble is girlfriend trouble!" He placed our fresh coffees in front of us and hurried away.

"It's the space," Rita said. The room we were borrowing we only had because the director of the building was a relative of Eduardo's. She'd graciously let us use the upper floor of their building since we'd begun. "I think she wants us out." I stopped stirring my coffee. "I think when she agreed to let us use the space, she assumed that you and Eduardo were in charge. I don't think she can cope with the idea that I, a black favela woman, could be running it here. She keeps asking when you or Eduardo are coming back. She keeps telling us to keep the girls quiet. They *are* trying to run an office below us. But the other day, one of her assistants asked if the girls have lice."

"They might."

Rita laughed. "All kids get lice at some time. The issue is that they don't want favela kids in their building unless they are supervised by a middle-class director who will make sure they behave and don't steal anything."

"They're just little kids!"

"Margaret," Rita said. "Don't play naive. I can't blame her in some ways. After all she's responsible for the space. She doesn't know me, only Eduardo. Why should she trust me?"

"She doesn't know me any better than she knows you," I said. "Why should she trust me either?"

"Be real, Margaret. You're a white, middle-class foreigner with a Ph.D."

My stomach hurt.

I arranged to meet Mary in the upper praça of Pelourinho. The praça was being renovated. All the large shade trees had already been cut and the old mosaics dug up and carted away. As a part of the renovation, one section had been excavated as an archaeological dig and the findings left exposed for people to view. I sat on one of the bright, new stone benches in the boiling sun and waited. Then I saw Mary moving swiftly through the piles of construction materials. She wore a flowing blue dress that matched the deep blue of her eyes. She looked healthy, happy—and exactly on time.

"Margaret!" she said as she reached me. She gave me a big hug. "It's so wonderful to see you. And here! We meet in Seattle and then we meet here. The world is a strange place."

"Yeah. How are you liking it?"

"I love it! And Rita's wonderful, isn't she? Bahia's such a fantastic place. I don't think I ever want to leave."

"Huh. Well, Mary..."

"Did Rita tell you that we're working on the nonprofit registration? Boy, they're slow here!"

"Mary." I took a deep breath. "Mary, I don't think we can have you work with Bahia Street any more."

Mary shaded her eyes. "But Margaret... I understand that you don't have money to pay me. I'm looking for jobs here teaching English."

"Mary. I don't think we can have you volunteer." Her silence was louder than the construction hammers. "It's just...it's that Bahia Street is too young. We shouldn't have taken a volunteer yet. We don't really know what we're doing ourselves yet. Rita's learning to be the director here. And I'm learning in the States. We were wrong. It's too early."

"But now is when you need the help. I've worked with other nonprofits. I know how to do it."

"Yes, you probably do. But we haven't settled on our infrastructure yet. Rita and I have to figure it out ourselves. Later, when we're more organized. Then maybe we can use you. Then we'll need volunteers I'm sure."

"But this is what I came down here to do."

"Yes, I know that. I shouldn't have agreed to it. It's my fault."

"I see."

"Do you want to go for a coffee or something?"

"Not really. There are lots of nonprofits around. I'm sure I can find one that can use my skills."

"I'm sorry, Mary."

To a Mailing List of 90: January 15, 2000

Dear Donors and Volunteers,

I am watching a thin line of bright along the misty horizon, a crack of space between the muted winter sky and pewter sea. This cloaked light, encased in cold and rain, brings a quiet that I somehow love.

First of all, the biggest news—for those of you who haven't heard already through the grapevine—all the girls passed!! We—and most of all they—have succeeded through their first year, and second year for Juliana! This means that Christina will enter the third grade and Juliana and Paula (Lidia) will go to the sixth. Rita was laughing with excitement when she told me.

I have just returned from Brazil, and it was one of those trips that leaves one exhausted, and yet full of an exhilarated energy. The girls are well. Christina used to be terrified of me and in general very shy and withdrawn. Now she is jumping all over the place, talking a mile a minute, full of energy and life. She was also reading to me happily—even putting voice inflection in her reading as she went. And to think that less than a year ago she was totally illiterate. Interestingly, Christina is developing a real skill and love of art. In her first term reports, she received an 8.6 out of 10 (6 is average) for art. Paula just gave a public talk on capoeira angola, which apparently went very well. I wish you could all know Paula. I am so proud of her, of her confidence and courage to get up in front of a group and talk. She could never have done this even a year ago.

It is so amazing for me to see the change in all of these girls; they are so bright and happy, full of ideas and stumbling over each other to tell me what they think about a whole variety of subjects.

We have made the decision to add three new girls this year. This is a bit scary since our expenses in Brazil will be almost double each month. In addition, we pay for the entire year's uniforms, books, and other supplies at the first part of the school year, so February is a very expensive month. The increase in the number of girls is possible, in part, because São Bento has given Bahia Street a sixth tuition at a 30% reduced price. Rita negotiated this tuition donation.

One of the new girls is eight and lives in the same neighborhood as Christina, while one of the others, who is ten, lives in the same neighborhood as Claudia.

I also have the sad news that we have lost two girls from the Bahia Street program. In both cases, the girls themselves did not want to leave; rather, it was their parents who undermined their ability to attend school and the tutoring. Claudia's mother has decided to move herself and her children to a distant, particularly violent neighborhood to be near her twenty-year-old, drug-selling boyfriend. Claudia came to visit Bahia Street for a final time just before I left Brazil. She stood tall, controlling the tears that stood at the edges of her eyes and said to us, "I realize I am losing my future."

There was nothing Rita or I could say or do.

Then, as she left, Claudia turned, holding up her well-thumbed workbook. "May I keep this?" she asked.

Because of these experiences, we have changed our selection process. Now we have a more focused screening of the parents. Even so, we realize that some of the girls may not have a chance to finish the program, and we are exploring ways to have as much impact on them as possible for the time they are with us. Studies have shown that both mortality and pregnancy rates go down with increased education. Thus, in continuing to develop the education program for the girls, we are bearing in mind the short-term as well as long-term effects their education will have.

On this trip Rita, and I hired another tutor, Ana, to teach the older girls. Ana is a certified teacher with extensive experience working with impoverished families in Salvador. She herself is negra, of a darker skin color, giving the girls, who tend to be dark, someone like them to look up to. She is very excited about Bahia Street, and I watched her the first day charm the older girls; she has an ability to understand what will make them excited about learning and to bring it to class (for example, Paula, who loves capoeira, has been having difficulty with her Portuguese, so Ana brought her books on capoeira to read, which Paula is now gobbling up as fast as she can).

We have been working for some time to try to register Bahia Street as an official nonprofit in Brazil and on this visit we made great progress. We drew up a set of By-Laws and Internal Regulations and the other requirements of the State, and selected a Board of Directors, which includes as the Treasurer an African-Brazilian woman who is both a qualified accountant and lawyer.

One of our interns here in Seattle, Karey, is going to Brazil to teach

English to the girls. She received a scholarship from the University of Washington for this trip, and she will be leaving in the next few weeks.

Here in Seattle, we have found an office! Intriguingly, it came through someone stealing my bicycle seat and my having to go to Recycled Cycles to find a new one. There I saw the "For Rent" notice and the rest followed. The office is literally at the end of a dock. It is very cheap because it is considered a "shed," but for me the location is perfect. The space is tremendous, and besides that, I may be able to kayak to work in the summer. I shall be keeping a nine-to-five schedule as much as possible, two days a week. Do ring before you come as I may be out at a meeting or on an errand.

I wish you all wonderful holidays, and for those of you who protested the WTO in Seattle, I hope you were able to avoid violence. It was incredible in the march to see groups for labor, the environment, and social justice all walking together and united. We in Bahia Street are working for change and social justice through providing educational opportunities and giving people a base where they can fight poverty, class, and racial barriers. Hand in hand with other groups, we do have a chance to change societies to create a better world. I wish you all warmth and intimacy with friends (and snow...maybe snow?) at this dark and contemplative time of the year. And we can think of the girls, proud, frolicking in the midst of their summer.

Um abraço,
Margaret

power and presence

On my previous trip to Salvador, I had gone to an exhibition put on by a local aid group. It featured lovely photos taken by street children and young people who worked on the streets. The aid group had given the children cameras and then presented the best, in middle-class terms, of what they shot. As I walked around this exhibit, I grew increasingly uncomfortable and wasn't sure why. Only later did I understand.

A middle-class aid agency had put on the exhibition. They kept all control firmly in their hands, hierarchies still in place. They gave middle-class tools (cameras) to children, adult to child, wealthy to poor. They taught the children to use these cameras just enough for the exhibition, but the real knowledge remained with the middle-class. The core message of the exhibition was, "My, how incredible it is that these poor children can use our middle class tools and make something lovely. Who would have expected that?" The smell of patronage was so thick I could taste it.

I began to think about the giving away of power. Generosity in terms of the donation of material things is comparatively easy. We keep the power because we never give away things we really think we need, and because through giving we increase our social power. We do nothing to destabilize the status quo.

Now that Bahia Street was more established (in other people's eyes, at least), it seemed that everyone wanted to talk with me about their own project for social reform among some economically impoverished group of people. They all wanted to be directly involved in the project in the other country. This was, of course, the flashy, exciting part. It was also where they felt powerful. One woman came to talk with me about an education project she wanted to do in Ecuador. On a visit she'd made there, she had seen the hardship people suffered and wanted to help. Her plan was to go to Ecuador and write the curriculum for a school's program—a school she would build and control. I suggested that she have people there write the curriculum, but she said she did not want to do that, as she had many ideas about what would work to educate the people there. I suggested that perhaps the people there understood what would work in the curriculum better than she did. She said she didn't feel that to be true. Finally, I suggested that she could organize a forum where the people there, who were experts in the area, could give their ideas. She could offer suggestions for a curriculum that they would write. Then the local people would control it, being the teachers, etc. The woman said, no, she didn't want to do that.

Finally, she admitted that she wanted to control it because she wanted to write the curriculum and to set up the school because she thought this would be fun. And, after more conversation, she also realized and admitted that she did want to be known as the person doing this, to get the accolades for the project, and for people there to look up to her. In the end I said, well, at least she needed to be clear why she was doing what she was doing, that it was not really for others, but mostly for herself.

This is a central difficulty: people start nonprofits for all kinds of reasons, and, generally, the primary reason is not that they want to change the world. Perhaps that is what they *think* they want to do when they start, but individual development aid projects have a great deal to do with personal insecurity and the desire for power. It is very clearly present in evangelical groups who go to areas, purporting to do "charitable" work, but who take with them a concrete vision of a world order that they want to impress upon those they encounter. Inherent in this approach is the desire for control. They want these people, who are of another religion and another lifestyle, to change their lifestyle and change their religion for one in which the evangelist has cultural— and spiritual—control. And, of course, the sources of power lie in the wealthy, and often white, first-class societies.

For those participating in secular development aid projects, this centrality of control is not so apparent. Our desire to help is not overtly evangelical, but it is there in more subtle ways. We have a concrete idea of what a "good" life for others is and what they need to have this "good" life. So, we force ideas upon them. We have the money and the institutional power to do this. We want to write the curriculum, design the housing project, the water project, the solar project— whatever it is that we think would be best for others.

In the end, however, we keep the control of society in our hands.

This is also why most projects help people just enough to give them tools to survive, but not to raise them to a level to make them equal with the ruling class. This would be dangerous because we would no longer have control.

Central to actual change is the real giving away of power and influence. This is very difficult on a personal level because we want to be recognized for our work, for the things we have done that have actually helped, and for the time we have spent on whatever project we feel strongly about. In most cases, this is the reason we participated in the first place.

But, I began to realize, giving away power is a learning experience of the deepest kind. Through giving away outward power, I realized I had begun to gain internal power: of myself, of not needing so much to control others. The insecurities I felt when we began Bahia Street had diminished, even if they had been replaced with a different kind of trepidation. Although I had not yet discussed it with anyone, I saw in the years ahead an encounter with the hardest part, as with a lover I did not want to leave me, the entire model of Bahia Street meant that one day I would have to let go. With love and openness, I must one day let go. I understood, theoretically, that if I knew this from the beginning, Bahia Street would not become a tool to mask my own insecurities and perceived inadequacies. And once I let go, I could begin other projects, take other roads. My life could be full of the many projects I could do.

I say I knew this theoretically, and I knew that the time of my slipping away from Bahia Street, of leaving it all in the hands of Rita and her staff, was in an unspecified future. But, for now, I had not published any research papers for a couple of years, and I had severely compromised my academic career. I understood theoretically the personal compromises I would need to make for a real shift in Bahia Street's power structure, but I wasn't so clear on how I personally fit into the plan. I was going to have to make some decisions at some point, and I wasn't sure at all what they would be.

For starters, I decided to get some furniture. I bought a sofa, bed frame, and a kitchen table at a garage sale. Mike, a white friend in Seattle, had agreed to pick the items up for me and was on his way.

"You think it'll be OK if I leave my car parked in front of your house?" he asked. He was speaking on his cell phone. He'd never been to the Central District before.

"Is it a BMW?"

"No, a Honda truck."

"You'll be fine."

I was learning how racial social apartheid worked in the United States. Near my house was an independent local grocery store. Everyone in the neighborhood used it, but no one came from outside the Central District to shop at our local store. So the separatism created a community. Each time I went to the store, I met the same people. I was growing to know the checkers. Kids from the local middle school came by in the afternoons to buy potato chips and pop. They hung around the front of the store and showed their school reports to the checkers, many of whom also lived in the neighborhood. The store played excellent music: funk, blues, and jazz.

The leafy neighborhood streets in other parts of Seattle were deserted most of the time. They made me nervous; I kept expecting someone to jump out from behind a bush or something. The Central District, however, was always occupied. The drug sellers on the corner two blocks away gave me curt nods as I passed. Even during the winter, in the evenings, and Saturday mornings, men worked on various old cars that lined the streets. Wilson, the enterprising fifteen-year-old son of the family across the street (not the drug house), had an after-school street-side business putting stereo systems in the trunks of hipster vehicles.

"Loookin' fine," the man around the corner said to me as I returned to the house laden with groceries.

"Not bad yourself," I replied. He straightened his shoulders in response to my compliment and returned to his engine repair.

Mike pulled up to the front of the house, and I went to the curb to help carry in the furniture. We had just opened the back of his truck when a tall fellow approached. He looked at us and slid his hand down the front of his pants. Mike jumped behind his truck. The man withdrew his hand and pulled out from his trousers—an electric drill. I couldn't help myself. I laughed.

"What's so funny?" the man asked.

"Your drill. What's with the drill?"

"It's for sale. Wanna buy it? Ten bucks."

"I don't think I need a drill."

"Really? It's not stolen!"

This made me laugh harder. "Uh huh."

"Really. Mrs. Williams down the street gave it to me."

I held out my hand. "I'm Margaret. And you are...?"

"Clarence. Live around the corner, two blocks down. Born here."

"Nice to meet you. Why're you selling the drill?"

"I need some cash to buy gas so I can see my old lady down in Tacoma." I gave him a skeptical glance. "Really," he said. "I'm forty-five. I'm a man. You aren't gonna see me walkin.'"

I looked him over appraisingly. "Forty-five, huh? You can't be forty-five. You look years younger than that!"

Now it was Clarence's turn to laugh. He looked over toward Mike, who was still standing behind the truck. "Your friend's OK," he said. "She's spiffed, but she's all right."

I offered Clarence my hand again. "Good luck selling the drill," I said. "See you around."

"After I get back from Tacoma, because this drill, I'll sell her tonight."

As I helped Mike carry the sofa into the living room, I ruminated on how race, class, and culture play out in the United States. And my reaction to it. Vashon was beautiful, but I hadn't been comfortable there; I'd felt out of place. Everyone there seemed self-satisfied, complacent. They were all white; they all looked just like me. They were all more or less middle-class, just like me. I had felt claustrophobic, as though I were suffocating. I'd felt as though I could only show one small portion of myself there; the rest of me would be relegated to sit dusty on a shelf in a closed back closet.

The Central District was alive, and I felt alive within it. Most of the families who lived in the area had arrived forty or fifty years before, many from Louisiana. Perhaps I now liked being the outsider. Perhaps I was addicted to the intensity of having to always be alert, learning from every interaction, never finding the expected. Perhaps the habit of being an anthropologist had grown so deep that I could no longer live in places where my curiosity wasn't excited daily.

After Mike left, I stood for a time on my front porch. It had been covered with indoor-outdoor green carpet sometime in the past. Water from years of rains had begun to rot the wood underneath. It felt even spongier than the floors inside. Then, on the night air, I heard the painfully sweet tones of a saxophone. I had recently learned that my neighbor was a well-known jazz saxophonist who had played with Miles Davis and other music Greats. The notes curled around the porch banisters and slid down the stairs.

Finally, I thought. Perhaps I had found a home. Then I reconsidered, not completely satisfied with this assessment. Was I merely enticed by the scent of new surroundings, ones I had begun to idealize because they reminded me of parts of what I had loved in Bahia?

But the Central District was, of course, not Bahia. Here I had a house far bigger than I would have dreamed of having in Bahia. Here I had space to be alone, to be myself—whatever that meant—in a way I hadn't explored for years. I heard the music again, restful. No blasting radios.

Peace.

To a Mailing List of 95: April 3, 2000

Dear Donors, Friends, and Volunteers,

I am at the office writing this and a man outside is repairing a boat. His noise sounds exactly like a dentist's drill, so my concentration is a bit diffused.

First of all, Brazil, of course. At the end of this month, I shall be going to Brazil for two weeks—I have been invited to give a paper at an academic conference on race and gender in Brazil, so my fare will be paid. My next letter will be full of news about the girls and the new school year. But for now, I'd like to share (with her permission) part of an email our intern Karey just sent:

"Teaching is going very well. I've gotten into a rhythm with the Bahia Street girls, and we're working a lot on speaking. They're always concerned with filling in the blanks in their workbooks, but sometimes I don't even make them write anything, just talk. But I'm working toward their being able to express themselves both in writing and in speech. I have these grandiose goals and the actual learning process is very slow, but I know we're all making progress. I started working with the younger girls, too. They were learning the names of animals, so we got down on the floor to imitate dogs, cats, ants, lions, etc.

This past weekend our capoeira group hosted the third annual event in honor of International Women's Day. There was a lecture given by two prominent local women in capoeira angola, and a discussion about women's roles in capoeira, and a reception afterward. The next morning women from two groups taught classes, and then we had a big roda directed by women. One of the women who taught was Paula, the oldest Bahia Street girl. I was so proud, and simultaneously so sore! She can teach, that one, and was quite demanding. She wanted us to go from a squat into a handstand (try it right now— it's so hard!). She could do it, of course, but I had to just laugh at myself. She showed me no mercy, even though I'm her esteemed English teacher. (Or because I'm her teacher...)"

We are moving the tutoring space in Salvador. For over two years, the Teacher's Association has most generously allowed us to use a space for the tutoring. In particular, Bahia Street thanks its president. Now, unfortunately, they require the space, so we are moving. Rita has found a temporary space at the Church of the Blacks, a Catholic church located near the girls' school.

Take care, and when I next write to you I will be full of Brazilian news.

um abraço
Margaret

twenty | trust

"Rumor has it that you've bought a house in the Central District."

"Yeah."

"And that you haven't got much in the way of furniture."

"I've got a sofa and a table."

"Chairs?"

"No."

The interrogator was Phyllis, an African-American friend who was doing her master's degree at the University of Washington in ethnomusicology. Her thesis was on Brazilian popular music, and she had spent three months in Salvador while I had lived there. I had helped her find an apartment. She had often invited me over for delectable cakes and other specialty food she foraged from upscale shops that I had never discovered in all the years I had lived there. Phyllis had coped with the culture shock of Bahia by reading copious numbers of English novels that she found in a few select secondhand bookstores. Her mother was a librarian, and Phyllis had inherited a talent for reading novels faster than most people read the morning paper. Her African ancestry was mixed with European and American Native, giving her a compellingly exotic look. She was also endowed with the perfect Bahia body type. When she had visited me one day at capoeira practice in Salvador, my usually fleet-footed compadres had stumbled all over themselves trying to impress her.

"I've got lots of furniture," Phyllis said. "And I've always wanted to live in the Central District."

"You have?" My heart jumped. I didn't want to admit it to anyone, but I was beginning to have real financial difficulties. For the last two years, I'd spent an average of nine thousand dollars a year on Bahia Street—and that only included the expenses I'd recorded. I had to commute to Portland each week for my teaching job, racking up more expenses, and I wasn't earning very much. My savings were being depleted, and now I had a mortgage. A roommate could really help. "Why do you want to move into the Central District?"

"I'm black, in case you hadn't noticed. It'd be nice to live around

185

some black people for a change." I felt an affinity for Phyllis, not only because she'd spent time in Salvador and understood some of my conflicts upon returning to the United States, but also because she, like me, was a native Oregonian. Most people in Seattle were newcomers who didn't really understand the Pacific Northwest. However, being black, Phyllis' experience of Oregon was an interesting contrast to mine. "Besides," she continued. "I have an auntie who lives in the CD."

"You do?"

"Sure. She's a lawyer. She lives near Madison Valley, in the part north of you—the middle-class part?"

"My part of the Central District is not middle-class."

"I am aware of that."

"You haven't seen the house yet, Phyllis."

"So?"

"It's pretty bad. I'm ripping up layers of carpet. Under the carpet is ancient linoleum. The bathroom has pink fixtures and the bathroom floor is covered with pink shag."

"Is the toilet solid?"

"I can't guarantee that."

"Does the house have ceiling fans in every room?"

"Well, yes, it does actually. I thought that was strange for here in the Northwest, I have to admit. It has a very strange light fixture in the living room as well, long pieces of amber glass hanging down."

"I know that light. That house was an African-American home, with different sensibilities than you have, Margaret. I'll feel fine."

"Why don't you come and see it, Phyllis? I'd love to have you move in, but I don't know if I could expect anyone else to live here. It's pretty trashed."

"I'm on my way."

When Phyllis stepped in the front door, she squeaked in alarm. "Why is your floor spongy?" she asked.

"That part's OK. They've just done something very strange. The floor is covered with three layers of carpet, with linoleum over the carpet. I'll be ripping that out soon."

"I see." Phyllis surveyed the dark, vacant rooms, lit only through the dusty patches where I had managed to chip the black paint from the glass. She walked into the bathroom. "Oh God, don't let me come in here drunk," she said. Then she turned to me. "Looks like you need a roommate to help you clean this place up," she said. "You obviously haven't a clue."

When I arrived back in Seattle after a week of teaching, the house seemed transformed. It was full of furniture, and it seemed so spacious. Brilliant sun streamed in every window. The walls looked spotless. "Phyllis! What have you done? How did you get the paint off the windows?"

Phyllis looked up from her novel. She was lounging on the sofa with her feet up on the arm. She had a bright new pillow under her head.

"Oh, hello. There are cleaning compounds, you know. I just washed it off. It wasn't paint. The people who lived here before were elderly, right?" I nodded. "The light probably hurt their eyes, and also they didn't want people looking in, seeing what they had that someone might want to steal."

"And the bars. They're gone!"

Phyllis raised her hand languidly. "I had a friend come by. He cut them off. The jail feel doesn't suit me." She got up. "Want some tea?"

I put my bags on the floor and dropped into a wooden chair in the kitchen, one of four now tucked beneath my little table. "Next week I'm gong to Brazil," I said. "It's spring break and I've been invited to give a paper at a conference there. You'll be all right?"

"Of course." I noticed that she'd replaced the damaged burner on the stove. "Oh Phyllis, I'm exhausted."

"That's not a surprise."

"And I don't know how I'm going to raise the money to pay for even next month of Bahia Street. We haven't paid the tutor this month, and Rita's not taking any salary. I don't know how she's doing it."

"You aren't either, are you?"

"No, but I'm in a better position than she is." Phyllis nodded in silence as she put the kettle on the stove. "Do you remember I mentioned Joyce, the professional grant-writer who said she might help me write grants? That would be great in theory. But, I don't know, Phyllis. Who's going to give us a grant for a project that helps six girls? 'Help us change the world. We're *really* doing it one girl at a time.'"

"Better than a lot of groups. They don't do anything at all." She handed me a steaming mug of tea. New mug, I noticed.

"Well, I don't know about Bahia Street either. You know the story about Madalena and how we had to hire a new tutor, Ana?"

"Yes." Phyllis put down her mug of tea and sat across from me.

"Maybe you can help me, Phyllis. I don't like her. I understood that Madalena wouldn't work, but personally, I liked her. But Ana—Ana doesn't like me either. I don't think she likes anyone who's white."

"Histories of oppression do that."

"But it's as though she has a huge chip on her shoulder. And it's more than that. Even for the short time I saw her at Bahia Street, she seemed to be taking over. I think she just wants to use Bahia Street as a jumping off point to further her career. She doesn't seem to accept that I understand Portuguese, so she kept saying things in front of me. I heard her tell the girls that she knows more about education programs than Rita."

"Maybe she does."

"Yeah, but Rita is supposed to be the director! It seems to me that she's just undermining her. And she recently wrote a grant for Bahia Street. Rita sent me a copy. It says that she and Rita founded Bahia Street and that 'an American woman' had given some financial assistance! I don't mind Rita getting all the kudos for Bahia Street, but this other interloper taking credit where none is due—it hurts." I sipped my tea, irritated. "I heard her telling the girls that Bahia Street was much less organized before she came, and that she ran it now while Rita just helped her. She also told the girls that Bahia Street would never accept a white child because whites are the oppressors, and that a poor, white child given education would just become a rich white oppressor."

Phyllis laughed. "We could do with Ana here in Seattle."

"No, we don't. She'd just alienate people."

Phyllis raised her hands as if weighing the issue. "Maybe. But, what about Rita? She doesn't want Bahia Street to be a separatist organization, I'm sure. What does she say?"

"I haven't talked with her. It all happened so fast while I was there. And then while I'm here, I don't really know what's going on there. We can't talk on the phone either since Rita doesn't have a phone. I don't know, maybe Rita is more inclined to follow what Ana believes than what we had decided before."

"Don't be ridiculous, Margaret. You've known Rita for how long now? Almost ten years?"

"Yeah. I guess I keep thinking that Rita and I are beyond race. That we are such good friends that we can ignore it. But it isn't like that, is it?'

Phyllis quietly stirred honey into her second cup of tea. "No, Margaret. It's not. But what you're talking about here is trust. Even if two people really love each other, the world will never let them forget they are of different races. You and Rita had better confront that." She laid her used spoon onto a pretty, blue saucer that she'd placed on the table for just that purpose. "Because Margaret, once you've figured this out, you and Rita can use other people's perceptions to your own advantage. If you and Rita are going to make any real change in racial inequality, you're going to have to go beyond other people's— and institutional—prejudice. I know race works differently in Brazil, but you're still looking at discrimination and inequality." She looked at me. "The moment any of us forgets that—white or non-white— when we slip into a comfortable malaise, we have accepted the status quo. And then, when we're not paying attention, that status quo will poke out its foot and trip us. You have to know, and stay aware of, the complexities of race relations before you can subvert them."

The symposium organizers paid for a room in a very pleasant middle-class hotel in Salvador. It was a comfort I decided I could get used to. I gave my paper two days after I'd arrived. The presenter of my panel, who clearly had been at that first presentation I had made years before, introduced me by saying, "And we would like to welcome Dr. Willson. Several of you will remember her first scintillating presentation here in Bahia." Scattered members of the audience burst into laughter. Embarrassing memories die hard when one's colleagues keep bringing them up over the years....

Don also came to Salvador for the conference, and we went to visit Keila at the tenement where Don had lived. It had now been slated to join the renovated streets of the rest of the Historic District. In preparation, it had been condemned. The transvestites had much difficulty in Salvador finding accommodation where they could live the lifestyle they desired and ply their trade. So, with the renovation trucks fast approaching, the tenement owner (who was also a transvestite) was still able to command high rents in the condemned building.

Keila had gone to Italy for a few years, her passage funded from her work with Don. She had worked there as a prostitute. This was the dream of most of the transvestites, to go to Italy and earn the huge sums they heard could be made among the Italians. Keila, who, like all the other Brazilian transvestites in Italy, had been an illegal immigrant, got caught and kicked out of the country. She had temporarily returned to the old tenement where she had lived before and where her friends still did.

Keila spoke a very colorful and clever Portuguese, and, while in Italy, she'd learned Italian. Not surprisingly, she also learned a great deal about Italian cooking. She invited Don and me to dinner one night. Don paid for the food, and Keila invited the entire building.

Don and I sat on folding chairs while she regaled us with stories of Italy, demonstrating particular points with her large spoon and screaming insults in Italian to friends in the hallway and the street. The fact that no one could understand her seemed to delight her only more. Physically, she was transformed. Now she looked like a very attractive, middle-aged, slightly plump, slightly dark, Italian woman.

While she was cooking, Don and I explored the tenement. Don's room was gone. We walked to the concrete wall at the back. In the gathering darkness we stared at the open area that lay behind the wall.

"Look," Don said. "The garbage has been taken away."

"Mmmm," I said.

"It looks as though they're just throwing garbage out there again."

We stood in silence a minute.

"What are you looking at?" I asked.

"Just gazing. Waiting to see if the rats will come out. Look, here they come. Still fat."

I glanced down the dark hole of the descending stairway. "I wonder if people are still living below," I said

"Keila says there are. Two. Crack addicts."

"If the rats ate them would anyone notice, do you think?"

"The owner would notice when the rent came due," Don said. We shared a nasty little laugh.

"I hate this place," he said.

"Salvador?"

"Yeah. Salvador."

"We should have taken more holidays," I said. "Gone to the beach more."

Don smiled and turned away from the rat vista. "We always say that," he said. "We should really do it someday." I nodded and we walked around the corner to where Keila was cooking.

"You look really beautiful since coming back from Italy, Keila," I said. She twirled in a small circle.

"Don't I though? I mean, I've always been beautiful, but now—" and here she injected some Italian phrase I didn't understand. "That means 'but now I'm absolutely stunning!'"

We laughed and she began to lay out the dinner. It looked delicious.

I stopped by the church where Bahia Street was now holding its classes and watched Ana work with the girls. She was very lively. She often hugged them. And it was clear she engaged their attention, but she ignored me. When I had first arrived at the church, the doorman wouldn't let me in.

"We're not open to tourists," he said.

"I'm a friend of Rita's. I'm helping her with the project with the girls upstairs." His face brightened instantly, and he ushered me in.

"Rita took pictures for my daughter's confirmation last week. She's a wonderful photographer."

I ascended the narrow stairway, and the air grew hotter and closer with every step. How could the girls study in this? When I entered the room, I saw they all sat on a single long bench, their books in their laps. The light in the room was dim, and the narrow windows were covered with grime. The room was clearly a storage space with stacks of church equipment covering most of the floor. When they saw me, the girls shouted a greeting. Rita gathered her knapsack, and we descended the stairs together.

"How can you stand being up there all day?" I asked as soon as we were in the stairwell.

"It's not good. The girls can't concentrate. But I think I've found us a new place. If we can get it, it'll be great. Not fancy, but with a small kitchen, a middle room, and a front room. We could have a classroom.

I'll show it to you." Rita waved a greeting to the doorman, and we walked out into the hot sun.

"I have to do some shopping. That OK?" I nodded and we walked up the cobblestone street. "I've been thinking, Margaret, these girls, they're sleepy all the time. They start to study and then they just fall asleep. I questioned them, and they aren't getting any breakfast. I think they're completely malnourished. Notice how small they all are? I don't think we can expect them to study if they're hungry. With the new room, I'm trying to think of a way we can feed them."

More money, I thought. Which we didn't have. But I didn't say this. Instead, I asked, "How's Ana?"

"Fine, I guess."

"Ah." We finished Rita's shopping for various school supplies, then stopped for a beer and evening cheese sandwich at our usual street-side bar near Bahia Street.

"I am worried about Ana," Rita said.

"Yes?" I said, looking into my beer.

"Her knowledge about nonprofits and administration is very good. And she has excellent connections in this city."

"Yes?"

"Well, this may sound crazy, but I think she's trying to take over Bahia Street."

"So she can get wealthy?"

Rita laughed. "Bahia Street has a name here now. She could use that to promote herself. And that's what I think she wants to do. She won't stay with Bahia Street—it's too small. But she wants to claim its success for herself."

Rita poured herself a beer and pulled on her fingers. "She's trying to get staff hired who are her allies, who will treat her as director instead of me. She's telling the girls that she's really the director and that they should listen to her over me. You know the grant we just wrote, the one I sent you?" I nodded. "Well, she wrote it mostly—I'm not much good at those things. So, now she says that if we get it, she should get a percentage of it and be in control of how it's spent."

"That's not good."

"Shortly after you sent me the information on that grant, I showed it to her. She wrote most of our application, but she also wrote another one to the same foundation, but for another group here. They wrote for a project, but they aren't going to spend it on any such project at all. They will give her a percentage and use the rest to buy a new building."

"You know, she doesn't like me; she will barely speak to me."

"You're white; of course she doesn't like you. And worse, you're from the United States. She detests Americans."

I coughed to clear my throat of the annoying lump that had arisen there. "I'm so glad you're telling me this," I said. "I—well—I wasn't sure if you agreed with her on things...."

"You know what I read?" Rita interrupted me, ignoring, or over-riding, my distressful insecurities. "She wrote that she and I started Bahia Street. She listed us as co-directors and put her name first!"

We sat in silence for a few minutes. I asked Nelson for some sparkling water. Rita asked him to bring a glass for her as well.

"Seems strange someone actually trying to take over Bahia Street, this little idea that you and I had a couple of years ago."

"Yes," Rita said. "Once we have done the work, with no salaries, of setting it up."

"So, Rita," I said hesitantly, "why can't you just fire Ana? I mean you hired her. Just say she doesn't fit and give her notice."

Rita shook her head. "It's not that easy. Ana is very well-connected in Salvador. She could make things very difficult for us." She paused. "I have to be more political. I have to let her go, but let her think that she is deciding to go."

I smiled. "You are becoming a director, Rita."

"I have to keep her as a friend—she is a friend. It's complicated." She looked up. "I may be able to have her move into a position as a consultant and then say we don't have money for that in a few months. She thinks we have tons of money because you're involved, but at least that would get her out of the classroom where she's causing so much unrest. And, she would like being called a consultant."

"So, we would basically be paying her some of our hard-earned money to do nothing so she doesn't destroy what we have worked so hard to create?"

"Yeah. That's about right."

"So, since you almost never use your salary, she is, and will, be making more than you... for doing nothing."

"Yeah."

"So I propose a compromise."

"What's that?" Rita looked at me guardedly over the top of her water glass.

"You take your salary so you can continue your photography for the joy of it rather than having to do whatever to support yourself while you do a full-time job at Bahia Street. And we pay her for as short a time as possible."

"Most people in Bahia hold two or even three full-time jobs, you know."

"Yes, I do know, but I'm not talking about them, I'm talking about you. If you get sick, or just too tired, this whole thing falls apart."

"True."

"So?"

"How are we going to pay for this, Margaret?"

"I don't know. I'll think of something."

"Becoming indispensable is a trap."

I shrugged. "You think I haven't figured that out yet?"

Rita smiled. "Sure, you have a compromise."

"To survival?"

Rita raised her glass. I raised mine. "To survival."

To a Mailing List of 110: May 18, 2000

Dear Volunteers, Donors, and Friends,

Our Bahia Street dock keeps moving as I am trying to write on the computer—a very strange sensation, especially on this anniversary of Mount St. Helens' eruption…

I recently returned from Brazil, and on the way, got stuck in Chicago for two days because of plane problems, but finally arrived in Salvador to give a paper on Bahia Street for a symposium on race, class and gender. Participants for the symposium came from all over the world, and it was a wonderful meeting of ideas and connections. Rita, Ana, and the mother of one of the girls all came to comment and discuss the paper I presented with others in the symposium. I might emphasize how unusual it is at an academic conference for the people being written about to actually partici-pate in the discussion (in fact it is essentially unheard of and made several people nervous.) It did, however, make for a fascinating and lively discus-sion and considerably expanded contacts for Bahia Street.

The rest of the time I spent visiting the girls and working with Rita. She is working very hard to find us a new space for the tutoring. The Church of the Blacks is generously allowing us to use an upper balcony of the church for the tutoring, but it is noisy and very hot, making concentra-tion difficult for the girls. We also do not have enough desks or chairs and the girls have to share a bench. The light is also not good. And the location, although about fifteen minutes walk from the school, is in the tourist center of Salvador and is very distracting for the girls. Rita has found a good space near the school but it rents for about US$250 a month. Because the school is at the center of the city, any space that is light, airy and secure will be comparatively expensive.

About the girls themselves: we now have eight girls in the program, including two new young ones—Aninha and Jessica, and three older ones, Dazá, Aqualuxe, and Luedge.

Paula (Lidia), Christina, and Juliana are all doing great. Paula and Juliana are going through some general teenager problems but are continuing to work hard at their studies. Ana, Christina's mother lost her maid's job when the family she was working for moved to São Paulo. She, Christina, and Christina's brother were on the street for a bit, but she has now found another job, and they are staying in the one-room *shack of a friend and her son. She now works six days a week from seven in the morning to seven at night for about $40 a month. This means the children are alone much of the time, and Christina often comes to school crying from hunger. We are still giving about $30 a month to Christina's mother and periodically feeding Christina when she comes to school. We have become increasingly aware that we must work with the families of the girls to help them improve their situations in order for the girls to have a chance to study and concentrate. Amazingly enough, despite all the difficulties, Christina is maintaining passing grades and almost never misses either the tutoring or school.*

Paula is going through a hard time right now. The family's three-room house is now shared by her father, her father's girlfriend, two brothers, an aunt, and a grandmother. She is having difficulties communicating with her father (not unusual for a teenager), and she has some health problems. Her mother (who lives away from the family) will not take her to the doctor, probably because she would have to take a day off to wait in the enormous lines for the free medical clinics for the poor. Rita is taking care of this problem at this time. Paula burst into tears when she was telling me about her fears and her worries; on top of everything else (and not surprisingly) her Portuguese marks are not high. She is terrified that because of this she will be kicked out of the program.

Juliana is still doing well in her classes, continues to be very directed in her studies, and her home life is stable with her older sister still able to (marginally) support the family through making and selling pizza on the street. We did learn something that has given us conflicting reactions. At the end of last school year in November, all of the girls failed at least one exam on the first try and had to take them again, at which time they all passed. Or so we thought. We now know that Juliana actually passed all her exams the first time around, but lied to us, saying that she had failed. This meant she had to study for another month and take a make-up exam. She did this because she did not want Paula to study and take the make-up exam alone. Of course she shouldn't have lied, yet it is hard to feel anything but compassion for such support for a friend. And we will never know how much this support helped Paula to pass.

Also, some news on Patricia. One of her brothers recently got shot five times. Amazingly, he was not killed, but is now a quadriplegic and will be confined to bed for life. I am not quite sure what will happen when he returns from hospital. The sociologist who originally introduced Patricia to Bahia Street is currently working with an Italian aid group to try and have them fund the construction of a small room for him on the side of the family's small home (which houses fourteen people). Patricia is still trying to attend public school.

I don't know the new girls very well yet, but they are both adorable. Aninha lives with her father and grandmother, who accompanies the younger girls to school and back everyday (we need to be very careful of the younger girls, as people might kidnap them and sell them for the sex trade or for their organs). They are all very excited to be in the project and are studying busily.

For those of you who are contributing directly to Bahia Street, in whatever way you can, it is hard to say how much this means. Thatcher Bailey, one of the people who made an AIDS hospice in Seattle possible, once wrote me an inspirational letter in which he explained that in this materialist society, we have an uncomfortable relationship with money, consumption, and greed. Through giving, we are literally transforming money into love. I didn't understand the truth of what he was saying at the beginning when we started Bahia Street, but I do now. Bahia Street is growing, and with it a love that unites people of different nations, classes, genders, and races. This includes all of us. Together we are making an important change.

Best of thoughts e abraços,
Margaret

twenty-one | tall poppy

"Bahia Street," I answered the phone.

"Hello. Do you speak Portuguese?" a woman asked in Portuguese.

"Yes."

"Oh, how wonderful. Are you Brazilian?"

"No, no, but I lived there for some time. Can I help you?"

"I was wondering if I could volunteer."

"We do take volunteers here in Seattle. What can you do?"

"I can do computers. But I live in North Bend." North Bend is a small town inland from Seattle, about forty minutes from the University District and the Bahia Street office. "And I don't have a car. Could I meet with someone here, do something here?"

I was silent. Public transportation from North Bend to Seattle was terrible. And I had been getting numerous calls lately from Brazilian women, none of whom could speak English, who had good computer skills, and who, at first glance, just wanted to do something for company. As I listened to them, however, I had begun to notice a darker trend. I suspected this was a similar situation. "Why are you in Seattle?" I asked her.

"I'm here with my husband."

"Your husband is Brazilian?"

"No. He's American." She sighed. "It's terrible. Oh, it's so good to speak Portuguese! I met John on the Internet. He seemed lovely. He came to visit me in Brazil a few times, and then he asked me to come here to live with him in the United States."

"To North Bend?"

"I didn't know what it'd be like! I'd never been to the States. I thought it was going to be beautiful. But it rains here all the time. I don't know anyone. I'm here alone all day. I have nothing to do, no one to talk to. I feel so alone. I'm so bored I could die!"

"Are you taking English classes?"

"John doesn't want me to. He says I should study it at home. He says he's tired when he gets home and doesn't want to drive me around to classes."

"How about getting a driver's license yourself?"

"I asked John about that, too. But I don't know how to drive. He says he doesn't like the idea of me being out on the road by myself. He says he likes me being home."

"Are there places you can walk around there?"

"I tried, but there isn't anything! We're way out in this suburb. Any stores are a long way away. And no one is in the streets. I can't talk with anyone." She began to cry. "Why did I come here? I just want to go home. I want to be with my family. I thought John was nice, and that we could have a good life here, but he's so controlling. He's worse than Brazilian men. He doesn't want me to do anything. Finally, after I begged him for months, he got me a computer. I spend all day on it. That's how I found Bahia Street. Oh, it's so good to talk with you!"

"Do you know any Brazilians here?"

"No. How am I supposed to meet anyone? I can't get out. I feel trapped, as though I'm in prison. I just want to go home!"

I sat back in my chair and rubbed my forehead. What was going on? Why was I getting so many calls like this? I must have received at least six or seven in the last couple of months. Women coming over as Internet brides and then being made into virtual slaves for American men who had no accountability about how they treated them.

"Has John hit you?" I asked. Silence. "You can get help from the police."

"I don't want any trouble with the police."

"Were you married in the church?" No response. "Are you illegal?"

The woman burst into sobs. "John said we would get a green card for me when I arrived. I thought I would then get work so I could be more independent. He was so kind in Brazil. It's not at all like I thought it would be. It's awful. I don't have any friends or family. I'm so alone. And it's so dark here. It rains all the time, and it's cold."

I talked with her some more, feeling increasing despair. What was I supposed to do? How could I help? Bahia Street was not a local social service agency, and the women who had been ringing would not go see anyone they considered connected to the United States government. Yet I couldn't just leave this.

After some thought, I picked up the phone again and rang Silvia, a professional middle-class Brazilian who worked for Microsoft. I had found it interesting that most of the Brazilians I had met in the Seattle area were from southern Brazil, nearly all white and middle-class, and most had come here for professional jobs. Microsoft alone hired at least a hundred. Silvia had been in the States for more than ten years.

I told Silvia about the calls I'd been receiving, and about the implications.

"I can't really do anything," I told her. "They need Brazilians. That's who they want. Brazilians who understand how the United States works, who can visit them and make sure they're safe, who can help them get legal papers and get some equality in their relationships—or figure out how to leave."

"Oh, how terrible!" Silvia said. "I would love to help. And I'm sure several other Brazilians at Microsoft would as well. We could even work with other new Brazilians, find furniture if they needed it. But mostly, we could just take them out, go for coffee, and give them support." She hesitated. "But, Margaret, I've never put together a group like this. I don't know what kind of regulations there are, what I should do. Could we do it as Bahia Street?"

"No. Bahia Street works in Bahia, but I would be happy to help you. I can come to your first meetings, and tell you how to register with the Secretary of State if you wish. It should be led by Brazilians anyway. That's who these women want to find."

"Oh, I'm so excited, Margaret. I'd love to do this. Maybe I can get my church to help."

"Whatever you want. Why don't I give you the phone numbers of the women who have called, and you can start calling them?" I felt so relieved when I put down the phone. It seemed that every part of every society needed something.

As it turned out, Silvia was efficient. She called a meeting at a friend's house, and about fifteen Brazilians came. They'd been energized, wanting to start a small group to help new Brazilians, particularly women who came via ads on the Internet. I offered whatever help they might want and had gone home pleased. Who knew what might come of this?

Late afternoon, a few weeks later, as the gray of a rainy day was closing into the dark of a rainy night, the phone rang. "Hello?"

"Margaret? So, you're trying to take over are you? After all the years

I've been working with the Brazilian community here, and you just want to take all the credit."

"Who is this?"

"You know who it is. It's Alice." Alice was a white Brazilian from the more European south of Brazil, who had lived in Seattle about thirty years. I had only met her a few times, but she had been helpful to Bahia Street. She was a respected community activist, and I had thought I had her good will. "You're stealing what I do. I've been helping the Brazilians here for years, translating forms, helping them in jail. And you think you can just take over."

"Alice, what are you talking about?"

"Don't act so stupid. I thought Bahia Street was supposed to be for girls in Brazil. You feel so big doing that, now you want to take over what I'm doing, too!"

"Alice, are you talking about the Microsoft group? I'm not doing it. I just offered to help. And it isn't about jails or anything. You could certainly join, too."

"I've been working here a lot longer than you have. I know the community. You're not even a Brazilian. You just want a big name for yourself through climbing on the backs of others who've worked here for years." I decided to make no response as my words just seemed to fuel her anger. After about thirty minutes, she hung up on me.

"That didn't sound good," Phyllis said from the living room, where she was reading a book on the history of samba. "Good friend of yours?"

"I think we'll have to screen our calls. I knew I'd offend someone someday doing this. It looks like I've done it."

I sat in a warm bath with a whiskey in my hand. The bottle was on the floor. About two weeks had passed since Alice's call. I picked up the e-mail again. It was written in a mixture of Portuguese and English. Someone had forwarded to me that afternoon. I took another sip of the whiskey. Phyllis and I had ripped out the filthy pink shag carpet. The linoleum it revealed was burnt orange and avocado. The pink toilet stared at me.

The letter started out asking for information regarding a group in Seattle, which called itself Bahia Street, that was active in raising money. Members of the Brazilian-American community were wondering about this group, the letter stated, since they had never heard of it in Brazil and couldn't figure out its exact location. They had spoken with Bahia Street people in Seattle, it said, (they had never spoken to me about any issue in the letter, I noted) and had concerns about the group because neither its website nor its people gave any credit to, nor seemed to know about, all the fine work being done in Brazil with children. This was a theme to which the letter returned several times. Bahia Street, the letter said, appeared to be completely the project of an "English anthropologist" who was living in the United States, a First World outsider who had come to Brazil, a Third World country, to tell people there what they should do. The letter sandwiched sections of my last donor letter between critical commentary: the writer found the name of Bahia Street demeaning, my referring to the girls as "adorable" racist and sexist, that rumors of organ stealing came from a misinformation campaign by the KGB whose propaganda I was now repeating, and that the idea of the girls becoming social activists was a foreigner's agenda forced upon the girls rather than anything that might be good for them.

The letter concluded with a request, in Portuguese, for the readers to let the writer know if Bahia Street was trustworthy, or if they had even heard of it. The insinuation was that the Bahia Street project in Bahia might not exist.

The name at the bottom of the e-mail meant nothing to me. Apparently the letter had been sent to a mailing list of undisclosed recipients—not to me of course—both in the United States and Brazil. I'd already heard from three people that the real author of the letter was Alice, and that she'd convinced someone else to put her name to it.

I took another sip of whiskey and tried to curb my raw anger and humiliation. I kept thinking how unfair and low this attack was, to never contact Bahia Street directly about any concerns, to never make any attempts to talk with me, but then to accuse, and—almost more damning—to insinuate, that Bahia Street was a racist group, lead by one white "English" woman, and very possibly a front that did no work in Bahia at all. And then not to have the decency to even inform me that the letter was being sent. Did she think I wouldn't hear of it?

But, this issue went far deeper than that, I realized. The Brazilian community in Seattle was fractured into several factions. People of one faction would not speak with the other, and some actively worked to destroy the businesses or success of others. I always trod very carefully and stayed only marginally involved with this community in order to avoid becoming entangled in these destructive fights. Local Brazilians had told me that they felt it unlikely that a Brazilian could have run Bahia Street in Seattle because he or she would not have been able to avoid taking sides. I had always known I was walking on eggshells in this community.

I cursed myself for not being more careful in my phrasing of the sentence on the kidnapping. I had been naive, just writing these letters to people I considered friends. Alice's KGB reference was nonsense, and some very courageous anthropologists and organizations were investigating the large organ and sex trade that certainly included Brazil; but I should have written that "the parents and Rita were afraid the girls would be kidnapped." That would have been more accurate.

After all this time working, and one small slip of phrasing would bring a smear that could potentially destroy us. I felt terrible for all the local Brazilians who had come to trust Bahia Street. Local Brazilians often told me that this was the first nonprofit to which they had given because it was the first one they felt confident would actually send the funds to the stated project instead of into their own pockets. I felt honored by their donations. This letter might destroy that fragile trust.

The funding of Bahia Street largely existed because of the good will of others. In terms of sustainability, its good name was our most valuable asset. Bahia Street relied heavily on our Seattle-area Brazilian donors, many of whom made our fundraising possible, not so much in terms of the actual money they gave, but in their generous offers of time, musical performances, and other talents.

I am vulnerable to attack, I reflected, because I trespass on the issue of identity. Brazilians in their adopted country of the United States are trying to be accepted by Americans, the vast majority of whom have never been to Brazil and, in most cases, know next to nothing about it. Yet how these Americans regard Brazil directly affects how Brazilians are treated here. So-called Third World people in the United States are treated completely differently than Europeans. Not surprisingly,

Brazilians I knew in Seattle far preferred Americans to think of Brazil as an exotic land of white beaches, great music, and gorgeous people than a poverty-stricken land of racism, death squads, out-of-control violence, and street children.

One Brazilian stated one aspect of the issue very clearly when she said that she had never understood racism until she came to the United States, because only then had she realized that others could consider her—pale-skinned with European features—anything but white.

I sighed. In many ways, it was remarkable that any Brazilians in Seattle supported Bahia Street at all, particularly since so few of them were even from Bahia or of African descent. It said something about their generosity—or about displaced communities—that as relatively recent immigrants they would even care. Indeed, I had noticed that middle-class Brazilians in Seattle tended to express more concern over Brazilian inequality than I had ever seen in Brazil.

I finally emerged from the bath, whiskey bottle in hand. Phyllis greeted me with a dubious gaze. "You look like a prune," she said.

"Better than being suicidal."

"Don't be a drama queen," she said, taking the bottle. "If you'd hoarded this bottle of single malt scotch any longer, I'd have had to kill you." She took out a glass for herself from the kitchen. "See? I knew you could still smile."

I presented the letter to my board. Joyce, the grant writer, had become a member of the board, as had Helen, a lawyer. I explained who had apparently instigated the letter, probably written it, and what seemed to be her motive, as much as I understood it.

"She sounds disturbed," Helen said. I shrugged. "We should probably send her a letter," Helen continued, "telling her we'll sue for libel. Libel is almost impossible to make stick, but it might keep her from sending more letters. Did you talk with the woman whose name is on the letter?"

"I tried," I said. "I rang her, but she won't talk with me. I can under-stand Alice, in a weird way; she thinks I've threatened her work. But this other person, I haven't a clue. I have no idea of her motives. And she won't talk to me, so I don't know how I can figure it out."

"We'll send the letter," Helen said. "And I'd screen my calls." I nodded. "Just don't engage her. Hopefully, the whole thing will die away. You'll lose some support, but I don't think there's much you can do about that now."

"Margaret," Joyce said. "You know these claims are crazy. We know it. Just keep doing what you're doing. The person who wrote this letter has a lot of other issues; she must be in pain. You're the tall poppy, daring to stick your head above the others. That's always dangerous. People notice you, winds buffet you. Let's just go on. In time, people will forget."

As the weeks went by after this letter and the several exchanges that followed, I watched for the fallout for Bahia Street. It appeared that everyone in the Brazilian community, or associated with it, had received a copy of the e-mail. We had an event for Bahia Street soon after; it had always been well-attended by Brazilians in previous years. This year was a disaster—almost no one came.

I opened my e-mail during this period to see a message from Rita. "Call me," it read. She included a friend's phone number and a preferred time to ring. I wondered whose Internet she was using. Perhaps an Internet cafe?

I dialed the phone with trepidation. After some deliberation, I'd sent her a copy of the letter. I decided that she had as much right to read it as I did.

"I sent her a reply," Rita said when she answered the phone. "She insulted me more than you. She never even mentioned me. It's as if I had nothing to do with Bahia Street. She acts as if you did the whole thing; you thought up the name, you designed the program. She just forgot about me. She's the racist, assuming that, of course, the African-Brazilian doesn't have any real power. Or worse, maybe she really never noticed my name. Probably the only black person she ever met in Brazil was her maid."

"You sent out a letter, Rita? Did you write this in it? To whom?"

"To everyone."

"What do you mean everyone?"

"I just cut and passed her address list. Everyone who received her letter has now received mine."

My heart sank. "Do you think that was a good idea, Rita? It

might just make her angrier."

Rita laughed. "We shall see," she said. "If she doesn't like Bahia Street, she should come down and talk with me sometime."

"Did you talk with your board, or a lawyer or anything?"

"Of course not. I was too angry." She paused. "Bahia Street is a fight, just like life. No shallow, inconsequential idiot is going to damage this work I've done."

"You didn't write that, did you?"

"Oh, I don't remember. I'm sure I gave her something to think about."

I decided not to tell my board about her letter unless I had to. But a part of me quietly exulted. African-Brazilian Rita from Bahia could credibly say things in defense of Bahia Street that I never could. Since I wasn't on the mailing list, I never received her letter. Oh well, I thought. Probably better I don't know.

twenty-two | a shadowed color of shade

On top of all this, Eduardo had decided to leave the board. He said he was leaving because his music business was taking so much of his time. He was becoming successful, and he and his wife were managing his music as a business. He was starting to teach in the local schools. And he had a child. I could hardly fault him, but his departure made me feel alone.

About two weeks later, early one Saturday morning, I was walking home from the local store, carrying a sack of milk and other breakfast groceries. Despite the early hour, Wilson was already working on a car. An old classic Cadillac, its front windows broken and covered with plastic; it hadn't moved in six months. For all I knew, it didn't have an engine. He'd had his head stuck underneath the hood when I'd passed on my way to the store. As I approached now, I thought I heard the motor cough and then purr. Wilson stared at it in deep concentration, a screwdriver in his hand.

"Wilson," I asked. "Did you actually get that thing running?"

Wilson flashed me a huge grin. "I certainly did! You know, I was laying in bed last night thinking about this engine. I kept asking people to help, how I could get it running, but then, last night, I realized I could do it myself. I laid there and figured out what I thought was wrong. A simple thing, really. I couldn't wait. So, this morning, as soon as it was light, I got out here. And I was right. I did it!"

"Congratulations, Wilson. That's fantastic." He waved his screwdriver at me as I crossed the street to my own house.

"Breakfast!" I shouted to Phyllis as I entered the front door.

She walked out of the bathroom rubbing sleep from her eyes. "You're not supposed to call me until the coffee is already made," she said.

"Sorry. You don't have me trained well enough yet." I ground some coffee while Phyllis put a CD in the CD player she'd brought. The fridge was leaking again, I noticed.

"Aren't you supposed to call Brazil this morning?" Phyllis asked.

"Yeah. I hope I can get through. Rita's got a new cell phone, but it never seems to work. And Telebahia, the telephone company there, they put this message on it asking you to leave a message, but apparently you have to pay to receive the message. Nobody, including Rita, does that, so even if I left a message, she wouldn't get it. But, if I can get through, it's good. She doesn't have to pay for calls she receives, just the ones she makes. So she uses the phone to receive calls and makes calls from a phone box." I poured the ground coffee into the coffee maker. "She sent me an e-mail."

"Rita has e-mail?"

"She sent it from a friend's house. We have to get her a phone line so she can have the Internet. Of course, the phones don't work most of the time, and the price to put in a phone line is insane. But Rita says with the competition from cell phones, that's going to change." Phyllis wiped the table and covered it with a red and purple patterned cloth. "Nice cloth, Phyllis. When'd you get that?"

"Oh, you know. I just got paid, so I thought I'd brighten this place up a bit." She began making toast. "What'd she want to talk to you about?"

"I don't know, but it's not likely to be good if she's sending me an urgent message."

"So, maybe you should call her before breakfast so you can eat."

"Good idea." I went into the dining room and dialed from the phone Phyllis and I now shared. Another expense helped by having a roommate. Astonishingly, the call went through.

"Hey Margaret," Rita said. "I think you have to come down. Can you?"

"What's up Rita?"

"It's about Christina. I'm really worried about her."

I felt a pang. I still felt most connected to those first girls we took, girls who had grown alongside us, especially Christina. I think we all held a special love for Christina. Her spark, her shy glances interrupted by flashes of illuminating joy when she laughed. She was perceptive.

"Something's changed," Rita said. "She's started coming to the Center dirty. She's got lice. Sometimes I find her crying. She won't study. She gets angry at nothing and shouts at the other girls. Lately, she spends half the afternoon in a corner holding herself and singing."

"Singing?"

"Not really singing. More like a chant, something unintelligible, like a low, toneless murmur." The line crackled.

"What'd you say, Rita? I couldn't hear you."

"I'm scared, Margaret. Sometimes, she comes with money in her hands."

"Money?"

"Yes. Ten or once twenty reais notes. How does Christina have money?"

"Oh Rita, that's not good. Have you talked with her mother?"

Rita laughed a short and uncharacteristically bitter laugh. "Her mother's part of the problem. That's why you have to come down. People in Christina's neighborhood know you better than they do me. You can talk with the neighbors and find out what's happening. And if it's, well, if it has to do with her mother or someone in her household…"

"What?"

Rita sighed. "Margaret, this is where you being the white foreigner can help. Whatever is going on, you can threaten them. Tell them that if it doesn't stop you'll call social services or the police. No one would do anything, we know that, but they might believe you have the influence to get someone to come. Margaret, you could probably make them afraid of you. They won't be afraid of me."

"Oh God, Rita." Phyllis silently handed me a cup of coffee and returned to the kitchen. I sipped it gratefully. "You know what's going on Rita, don't you?"

"Not exactly. I hope it isn't as bad as I think. So you see you have to come."

"Yes, yes, I see that. I'll figure it out. I'll come down in December."

"She won't even talk with me, Margaret. I'm not sure she's going to school anymore, but she comes to Bahia Street every day. And she never wants to leave. She starts crying when we shut the doors. At eleven, I'm afraid Christina's struggling with the kind of knowledge that makes people old."

Then, so quietly I almost couldn't hear her, Rita said, "I wish she weren't so pretty."

I slumped into one of the kitchen chairs. Phyllis served me toast and scrambled eggs.

"So, you're going to Brazil," she said.

"Oh, thank you, Phyllis. You could understand what we said?"

"Enough from your side." She sat across from me. "You have that anthropology conference on the East Coast, don't you? You could go directly from there."

"Oh boy. I suppose so. If I give essay finals and do the grades at the conference."

Phyllis patted my hand. "While you're gone, I'll feed your cat."

I was in my hotel room in Salvador pretending to write notes on my laptop, but I was really just staring at the wall. I never stayed with Rita anymore. The shootings had increased dramatically in her neighborhood. She said that next time I came it might be better, but right now she was too worried about my safety. I was worried about *her* safety. I decided not to tell other friends I was coming to Salvador because I knew that then I'd be swept up into a social whirlwind and not get any work done. I'd just booked into my usual cheap hotel.

It was strange how, in the outer physical reality of the world, the spaces and conditions of Salvador and Seattle were so far apart, yet in my mind, within the confines of that internal space, they joined in a turbulent mix. The Salvador communities like Rita's and Christina's were changing. Could we even call them communities anymore? Each person was fighting for survival alone. When murder becomes the norm, everything else gets twisted. Torture loses its meaning; the suffocating scent of death stifles any shred of humanity. I looked into the eyes of these twelve-year-old boys, all of whom now carried guns. Most sniffed glue. I saw nothing but my reflection in their eyes. They knew they could die tomorrow. They literally did not care if they killed you, if you screamed in torture, you and the rats. It was all the same.

I sighed. I'd blown my paper at the anthropology conference. I'd given it on drugs, gangs, and violence in Salvador. The people listening, hardened anthropologists, were visibly disturbed by what they heard. My images were too raw. The listeners distanced themselves through abstract comments: "Impressive ethnography, Margaret." I was too edgy; I was too deep inside for distance.

After so many years in Salvador, I had seen a lot. I knew horrific violence was perpetrated against children, that it happened all over the world. But why Christina? Of what depravity are we humans capable?

I had talked with Zezé, Lula, and Jorge. It didn't take long. Everyone, it seemed, knew what was going on. Christina's mother was jealous of her. She wanted to go out dancing and didn't want to take care of her kids. But she wouldn't give them away either. While she worked, she left the kids in a shack alone with her new twenty-year-old boyfriend. Some months ago, he had started raping Christina. He gave her money. I gathered, although no one would say this directly, that he was pushing her to be a prostitute since this would make them all money. Since she was so pretty and all. Her mother knew all about this and seemed unconcerned.

"Why didn't this neighborhood do what Claudia's did with her mother's boyfriend?" I asked. "Run him out?"

Jorge looked at his hands and I could hear humiliation in his voice. "He's in a gang, Margaret. He'd probably shoot us. Or somebody else would."

I now understood more why Rita couldn't talk with the family. So I played the big bad gringa. I gave Christina's mother a dark warning of unspecified impending doom if anything happened to Christina. Then, by spreading rumors, I let it be known in the neighborhood that I had contacts with the military police (a lie) and that I could get her children taken away, even get her sent to prison. I could only hope she believed this enough to get her boyfriend to stop.

"Her mother wants to destroy her," Rita had said to me later that day when I'd met her at our coffee cafe near the center of town. "Because she's so pretty. She's competition. And also because Christina's so smart. Christina now has more education and possibilities for her future than her mother ever had." Rita waved to Reinaldo. "Two medium coffees, Reinaldo. With milk. And could you get us some water, too?"

Reinaldo nodded to me. "Why, hello again. My God, you two don't look happy. Again."

"Yeah," Rita said. "Just get us the coffees."

"Rita, do you think this would have happened to Christina if she hadn't been in Bahia Street?"

"Oh, I don't know, Margaret. It's a question, isn't it? But, yes, probably. This kind of thing is disturbingly common. When people get too poor in the cities like this, when they see other people with so much while they're starving... I don't know, Margaret. Our city is falling apart."

Reinaldo brought our coffees. "Here," he said. "I brought you some cake too. It's on the house. Looks to me like you need it."

"Oh, Reinaldo, you're so thoughtful."

Reinaldo pretended to wipe the counter in front of us and then left.

"Recently, when Christina comes to Bahia Street, she's had bruises on her. I think her mother's begun beating her when she realized we'd found out what was going on."

"Rita, isn't there any way we could just take Christina away from them? I don't know. But isn't there something we could do?"

"No." Rita poked at her cake. "And anyway, Christina would do anything to please her mother." She looked at me. "Margaret, more than anything in the world, Christina wants her mother to love her." We ate our cake in silence. I wasn't hungry, but I ate the cake to please Reinaldo.

"And, Margaret," Rita said as we left the coffee shop, "don't go back to that neighborhood for awhile, OK?"

A month later, I was back on the train heading to my job in Portland. Such beautiful countryside but all I kept seeing was Christina. The run I always used for my commute didn't serve lunch, so the dining room was empty. I had developed the habit of making the empty dining car my moving office. It had a large table, a small lamp, and I had four hours of uninterrupted work time.

I had to read forty essays before class that night. I spent three days a week at the university; I spent two, and weekends, with Bahia Street. And I was doing a rotten job at both. These were some of the best students I'd had. They were well-read, curious, analytical. I raced to class, hastily prepared, sticking only to strict office hours and then leaving, spending no extra time with either students or faculty. As for research or publishing—I couldn't even think about it. The best I was doing was giving papers now and again.

Bahia Street was like a fragile flame continually threatened by a wind gust. How could I expect others to devote time when I hardly could?

I had lunch with my friend Robert the next day between classes. Robert was about ten years older than me and a therapist. He had also devoted his life to Vipassina Buddhist meditation. In the late 1980s he had begun to teach. Some years ago, during a Christmas visit home, my sister had dragged me to a week-long silent meditation retreat. All week I was annoyed, frustrated, chafed by this waste of time. But afterward, I felt a stability I hadn't known before. I found it easier to laugh.

So I had returned almost every year. And over the years, Robert and I had become friends.

"I'm feeling overwhelmed," I told him over my tuna sandwich. "I'm not doing a good job at anything."

"From the depths of self-incrimination." He took a bite of his own sandwich. "You're doing a lot, trying to satisfy a lot of people."

"I'm trying to be a decent teacher, but I'm not sure I'm teaching anyone."

"Oh, you are. You teach me every time we meet."

I laughed. "Thank you, Robert. You are very kind, but I mean a real teacher."

"So do I."

"No, Robert, you teach meditation. You know what I mean."

"I know you have a great deal to teach all of us." He put down his sandwich. "Margaret, I consider myself privileged to be in front of groups of people who have the courage to explore the depth that comes with meditation. I am on the same road as they are; I have just devoted more time to it over the years and have some insights that I'm pleased to see that people sometimes find useful. But I am still vulnerable. I work to understand how my mind feels anger or depression. I watch it, but I still feel them both. And everyone who comes to me hoping to learn, to find deeper understanding, teaches me. You teach all the time. And you have a lot to give."

"It doesn't feel like that now." I picked at my sandwich. "I don't really want to teach at university anymore. Bahia Street is bigger now, it takes a lot. If I can give more to Bahia Street, I feel I have to. But I can't just leave my job."

"Why not?"

"It's my career. Also, Bahia Street isn't going to pay me much. It's not what you might call a secure employment option."

"Well, only you know that." Robert calmly took another bite of his sandwich. "I think you already know the path that will be the most rewarding. You just have to relax so you can go there."

I glared at him. He smiled back.

"Meditate on it," he said. "Open your senses to what comes. I'm sure you'll know then what you want to do."

To a Mailing List of 150: December 15, 2000

Dear Donors, Friends, and Volunteers,

I wish to start this letter with a note of appreciation to our vice-president, Eduardo, who has decided to leave the board. His energy, charm, insight and experience have all greatly influenced what Bahia Street is today.

Well, it is that time again: holiday season and the end of the year for students in Brazil. The girls have taken their exams, and one could hardly be prouder of the results. Paula, Dazá, and Luedji passed everything on their first try. This is the first time so many of the girls have passed everything on their first taking of the exams and represents a wonderful achievement on their parts. They will now go to the equivalent of the eighth grade.

Juliana, who has always been very studious, passed everything except math, a subject in which she has always had difficulty. Juliana began to cry when she learned this, but Rita and her tutor reassured her, supporting her solidly while she studies to retake the exam. Juliana is both very kind-hearted and has a fierce desire to succeed at anything she tries. This combination endears her to many, including her teachers.

Of the younger girls, Aqualuxe passed everything; Aninha and Jessica need to take the math exam over but passed the year because their other marks were quite high and their math scores were just below passing. This again is wonderful news, and they are all very proud of their achievements.

A central principle of Bahia Street has always been the strength of a partnership, where peoples of varied countries, races, and classes can learn from and help each other. It has been vital that our infrastructure reflect the changes we are trying to effect in society, both in terms of class and race. This means that all people working directly with the program in Brazil need to have first-hand experience with the conditions and challenges the girls are experiencing. The idea is also that these same people in Brazil will gradually take increasing control of all administration and, if possible, even finances.

As a model for change, Bahia Street is exciting. It is doing what few "development" projects are able to do—namely, to effect change in an international partnership that gradually passes power from the part of the organization granting the funding to the part of the organization doing the on-the-ground change. In this way, Bahia Street is empowering not only the girls, but all of us involved in the infrastructure as well.

Abraços,
Margaret

part three

laughter lessons

twenty-three
leaves of understanding

"Oh, oh. Here she comes."

Rita and I were sitting at the comida a quilo where we often went for lunch. We had invited Karey to join us.

There was a slang term common in Bahia at that time, *amizade colorida*, meaning a friendly relationship with spur of the moment privileges. These *coloridas* did not have the quality of the "one-night-stand" in the States. Literally, colorida could be translated as having "color in your cheeks"' in keeping with the Brazilian idea that it is healthy to have sex.

So, as Karey approached, Rita said, "Karey's cheeks look colorida, but not the way we would hope."

Our intern Karey was having trouble in Salvador. Rita had asked me to talk with her and give her some support when I arrived, but I wasn't sure I could help. Karey expected the girls to be as adorable in their behavior as they appeared in their photos. She wanted to control them in class. She couldn't. Nothing in her life's experience had prepared her to deal with children this disturbed. We should not have interns, I told Rita. It's a disaster.

Life was altogether hard for Karey in Salvador. She wanted to do her capoeira, but people took her money for nothing, deceived her in various ways (a well-established capoeira art form in itself actually). She said she was lonely and that she constantly felt out of place. Being Jewish, she had thought she could find connections in a Salvador Jewish community, but their practice was so different from what she knew in the States that she only felt alienated.

Karey also couldn't handle the street comments from the men. She reacted the way most United States women would, feeling that these comments were meant to humiliate her. I wasn't sure I could teach her, as Luzia had for me, to take a street power for herself, to play with flirtation, trade power play for street power play and to keep her strength for herself.

Rita liked Karey and also felt responsible for her. She wanted Karey to feel happy, to relax into Bahia. Neither of us was sure what to do.

When Karey reached our table, she slammed herself down into the chair beside us.

"Brazilians are barbarians!" she burst out. "How can this country consider itself civilized? I don't see how I can possibly live here. I don't want to even stay here anymore!"

Rita glanced at me as I glanced at her. "What seems to be the problem?" I asked Karey.

Her eyes took the shiny look of gathering tears.

"Last Saturday was Passover, so I went to the synagogue, but no one was there. I found the rabbi and asked him where everyone was, what was happening. He apologized, saying he was sorry I hadn't heard, but there was a very important soccer game this weekend, and as no one would have come to Passover at the same time as a soccer game anyway, they had postponed Passover celebrations until Tuesday!" She slapped the table, a hard snap that echoed around the room. Other customers glanced at us, then looked away. "They moved Passover for a soccer game! What kind of country is this?"

Rita looked at me, and I could see that she was trying not to smile.

"In Brazil, we have many faiths," she said, "but soccer is the central religion." Karey turned her head away. "And," Rita continued very gently, "this is Bahia. People take their spirituality inside them. But the outside ceremonies, we are relaxed about that. It doesn't really matter what day we celebrate Passover, does it? If Tuesday, the synagogue has more attendance, more people concentrating on their spirituality, then that seems, for people here, the sensible thing to do."

Karey twisted in her chair and her face closed in on itself in pain. I wanted to hug her, but I could feel her pushing us away, making even thicker the sultry Salvador air.

Two days later, Karey left Brazil and returned to the United States. Rita and I went out for a beer. We both felt we had failed. Nelson brought us an ice-cold beer, telling Rita to touch it to confirm that he had brought her the coldest he had.

I had been a bit nervous about walking to the bar at night. Everyone in Salvador had been telling me about the recent police strike.

"What do you expect?" Rita had said. "The police haven't had a pay raise in seven years. They can't survive on their salaries; they have to take bribes to exist!" The police had tried to negotiate with the local government but had gotten nowhere, so they decided to strike. The ensuing chaos had led to pitched gun battles in the streets, massive looting, seventy-eight deaths, and, no surprise, all schools being closed, including Bahia Street. "We just stayed inside," Rita said. "Don't worry. Everything's fine now." No one else seemed particularly nervous either, so I decided to relax—or more accurately, relax in the alert street-smart awareness I always adopted in Salvador.

"These interns are so difficult," Rita said as she poured our beers. "On one hand, I feel I should have taken better care of Karey, but I don't have time to look after someone here." She downed her small glass of beer in one gulp. "My, that tastes good," she said. "Perhaps we could get a special group of apartments close to Bahia Street for visitors and young students so that after the excitement and exoticness of the first few weeks wears off, I could protect them a bit from the struggles and loneliness that that seems to come from actually living here. Particularly since the interns aren't living with a wealthy family who can make life resemble what they know in the United States."

"Life here, even with a middle-class family, bears almost no resemblance to the United States," I said. "Particularly for people from Seattle." I waved to Nelson and asked him for a prosciutto and cheese sandwich. Rita said she'd have the same.

"A middle-class family here is only going to be overprotective of them," she said. "The interns would miss the entire point of coming here. What would they do? Take a bus from their fancy condo to teach in the scruffy center of town?"

"No, that doesn't work. But what can we do?"

"Not have any interns?"

"We've said that before as I recall," I said.

"Yeah." Our sandwiches arrived. "Thanks Nelson. That was fast," Rita said.

"Always fast here," Nelson said.

"In more ways than one," Rita retorted. He flipped an impolite hand gesture and Rita laughed.

"Do you want me to be there tomorrow when you talk with Christina's mother?" I asked.

Rita's meeting with Christina's mother was designed to convince her to let Christina and her younger brother stay with Rosa, the same caregiver we'd used before.

"No," Rita said. "I'm going to tell her that we'll pay for the caregiver, but not give any money directly to her."

"And if I'm there, she'll think you should be giving her twice as much because you have this white gringa supporting you."

"Exactly. The boyfriend probably won't want Christina to leave."

"Is he still raping her?"

"It appears not." Rita waved to Nelson for another bottle of beer. "We don't really want him to know you're here anyway, do we?" Nelson brought the bottle and placed our empty one beneath the table for counting later when he calculated our tab. "So Margaret," Rita began as she waited for me to finish pouring our next beers. "I want to talk with you about an interesting thing that's happened with the public and private school girls in Bahia Street."

Although the Bahia Street Center itself was now as good as the best of the private schools in Salvador, we had come to realize that we could no longer afford both private school tuition for all the girls and the expenses of the Bahia Street Center. So, the previous year, we had decided to continue with as many students as possible in the private school, but at the same time also offer the Bahia Street program to a select group of public school students. In this way we had been able to do a year's comparison between the private and public schooled girls in the program.

"The younger girls in the private school continue to have problems with discrimination," Rita said. "Other children harass them. A gang broke the glasses of one girl, some children beat up another. The teachers are generally 'nice' but often condescending toward the girls. Our girls continually try to copy the middle-class girls and end up feeling that they are inferior. But they did form a very strong bond between them. They always watch over and defend each other."

"And for the public school girls?" I asked.

"Ah, now that was completely different. These girls were getting a good quality education at Bahia Street, of course, unlike anyone else in their public school. So they rose quickly to the top of their classes. They became leaders—even the very young girls. And the most startling part was that all of these girls passed their end-of-year exams with grades equal to or above those of the private school girls."

"That's incredible, Rita."

"It goes further than that. The Bahia Street girls in the public schools also got stronger, more sure of themselves. They were more excited by what they learned and more political about the relationship of race and class in Brazil. Other students in their classes asked them to help them study; they were actually getting other students to *want* to study. Teachers told me that the Bahia Street girls are making them want to teach again. Can you believe that? They said that these girls are inspiring their entire class. And I can tell that the public school girls are happier and feel much better about themselves than the private school girls."

"This is outrageous, Rita. We should stop paying all this money for private schools."

"I have all this trouble with the girls in the private school," Rita said. "They think they're better than the other Bahia Street girls. It creates a division at the Center. But they aren't getting any better grades."

"It says a great deal about the quality of the education they're getting at Bahia Street, Rita."

"We're getting through to them on one level at least," she said. "When I asked Diana, the little ten-year-old, what she'd learned this year, she said, 'I have learned to study hard and to never have sex without a condom.'"

"What's this I hear about a condom?" Nelson asked.

"Put it on your nose," Rita said. "And get us another beer. A final one for going home."

I went to visit Tatiana in Penambuas while I was in Salvador. It had been years since I had seen her. She looked twenty years younger. I had never thought of her as anything but old and tired before, but now she was beautiful! Lively, full of spark, life, and flirtation. Her husband had died some years before—no great loss to anyone. All the girls were gone to Europe, she told me. Alexandra had moved from Holland to Germany, was studying to be a dental assistant, drumming with a band, and had a boyfriend. Ana had met an older Belgian fellow in Salvador who had two teenage children. She married him and moved to Belgium. She was just finishing a course on chocolate-making and cake decorating. Her plan was to start a business in Belgium. Alexandra had paid for Soraia to come to Europe; now Soraia was taking classes in Dutch and living with a Dutch fellow she had met who worked with computers. And Andrea. She met a Greek fellow in Salvador and went to Greece with him. But after a month, she got bored and left him, joining Alexandra in Germany. Andrea was now dancing with Alexandra's band and had recently been in a television ad. She wanted to be a model. She had the body for it: very tall and slender with a chiseled, beautiful face. And those bright eyes. I hoped they were still the same.

I walked around the neighborhood with Tatiana with a light step, knowing that these girls, at least, had been lucky. They looked after each other. None had ended up someone's slave or alone like the Brazilian women who had rung me in Seattle—or the even worse stories I had heard.

The girls all sent money to Tatiana. With it, she had bought the property across the street and built four apartments. The original house now had another floor. Tatiana had also established, and now ran, a little street bar down the road, selling drinks, peanuts, and other small snacks. With her newfound status, she also seemed to have acquired herself a very attractive younger boyfriend.

"You always had the core of a businesswoman in you," I told her, "making something from nothing as you sold sonhos, those sweet dreams, from the crumbling front window so many years ago."

"We're strong women," Tatiana said and laughed.

To a Mailing List of 200: February 6, 2001

Dear Donors, Friends, and Volunteers,

I now sit in the Seattle Bahia Street office where a chill sun warms my back through the window. So far removed from the intense heat I just left. Salvador was all in preparation for Carnival, with workmen stringing lights along the avenues, huge bleachers rising on Campo Grande, and a certain anticipation moving alongside the hot wind that passes your shoulder and touches your cheek.

These last few weeks were possibly the most fulfilling time I have spent in Brazil. Not for the sightseeing or the swimming, but for the connections of solidarity and united purpose. The Bahia Street Center is in an old Portuguese-style building with a music studio in the basement and a family who lives on the top floor. Bahia Street has the middle floor with three rooms and a kitchen. It has old hardwood floors and tall, wooden-shuttered casement windows. All are in bad shape with paint peeling and cracks in the plaster, but the girls have been decorating, covering one entire wall with newspaper and magazine clippings. On the other walls are their own drawings. At the back is a small kitchen with a stove and a secondhand refrigerator that Rita has procured. The main room, which has a door leading to an open back walkway and a large window, has become the classroom. Rita bought ten desks, and at the front is a blackboard, along with a strange-looking plant the girls have placed there for decoration (strange because its one spindly stem sprouts a single sickly leaf at the top. Rita says she thinks the girls relate to it in some way).

Of all the girls, Christina did not pass her exams due to problems with her family. This means she cannot return to the private school, but we have placed her in a public school which has afternoon classes that follow our tutoring sessions. She will go to the tutoring each morning, then be taken by Bahia Street volunteers to her public school so we know she gets there. Because of family conflict, we have also, with her mother's permission, placed Christina and her brother with Rosa, the nearby caregiver who looked after her before.

So, with the new Bahia Street Center, we are enrolling twenty girls this year. This is possible, in part, because of increased donations and also, in part, because Rita has secured for all younger girls a much appreciated 40 percent reduction in tuition from the school. We now have five teachers

225

in place at the Center. Three teach the older girls math, Portuguese, science, geography, and history while two tutors teach elementary skills to the younger girls. Sally, an English woman who lives in Salvador, gives English lessons to the girls (and to Rita who is studying English as well). Sally is charging Bahia Street a fraction of her usual fees in support of the program.

Geldon, the math teacher who started last year, was teaching a summer preparatory math class for the ten older girls. We decided to hire two male teachers this year, not only because they had excellent qualifications, but because it seemed important that the girls have male role models as well as female ones. The girls all seem to have crushes on Geldon and are competing with each other for the best homework to present to him—a situation that can only improve their math skills. Geldon is also very good at engaging them, and, as Rita and I worked in the front administration room, we could hear them laughing and shouting out their responses to his questions. A sense of happiness pervaded the place. Everyone, from the girls to Rita to Iolanda, our part-time secretary, was full of sun, laughter, and excitement. We are now letting our dreams run away with us and thinking how wonderful it would be if we could actually buy a building for the Bahia Street Center so we could fix it up and wouldn't be dependent upon a landlord. But, that is for the future…

We also have a part-time, volunteer Spanish teacher, Margarita, a student from Spain who has been studying at the Federal University of Bahia (UFBA) on an exchange program through the University of Essex. She studied at UFBA for six months and is now volunteering with us for six months as a part of her international development studies course. I would like to share with you a letter she wrote to me where she described her background, which influenced her interest in Bahia Street.

"…my mother took me out of school when I was eleven years old…My parents never read a book in their lives. I do not blame them for anything because their situation was a consequence of the Spanish Civil War. They did not have an opportunity to receive an education because Spain was so destroyed after the war that children from the working classes, like my parents, could not go to school, they just worried about surviving.

For many years I was semi-illiterate… When I was much older and went out with other young people who were studying at university, I saw the intellectual difference between us. This made me feel bad and inferior to them. This is why, when I was twenty-one, I returned to education…I believe that education makes people free, and knowledge makes people feel and be equal…For me, it was difficult to get where I am now, into higher education, but it was not impossible, like it is for many poor and street children in Latin America…. I would not have managed to break the cycle of illiteracy in which I was living when I was a child if my circumstances were the same as poor children in Brazil. The only hope for these…children…are the non-governmental organizations…{Because of this} I would like to work with Latin American children and help to break the cycle of illiteracy, which is one of the consequences of poverty."

Things are going well at Bahia Street, but we have two programs that we desperately need to start but do not have the money for. The first is the Nutrition Project. The girls are coming to school hungry. We have been feeding them snacks of fruit, but this is not enough. In order for them to study, they need to have at least one decent meal a day, something they are not getting at home.

Rita has set up a wonderful way to feed the girls for minimal cost and help another local nonprofit as well. A few doors down the street from the Bahia Street Center, a woman has started a project to feed children who sell on the streets. These are not street children; they have homes and parents, but their families are so poor that the parents send the children out into the streets every day to sell whatever they can—candy, pencils, pens, telephone cards—to contribute to the family income. These children are sometimes as young as six, and they spend ten to twelve hours a day on the streets and generally do not eat anything. This woman is getting donations of food from local restaurants and offering a hot lunch that includes rice, beans, meat or fish, salad, juice and coffee. She is charging the children only a few pennies per meal. An excellent program, but she is having a difficult time making ends meet.

Rita has agreed to pay this woman about US$0.45 per girl in the Bahia Street program if she will include them in her lunch program. This is considerably more than the woman is charging the street sellers, but probably less or certainly equal to what we would pay if we were to buy the food and prepare it ourselves. In this way, Bahia Street money will be helping two groups at one time: we are feeding our students and contributing to a worthy local project nearby.

The other project that we need to start immediately is the Total Health Project. In the shantytowns where the girls of Bahia Street live, open sewers run through the middle of the streets. Rats and cockroaches roam freely both in and outside the poorly constructed shacks. Tuberculosis, AIDS, malnutrition, drugs, alcohol, and gang and police violence are endemic. Women and girls must cope with brothers, fathers, and friends being killed, and live with the constant threat of physical and sexual violence.

It is vital that a health program be incorporated into the Bahia Street curriculum quickly. The girls need to know the risks their environment presents and how to deal with violent threats. Bahia Street needs a visiting nurse and counselor as well as a health curriculum to help them deal with physical and emotional health issues as they occur.

The Bahia Street Center is a haven for the girls who study there. It must provide them not only with excellent academic support, but also deal effectively with their physical and emotional well-being.

In the meantime, let us here take joy in what we have, in the people we love, in our homes, and our luck to be living in relative peace.

Warmest thoughts to all and thank you so much for your support.

Margaret

twenty-four | love

On the morning of September 11, 2001, the phone awakened me at seven in the morning. It was my sister on Vashon Island.

Her first sentences garbled flat against my drowsy ear. She began to cry and blurted out unintelligible sentences.

I was now fully awake. "What's wrong? Are you hurt?"

"No, not me," she said. "It just—everything's falling apart."

"Is your husband hurt?"

"No, no, you don't understand, it's, oh my God. What are we going to do?"

"But you're not hurt? You're OK? Everyone else is OK?"

"Yes, yes, but no, none of us is."

My mind raced to the most horrific unimaginable scenarios I could conceive. "Did Mount Rainier blow up? Has someone dropped a nuclear bomb?" No, I thought, such explosions would have awakened me.

"No, no, they just crashed right into them…"

"Are you personally in danger, right now?"

"No, no…"

I felt the fear slide out of my body, replaced by an open awareness, cold, sharp, alert. It was the same balance I knew from skirting gun battles and knife fights on the streets of Salvador, from times spent in Papua New Guinea waiting for local marauders to attack, of odd experiences with crazed men in the South Pacific when I was young, of being in the Underground in London when a bomb scare was announced; all circumstances when I knew my survival hung on a single move, mistake, or on sheer chance.

"It's OK," I said to my sister. "Breathe. Focus on the plant beside you."

Gradually, she calmed down and told me of the New York and Washington, D.C., plane attacks. After we had talked for some time, she hung up and went, I knew, to visit her best friend down the road, to walk and think.

Later, I saw the television footage of the attacks. I permitted myself to view it once. Then, I turned off the television and turned on the radio. Beginning about ten in the morning, U.S. Pacific Standard Time, the phone began to ring. Rita was the first to call.

"Are you all right?" she asked.

"New York is on the opposite side of the country."

"I know, but…I don't know, you could have been visiting. And your brother's a fire fighter, isn't he?"

"Yes. But we were all here."

"It's strange, Margaret, but I feel more empathy for the people of the United States than I ever thought possible. They now must understand—what we went through with the dictatorship, what went on in Chile, Argentina. How it feels to know fear with no escape, to have something fundamental shattered, to realize how fragile we are, every one of us."

"Yeah." I gave a rueful laugh. "Americans, particularly white native-born Americans, have never experienced and probably never understood, that our borders are permeable, that even the United States is only a piece in a larger whole."

"And now they do," she said. "They're the same as us. In a sense, I can feel empathy because you are now equal to us. Americans, like most of the rest of the world, now know in their gut the absolute insecurity of real disaster. You know I love you."

We sat quiet. As I hung up the phone, I was crying.

Soon friends from Europe began to ring and, as the time zone caught up to her, a friend from Australia. A garbled message from Jorge's family, clearly trying to put through their first international call. From everyone and everywhere, the message was the same. It was love.

I felt enveloped in a warmth I had done nothing to deserve, brought by the catastrophic deaths of people I never knew.

My overseas friends had always tended to separate me from my nationality when they wished to reinforce our rapport. "You're not really like an American," they'd say. Or, "You're the first American I've liked; you're different." "You're almost like a European." "You're almost like a Brazilian." "You're almost like an Australian."

Eventually I concluded that I must either be an impressive chameleon, or that their image of an American and my persona—perhaps the first American these people had ever really known—were different. These friends—who almost universally disliked the United States, its foreign polices, its international business practices, its tourists, its governmental attitudes of superiority—felt the need to justify their friendship with me, one of the nationals of this disturbing country. And, the only way they could do that was to separate me, to accept me as the exception.

But the days following the New York attacks were different. We were all equals in a turbulent and dangerous world. A Scottish friend who had recently become a teacher at the London School of Economics called.

"I've just come from the student bar," he said. "Everyone's crying, hugging. There's a sense of unity spanning the Atlantic that I never thought possible. I recounted the time the pub blew up from an IRA attack right next to me, a memory I never discuss. A French woman talked about an Algerian bombing in France. A student from Ethiopia talked about the horrors of his wandering from war camp to war camp as a child fighter. And the American students, they were scared, they were crying, but they were hugging, being hugged. And they understood."

I listened to these calls for a day and a half. The effect was a strange sense of quiet, peace, almost joy. Certainly power. I listened to stories of the courage of individual New Yorkers, and I felt proud of them.

Some years later, while I was preparing to write this book, I reread the notes I made during those days and came across a paragraph on my thoughts of the future. I could hardly have been more wrong:

"These people who attacked New York and Washington, D.C., whoever they are, don't know the international power they have unleashed. The death, horrific death, of this attack, perhaps it is not in vain. Perhaps from the ashes of this catastrophe will come a new unity, a real and collective unity where the United States can build on this empathy. Attacks like this come out of inequality and oppression. Today I see governments and people standing together. With this compassion, much peace could come."

Several months later, I was sitting in a café in Little Venice, an area in London of Georgian homes, elm-lined streets, and canals. This café was actually in a boat moored on one of the canals. It had two tables and a warm wood interior, and sold coffee, tea, and sandwiches. The idea, I gathered, was that most people would take their lunches away with them or sit outside in the summer. That day, however, the boat rocked on rain-filled bursts of wind. I was alone with a waitress who said she was from Romania.

I had given two papers in the previous week, one at the University of Manchester, the other at Oxford. I wrote about Bahia Street's infrastructure and why it worked. I gave the papers to see people's reactions. And also, to get my train fare paid to various parts of the country where I wanted to visit friends.

Oxford scared me. I had only been there a few times in all the years I had lived in London. I wasn't sure what to expect, as I had been invited to speak by someone I didn't even know. This meant I had no friends to pepper the audience, upon whom I could rely to feed me provocative sounding questions on subjects about which I knew a great deal.

When I arrived, I met the director of the Women's Studies Department, a very pleasant woman who took me to lunch at one of their formal dining areas reserved for faculty. Several people lunched in their black, long academic robes. I was sure I was going to spill food on the table, knock over my wine, or commit some equally embarrassing gaffe. Across the table from me sat an older man who said he was Professor of Spanish.

"What's it like in the States right now?" he asked.

"Strange. Everyone's scared. Most people have no idea where Afghanistan is, and now we're attacking it."

"And how are people reacting to all the civilian casualties we keep reading about?"

"Well, actually they aren't reading about them. I haven't seen anything in the U.S. press about these casualties, at least not in the big newspapers or our Seattle papers. We only hear about the Americans killed—and not much on that."

"Hmmm..." The professor chewed on his chicken and seemed to be reflecting upon profound thoughts, or perhaps his own memories.

"Most of us who have been overseas are reading the Internet, getting news from the press outside the States." He nodded. "People are scared," I continued. "I think they just want to feel safe again. Or, at least safe from outsiders, strangers from places they never knew existed before."

"I see." The professor ate the rest of his meal in silence. I tried to chat with others over the uncomfortably wide table. Finally, the professor stood and offered his hand for me to shake. "I enjoyed meeting you," he said. "It is always interesting to meet a member of an oppressed people."

I held his hand, somewhat confused, and then watched him walk from the room.

As a part of my role with the Bahia Street Trust, I spent much of my time in London having morning coffees, lunches, and afternoon teas. It was all very genteel. One evening, I attended a "charity do" with Alex and Susie. Alex explained that if we wanted others to give money to Bahia Street, then we had to attend their functions. "It's reciprocity," he said.

The party was at the house of the editor of one of London's major newspapers. She was the first woman editor of a major daily, and she had recently raised a large amount of money for children in Sudan through a single appeal in her newspaper. Susie advised me on what to wear.

We arrived and everyone seemed to know everyone. I knew only Susie and Alex who, upon arrival, immediately became involved in several simultaneous conversations with other people. I wandered away, looking for someone who appeared lonely and in need of companionship. But everyone seemed busy chatting; all the conversation clumps seemed locked, iron clad. Finally, I broke into a circle of three women chatting about fundraising for the charity in which they were apparently involved. All three looked like fashion models, polished and trim.

"Well," one said, "we're going to do another edited volume. The first one was such a success."

"Yes," the blonde woman standing beside her said. "Everyone wrote for the first book: three Booker Prize finalists, a best-selling novelist. It's sold two hundred thousand copies so far."

"What was the book about?" I asked.

All three women looked at me. "Why, it was a collection of short stories. We just let the writers do what they wished. And what a fantastic result! You are with that group Alex and Susie are supporting, aren't you?" I told them I was. "Well then, you should do the same thing. It can make thousands for your group."

The first woman laughed. "I had dinner with Erik the other night and told him he had no choice but to write in the next volume. You know he's up for the Fischer Prize?"

"And is he doing it?"

"Well, you know, I think he will. He does owe me after all, doesn't he?" All three laughed.

I didn't ask how she had indebted this writer. "Pet piranhas," my friend Gus had called such fundraisers—who had helped him raise an astonishing sixty million pounds for a university building project. "You want them to be aggressive, willing to take on anything, get what they want from anyone, regardless. But then you have to, at least marginally, keep them on a leash, make sure they can't turn and bite you."

"Is this my future?" I thought as I wandered aimlessly through the room. Not my best skill. I was walking, solitary, when I should have been chatting up the rich and famous, who were clearly in ready supply. If only I could recognize them. Why didn't I put together a book like the one the fundraisers described? Because (I answered my own question) I didn't know any famous writers who would draw an audience by their name alone. This part of Bahia Street I had never thought much about.

Bahia Street was becoming a success, even outside my mailing list letters. Rita was managing more and more on her own. The staff in Salvador was getting better and better. I was still helping Rita figure out how to do accounts (something I was just learning myself), but in general, my hopes of passing power and control of Bahia Street to Rita were close to being realized. This was what we wanted.

But where did this leave me? We still needed money. Was I just supposed to raise money, become uninvolved with the process of the change? Perhaps not completely. Rita called me several times a week. We consulted with one another. I offered her advice I thought was useful to her. But what about the future? How long would she need me and my advice? The aim, after all, was that she *wouldn't* need me. So, was my future a lonely one, one of begging people for money to support a wonderful project with which I had less and less connection? Would I become like these fundraisers, where everything, every contact and friend, was leveraged to a specific end?

By now I was thoroughly depressed and unable to talk with anyone. Then, outside in the garden, I saw a man standing alone. He had a pleasant face, and no one seemed to be interested in talking with him. So I approached him and said hello. He gave me huge and charismatic smile.

"Look at this garden," he said. "Their gardener's very clever the way he, or she, has placed these leaf textures and color, mixing gray and gold with those muted black greens I so love."

As we ambled the garden together, his enthusiasm captivated me. I listened, fascinated, as he showed me how the plants were set together to complement each other, not only for color and shape, but also for the way they balanced soil composition and gave needed shade or space to each other. I said very little.

Suddenly our hostess swept up upon us. "Oh, Darling! There you are! I have some people here you simply must meet!" She took his arm, gave me a swift smile, and hastened him away.

"Darling" looked at me over his shoulder and gave me his wonderful smile. "Nice meeting you," he said.

Alex came up to me, laughing, drink in hand. "You are amazing, Margaret."

"What?"

"You're so good at this. Pick out the star of the room and chat him up. And seem completely comfortable. Everyone else was too shy, or reserved perhaps. The difference between you Americans and us English."

"Who? What?"

Alex laughed even harder. "Are you telling me you didn't recognize him? He's a famous movie star. The reason most people here even came." Alex told me some name I didn't recognize and don't remember. "Well, part of your charm, Margaret. You treat everyone equally. You gave him your card, didn't you?"

"Oh, yes, of course," I lied. Alex nodded, smiled, and walked away. I watched as he slid gracefully into conversation with another group and realized how glad I was to have him and Susie around.

To a Mailing List of 300: September 11, 2002

Dear Friends, Volunteers, and Donors,

I look at the date as I begin to write this and realize it has been a year since the attacks in New York and Washington, D.C. Rita called me that day, worried, hoping that I was all right. We talked about the future of Bahia Street, of how uncertainties among world powers affect poverty in countries like Brazil, and how, within the insecurity, danger, and fear, so many of us continue to do those things in which we believe. There was a closeness between us, a realization of unity of purpose that stretches across national boundaries and ethnicities. I remember we felt it also when we both lay flat on the floor of Rita's apartment in Salvador listening to gun shots, witnessing our mortality.

That day, Rita and I also talked about the sad difficulties Aninha is facing. Aninha is eleven, one of the brightest of our younger girls. She studies very hard and has a joyful spark that makes the other girls want to have her as their friend. She and her three siblings lived with her father and grandmother. When their mother died, her father took responsibility of all four children. Her grandmother has been a constant volunteer for Bahia Street, walking the children to and from school, continually concerned for their safety and well-being.

Last month, Aninha's father was assassinated. Two hired killers shot him as he came home one night. He was not involved in any gang activity or drugs and, as yet, Rita has been unable to determine why he was killed. She suspects it was mistaken identity.

Aninha stayed home for a week, but then she returned to the Bahia Street Center, accompanied by her grandmother, who has also been spending considerable time there since the death. She is helping around the Center, and everyone there is trying to give her as much support as possible. The worry, beyond Aninha and her grandmother's grief and helping them deal with the violence of Aninha's father's death, is that the family now has no financial support. Rita is helping Aninha's grandmother in trying to find some kind of work. In the meantime, Bahia Street has given the family a loan to help them survive.

Rita had also warned me that our wonderful English teacher, Sally, was thinking of quitting. Then I received a letter from our Spanish teacher, Margarita, about Sally's situation that was such a delight I have to share it with you. Margarita wrote:

"I am writing to you to let you know that Sally, the English teacher, has decided not to leave Bahia Street.

The little girls wrote some letters to her asking Sally not to leave and telling her that they love her. I helped some of the girls to write their letters in English in order to make Sally feel more emotionated. They also played a theater with puppets for Sally telling her 'Please, stay. We love you and we promise to you not to shout in class and to be good.'

Sally could not go away."

I had to smile reading this. I don't think any of us could resist such a plea. Sally didn't have a chance.

I have recently returned from London. I went there, in part, to further organize the Bahia Street group there. They have been working for a year now for Bahia Street. Of these funds, not the largest, but possibly the most cherished, is the 150 pounds raised by girls at the Francis Holland-Clarence Gate School at a cake sale. The sale was organized by thirteen-year-old Clara, daughter of Alex, one of our board members in London.

And a day after my return, we are kicking off the campaign to buy a Bahia Street Center building! The Brazilian currency is so low in comparison to the dollar right now; we can buy a wonderful, large building in the center of Salvador for about $25,000. Our goal is to raise $45,000 to cover upgrading of electricity, renovations, legal fees and other expenses, such as title searches, etc. This building is part of the plan to enable Bahia Street in Salvador to expand and, at the same time, become increasingly self-sustainable.

A winter sun is pouring over my shoulder as I finish writing this, that wonderful warmth interlaced with a crispness we get this time of year. I wish you all a wonderful next few months and look forward to seeing you soon.

All the best,
Margaret

barriers of glass

I went to visit Jorge's family during my next visit to Salvador.

"A toast!" Lula said. He had recently had surgery for prostate cancer.

"Now, only a sip!" Zezé waggled her finger at him. He was not supposed to drink alcohol, but to Lula, that translated into "not much alcohol." Their little house near the beach was almost finished and they would be moving soon.

We sat on the front verandah—perhaps for the last time, I thought—and drank beers in the warm late afternoon sun. Jorge came by with his girlfriend.

"I'm going to be a father!" he shouted to me, his eyes dancing. His girlfriend had quit school to have the baby. Jorge was working as a night guard at an office building. He'd built them a little place across the lower sewer behind his sister's place. It had two rooms. "And I own the land legally!" he told me proudly. "We didn't invade it or anything. They can't take it away from us."

I congratulated him and laughed to dislodge the lump in my throat.

"Did you hear that Dona Cida is sick?" Jorge asked as he handed me a beer. "Something to do with her heart."

I shook my head.

"That's a woman I admire," Zezé said. "She grew up a hard life with almost no opportunities and then devoted her adult life to helping other women. She teaches about childbirth; she's like a midwife. Did you know that, Margaret?"

"Yes," I said. "I do know that. I admire her, too."

"She's been sick for a while, apparently. Gato's gone to their village to take care of her. And one of his brothers, the one who used to be the policeman, he's out there, too."

"Her medical knowledge certainly helped you, didn't it?" Jorge said. "The time you were out there and fell off the bike." He turned to the others. "Did you ever hear about this? Margaret was visiting and borrowed their bike, only she neglected to notice that it didn't have any brakes. She takes it for a ride on one of the trails, starts to go down a hill—there was barbed wire on both sides of the trail—

and couldn't stop. You hit a rock, didn't you?"

"Yeah," I said. "It was probably what saved me since the trail went straight into a ravine after that."

"So, she crashes, rips all the skin off one arm, the muscle off one entire thigh—wasn't that right?—tore herself to pieces. When she got back to Dona Cida, after the shock wore off, she couldn't walk anymore."

"You act like you were there, Jorge," I said.

"I almost feel I was since I've heard it so many times from Gato and his family." He shook his head and took a sip of his beer, timing his story. "There's no road to their village, so Margaret was stuck, no doctor, no hospital, nothing. Dona Cida took you to a neighbor who stitched up your knee, right? The bone of your kneecap was all exposed." I nodded, and my leg twitched in a muscle memory. "They stitched it with a needle and thread, no anesthetic. Dona Cida, she knew her medicine, she went into the bush and came back with herbs, made a paste that covered your wounds, and took care of you for, how long? Three weeks before you could walk. Made you special food and everything!"

I stared at the shadows that slid across the broken bricks of the shack across the street. ""She saved my life," I said.

"She did," said Lula, "with the tropical infections—"

"The Killers!" somebody shouted from the street below. "The Killers!"

"Oh, my God," Zezé groaned. She pulled me to the ground.

Jorge grabbed his girlfriend and pushed her quickly inside. We followed, running and crawling, staying as flat as we could. We heard submachine fire moving down the street. We all scuttled to the back of the house, and lay beneath the washing trough. The gunfire grew deafening, then moved by. None of us raised our heads until the sounds died away.

"You OK?" Jorge asked his girlfriend, holding her protectively under his arm. She nodded. We slowly crawled to the front of the house and looked down the street. Deserted. Then we saw others peeping from windows and doors. Neighbors began softly calling to each other to confirm that no one had been hit.

"I'll be so glad to leave this place," Lula said. "It was a reasonable neighborhood when we came here, forty years ago, but now it's fighting, all the time."

"It's drugs," Zezé said. "Did you hear about the mother, in that house almost next door? She decided that her son had cheated her in a drug deal and ordered him shot. Her own son!"

"What was the gunfire for?" I asked. "Who are the Killers?"

"Drugs," Zezé said. "Or something like that. One gang upset with someone else. Hired assassins with too much firepower. We'll find out later. The woman next door, her son was fifteen. He's dead now."

Below me, the street had returned to normal. Children picked up their balls and began an impromptu soccer game.

"You want another beer?" Lula asked me.

"But no more for you," said his wife.

These threads, fragile strings, I thought as I accepted the beer from Lula and watched his wife hand him a soda. These are the weave of our lives. And the threads that most keep us from falling into the abyss are those of friendship, of love. These we must continually care for, mend when they become frayed. I sat on the verandah on the metal folding chair that Jorge offered me. I should go visit Dona Cida, I thought.

Rita and I decided to overtly use Salvador perceptions about our differences in race and class to our advantage for the benefit of Bahia Street. A Rotary group in Seattle had expressed interest in spearheading a project for Bahia Street, but they needed a partner in Salvador for them to get the matching funds from the International Rotary. That meant that Rita and I somehow had to make contact with a Salvador Rotary club. The Rotary clubs in Salvador were almost entirely white and middle- to upper middle-class. They would never invite black, favela-born Rita to one of their meetings. So, I—white, foreign Dr. Willson—rang a club and asked if they would like me to give a talk about an education project in Salvador. They were delighted, and invited me to a dinner meeting in an upper middle-class area of Salvador, miles from the center of town and Rita's home. I neglected to mention that I would be bringing Rita with me. We took a bus. Brazilian politeness would never allow them to refuse her entrance in such a situation.

When the time came, I introduced myself and then turned the talk over to Rita. Within five minutes she had charmed the entire group, slicing through class and racial barriers with her sharp perception and inclusiveness.

"I have come to talk with you about poverty and inequality," she said. Everyone looked at her guardedly, waiting for the incrimination. "Poverty in Salvador affects all of us, you as much as me. We all need guards in front of our houses because of robbery and street attacks. For all of us, rich and poor, each day is a dangerous adventure of potential violence, muggings, kidnapping for ransom, and of virtual imprisonment in the secured spaces we call home. The poor, seeing only starvation and death, grow increasingly angry and violent. We cannot place the blame for this on any single person—we are all born into a class and ethnicity—but instead on a status quo in society that directs us to take our places in this hierarchy of inequality, not questioning the distress it brings for us all. Equality in our society will help all of us to live freer and more fruitful lives. We need it for all of our children, yours and mine." She paused. She had them. "Now," she said, "let me tell you about the remarkable program we have in our city; it's called Bahia Street."

Afterward, the group clustered around Rita, asking her questions and offering their help. When it came time to leave, perceiving that we had not come by car, one of the Rotarians, Elino, offered us a ride. Elino was near seventy, white and middle-class. It was pouring rain.

I was staying in my hotel near the city center, relatively near Elino's apartment; Rita's house was vaguely on the way. Most people would have dropped her on the busy street that ran beside her neighborhood, but Elino, with much courage and chivalry, said he would take her to her door. Rita protested, but Elmo persisted, bumping up and down the twisting narrow streets past the falling-down shacks.

"Can you find your way out?" Rita kept asking, knowing he had never entered this neighborhood before.

"I think so," he replied.

Then, right after the heavy metal door in front of Rita's house had clanged shut, a torrential downpour exploded, outstripping by far the "normal" heavy tropical rain bursts of Salvador. The rain became a waterfall; we could see no more than five feet in front of the car. Lightning sliced the dark on all sides.

"Is it true her neighbor is an assassin?" Elino asked.

I glanced at him. Why was he thinking of assassins in this storm? Then I remembered that Rita had mentioned her neighbor during her talk. "Yes," I said, "he is. And he's eighteen."

I knew the way to the end of the bus line, but because I had always previously arrived at Rita's by bus, I wasn't at all sure which route we should take after that. We got completely lost. The rain got worse. Lightning shot blue into the street beside us. We could smell it. Elino grew increasingly distracted and began to drive more and more erratically. Then a young man ran by.

"Let's ask him the way," I said.

Elino looked at the man nervously, who was about eighteen and had already passed us anyway. "No," he said. "No, I don't think that is the sort of person we should stop for directions."

And then, he looked at me, the rain, and we began to laugh. What assailant in his right mind would be out on such a terrible night? The only people out were lost sods like ourselves. We laughed and laughed, the car splashing along the muddy, rutted lanes.

Suddenly, we burst unexpectedly onto a busy street, and both Elino and I recognized where we were.

Elino smiled. "Ah, what an adventure Rotary is," he said.

"Hey, Margaret!" Phyllis bounded up the stairs to my front porch in Seattle. I was drinking a lemonade and watching the renovation on the house across the street that had formerly been the drug and prostitution center. It had been bought by a family of Ethiopians who had divided it into three apartments but kept the classic outside lines of the house. The entire crew also seemed to be Ethiopian. Phyllis sat in the chair beside me and handed me a flyer. "Isn't this your old capoeira teacher?"

I took the flyer. Our capoeira teacher had left Salvador some years before and moved to São Paulo, where he'd attracted a more middle-class clientele and made a livable salary. Indeed, it appeared that he, now clearly much better known, had been invited to the United States to give workshops. A local capoeira group had invited him to Seattle. He was to give a workshop that afternoon.

I had tried to play capoeira when I had first come to Seattle, but had soon stopped. It wasn't the same. Capoeira was rapidly becoming popular overseas as Brazilian immigrants introduced it in their adopted homelands. Some of them actually knew how to play; others did not, but the Americans they taught didn't know the difference. Some

Americans, who didn't have a clue, were also purporting to teach it. But even the knowledgeable Brazilians were teaching an audience that knew nothing about Brazilian society or history. The play was couched in terms of "takedowns" and competition instead of the complexity, balance, and chess-like strategy of the game I had known in Salvador. Besides, the emphasis the Seattle teachers placed on continual back flips was not going to work for me, so I had dropped it and watched the groups from afar.

I felt a rush of warmth when I saw the flyer, though. I hadn't seen our teacher for years.

"I would love to see him," I said. "Let's go."

The capoeira workshop was being held in a school nearby. Throngs of young students stood outside. I saw my teacher, his hair now in long dreadlocks, looking older, but just as fit and elastic.

"Danger!" he shouted when he saw me. "I thought you lived somewhere around here. I was so hoping I'd see you!" We gave each other a big hug. I was aware of the students, none of whom could speak Portuguese, staring at us. "I wish I'd known," our teacher said. "We could have gone out. I only have a few minutes before the workshop." He led me over to a patch of grass, and we sat together.

"I just found out today," I said, indicating Phyllis, who was chatting with someone else who appeared to be a friend of hers. "How is everybody? Have you heard from Fernando? Luiz? Pedro? Luzia? Anyone?"

"Fernando got his master's degree, did you hear that?" I shook my head. "He's beginning to teach for me now. Luzia, I don't know. And did you hear about Dona Cida, Gato's mother?"

"No."

"She died last month."

"Oh." I hadn't gone to visit her.

"She was a wonderful woman," he said. "Very clever. Gato's devastated." One of the organizers of the workshop waved at our teacher and he rose. "Are you going to play?" he asked me.

I laughed and shook my head. "I haven't played for years now," I said. "It's just not the same in the States."

He shook his head. "You should play."

I waved him off, watching the students walk in, wishing I could play and feel the energy of the roda.

244

"I'd have to train for ages to get strong enough again," I said.

I rejoined Phyllis, and we followed the crowd inside. Our teacher showed them some moves, stunning them, as I had been stunned so many years ago, by his electric energy. He passed us several times, inviting me with a gesture to join.

They began a roda, and I heard the long call I remembered so well, the chants so familiar, the postures I could still feel in my body, the energy that permeated the entire space.

We stayed for some time watching, then I went to give my respects to my teacher as the leader of the roda before I left, thanking him for letting me partake as a visitor. It had been eleven years since I had first entered a roda myself. So much had happened in that time. I blinked in the bright sunlight as we emerged from the dark schoolhouse. Playing the dance, dancing the game: what was true in the capoeira roda was true everywhere.

"Oh, that food does look good!" Phyllis placed another tidbit on her plate from the buffet line and moved to the next delicious-looking dish. I followed close behind. We were at Karey's wedding reception. Karey and her husband had decided to invite the wedding guests to bring the dinner as a potluck instead of gifts. A brilliant idea, I thought. It saved them money, it allowed her friends to make her something meaningful, and besides, getting mostly Jewish people to make food for a Jewish wedding? What could be better? Karey asked that people who wished to give further presents make a donation either to a Jewish cause for peace or to Bahia Street.

The room was joyful chaos. Karey had tried to combine both her Jewish faith and her love of Brazil, still undimmed despite her experiences in Salvador, in the festivities. She had hired Eduardo to play, and he and his band were valiantly trying to render a suspiciously Brazilian-sounding version of Jewish wedding songs.

Upon her return from Brazil, Karey had met, and was now marrying, a nice Jewish boy. She and he had also become involved with a local Seattle political group working for peace between Jews and Palestinians. She took this brave position, particularly for a person of Jewish heritage and Jewish faith, and participated in protests against Israeli policy in Palestine. She stood up to other Jews who spit on her in the street. She even traveled to Palestine for a month or so in an effort for peace. She and her husband had invited both Jews and Palestinians to their wedding. We all danced together, hugged each other, laughed together. It was an exhibition of the possibilities of a future of equality, but it was also unadulterated friendship. Karey did this in the face of strong opposition from members of her own family and others in her community. Her mother refused to attend her own daughter's wedding.

Karey had had a hard time in Brazil, and on that day we'd sat together with Rita at the lunch table in Salvador, my heart had gone out to her. But she returned to the States with a strength I had not seen in her before, a courage that comes only with depth of understanding. I was proud of her.

It's strange how times and the world change, how what we think is secure is not, and how dangerous is complacency. When Rita and I first started Bahia Street, we spoke about the political dangers inherent in the project for her. During the military dictatorship in Brazil, the people who protested and survived were often those with international connections who could get them out. Many people lived in exile for years. Both Rita and I understood how easily a shift in government could occur again. And how political was the agenda of Bahia Street.

So when we started, I told Rita, "Rita, get a passport. If anything happens, if the situation in Brazil changes so that you are in danger in any way, if you fear the oppression of your government, I will ensure that you get a ticket to Amsterdam where you do not require a visa. You can stay with friends there until we figure out a way to get you a visa to the States. And, don't worry about the money. We can take care of that."

How the world had changed in so few years. Each time I now returned to the States, Rita worried about me. She had lived through the emergence of the dictatorship in Brazil and was now terrified that this was what was happening in the States. I told her things were not that bad yet, but she was not reassured. One day, when we were speaking on the phone, she said to me, "Margaret, make sure you keep your Brazilian visa up to date. That way, if things get bad there, you can get a flight down here immediately." She paused, knowing she was echoing words we both remembered. "And don't worry about the money. When you get here, we can take care of you."

To a Mailing List of 420: January 8, 2003

Dear Donors, Friends, and Volunteers,

A brilliant winter sun reflects off the wind-touched waters beside my office. It makes silent, undulating shadows, creating an illusion that the walls themselves are moving. It blurs those boundaries between what is solid and what is air, reminding me of how quickly impermanence affects our bodies and the world in which we live.

And with Bahia Street I am also writing about reflections. I just returned from possibly the most joyous visit I have made to Bahia in years. Everything at the Bahia Street Center is going well. The infrastructure is continuing to improve. Rita now has an administrative assistant, Val, who answers phones and does the computer work (the Center has an ancient computer that Val makes do remarkable things, including Excel.) And this year, we will enroll thirty girls in the program! (Cough cough—this terrifies me a bit.)

I arrived at the end-of-school year and was greeted with remarkable results from the girls. All the younger girls passed their end of year exams with grades of 8 or more (out of 10). This result reflects impressive hard work on the part of the girls, increased rigor in the selection process, the excellence and dedication of the teachers, and the dedication of Rita herself. I think we can all be proud. This represents a huge success for all of us.

Those who passed with the highest marks included Aninha, the girl whose father was assassinated. That she witnessed his brutal killing haunts her. The new Total Health Project has allowed us to give her particular help and hire a visiting nurse, as well as Fio, our new Director of Curriculum. Aninha's grandmother comes often as a volunteer. Fio is being particularly caring, as Aninha seems to want male attention. Gradually, she has grown calmer. She has discovered a fascination with science and loves to do experiments. Aninha recently told Rita that she didn't know how she would have stopped crying if it weren't for the teachers and her friends at the Center. Everyone is impressed with her courage and determination.

Christina also passed, remarkably, but she still has psychological problems and is violent toward the other girls. Her mother moves from shack to shack, surviving as she can. Christina eats at the Center, takes showers there, and continues to come. The Center is clearly the only security in her life. We have also not been able to locate her younger brother, and now the mother is pregnant again. How this girl passed with the grades she did is a mystery, but it reflects a determination deep inside her. We can only hold her close to our hearts, watch carefully, and hope.

The older girls this year were all in the eighth grade and studied in preparation for an exam to try to get into a special school. This school is actually a "public" school (i.e. funded by the State), but the exam for admission is so difficult that only children who have attended the best private schools generally get in. It has one of the best records of students passing the university exam in the city. It also has an excellent reputation for all kinds of professions and creativity.

Our aim is to get as many of our girls into this school as possible, as we have realized that we cannot afford to pay for the specialized tutoring that these upper grades require. The girls admitted to this school will remain connected to Bahia Street, but their primary academic focus will be this new school.

The girls took the exam on the Sunday I arrived in Brazil. At lunch, on the day I was leaving, Rita received a call on her cell phone. It was Dazá, one of the brightest and most motivated of our older girls. She was crying and shouting and laughing so much that I could hear her across the table. She passed the exam. Rita herself began to cry and, I must admit, so did I. We don't know the results of the other girls yet, but Dazá is on her way.

It would be wonderful if we could buy our own building, particularly since we will now be paying about $500 a month in rent (including lights and water), money which could be used on our own building. I would consider, with advice, borrowing money here to buy a building if the payments would be about the same as the current rent. Anyone have ideas on this?

With these short days and interruptions, I see that the sun is setting beneath the clouds, creating shafts of temporary color between the shifting gray. I hope you have all survived the holidays with good cheer and fortitude, and that this New Year brings to us all moments of laughter and awareness, peace, and the companionship of good friends.

Margaret

twenty-six | storms

A profitable commerce had started in the States of companies setting up programs for students or other young people to travel overseas for three months, have an overseas experience, and help, supposedly, local nonprofits by participating in short-term projects. Many charge these students about $12,000. The problem is that these companies, and the students, expect the local struggling nonprofits to provide the space and supervision for these projects to take place. Bahia Street was on their list (they likely found us through our website), so now Bahia Street in Salvador was being inundated with eager young foreigners wanting to teach the girls, do photo projects, whatever. And the girls were trying to study for their exams.

I came into Bahia Street one afternoon to find Fio almost in tears.

"What's going on?" I asked. "Fio, what's wrong?"

He waved his hand and walked into the other room. After a few moments, he returned. "I'm sure they don't mean any harm," he said.

"They're arrogant," Rita said. "They wouldn't treat a school in their own country like this."

"Are you going to tell me what happened?"

Rita sighed. "More students wanting to be volunteers. We have to control this somehow, Margaret. We told them we didn't want them right now, but they just walked in anyway. They speak in English so nobody knows what they're saying. They walk into the classrooms and then the girls get all excited. It takes us the rest of the day to get them settled down again."

"Why didn't you just tell the students to get out?"

Fio scratched his ear. "Well, I told them we're busy, it wasn't a good time."

"I don't think they understood us," Rita said.

I felt anger rise in my stomach. "What are we? Some kind of tourist site so these groups can make money off us?"

"It's not the students' fault," Fio said.

"Yes, it is, in part," Rita said. "They're just ignorant. They have this sense of entitlement that they can just come in, that because we're a Third World country, in their eyes, they're somehow superior to us." She turned to me. "They're not all like that. One black American woman, Janelle, she's good, makes an appointment, only talks to the kids outside class, speaks Portuguese, is very respectful."

"Are the whites worse than the blacks?" I asked. Both Fio and Rita laughed.

"No," Fio said, "the blacks are worse, if anything. I think because they're black they somehow think Bahia belongs to them."

"Oh boy." I sat down. "We have to figure out some way to control this."

"We could start by making a rule that everyone who comes in here has to speak Portuguese," Rita said.

"But that means most of them won't be able to say anything," Fio said.

"Well, if they speak English, you can't understand them anyway," I said, "so I agree with Rita. To show respect, they should speak only Portuguese. It undermines your authority as well, them speaking some language that the directors of the Center can't understand."

Rita nodded. "She's right, Fio. And Margaret, we have to be more vigilant with the lists of people allowed to visit; maybe we could make, once or twice a week, a time for visitors to tour the Center. But now I have students coming all the time. I don't know if you've talked with them in the States, given them permission to come or they've just found out about us somehow here."

"I e-mail nearly everyone to say we do not take volunteers because all our staff is local. I should put that on our website as well."

Rita laughed. "Who would have thought social justice tourism would be a problem we would face?" Just then, three students walked in, one white, two of partly African descent, one of whom was very light.

"Hi!" one of them said in English, "we've come to observe some of the girls in their classes."

"They're studying now," I said, also in English. "Rita, the director here, doesn't permit outsiders in the classrooms. I'm sorry. If you'd like to make an appointment to talk with her, you may. But also, we have made a rule here, that everyone only speaks Portuguese while at Bahia Street." The young women looked at each other.

"These students came the other day," Rita said. "Their names are

Alice, Isme and the white girl's name is Jen."

"Alice?" I looked at Alice. "Didn't you e-mail me a few months ago, asking about Bahia Street, asking if you could volunteer and visit? I replied that we didn't take volunteers, but you could contact me again if you wanted to make an appointment to see Rita?" I now spoke in Portuguese.

"She never told me that," Rita said.

Alice looked confused, so I repeated my question in simple Portuguese very slowly.

"Well, yes," Alice said in English. "When you said I couldn't come, I decided I would ask people here, to see what they'd say. Someone here gave me Bahia Street's address, so I just came."

I translated for Rita and Fio.

"You don't understand," Isme, the lighter of the two girls of African descent said to me, also in English. "You're white, but we're black, so people here don't even notice that we're different. You look different, but we're really the same as people here. We can sit in the classes and the girls won't even notice we're there."

Rita and Fio pretended to be busy with some papers on the table.

"They do notice you're different," I said in Portuguese. "The way you stand, your clothes, the way you move, everything shows you're a foreigner. You're a First World person. That makes you inherently different."

"I am not a foreigner here!" Isme said in English, but using the Portuguese word for foreigner. "You are, but I am not!"

"The word 'foreigner' is not insulting," I said. I looked at Rita and Fio. "Excuse me," I said to them, "I have to explain this in English." They gave me bemused smiles and nodded. "The word 'foreigner' is not an insult," I said again, "it just means you're not from here. 'Gringa' also means outsider, specifically from a First World country, and sometimes it is an insult. But 'foreigner' has no such connotation at all."

"I am not a foreigner! We're just like people from here, we're all from Africa."

"A mix," I said. "Your ancestry is clearly mixed. As with many people here. But you are not Brazilian. That is the difference, you and me, we are both United States Americans."

Isme looked at me. "You have no idea what you're talking about.

251

No one here sees me as a foreigner. Rita and Phil, to them I'm just the same. I have an intuitive understanding of Brazilians that you will never have!" She turned to her friends. "Let's go. We can come back when she's not here."

They walked into the street and I slumped at the table. Fio came and put his arm around my shoulder.

"What was that all about?" he asked. "They didn't like you."

"No," I said, "no, they didn't." I sighed and told them the conversation. "I was stupid," I said. "I guess I just got angry. I got mad when I saw you both so upset, but I should have kept my mouth shut. They're young, they don't know any better."

"They're old enough," Rita said. "Other local nonprofits here are having the same problem we are. We're supposed to be international training spots for these kids. The people running these programs also don't understand, or don't care, that it takes our time when we should be running our programs. And no one has yet offered us any money."

"We should set standards," Fio said. "I was just startled when they came in before; I wasn't expecting them. Things have been confused because Jamin came in sick this morning and Jessica's neighbor got shot last night—she talk with you yet about that, Rita?" Rita nodded. "There was just too much going on."

Rita smiled. "You're just not very fierce, Fio."

"No," he said. "But I will be." He pretended to growl. "You give me the script, and I'll just become Muhammad Ali." He flexed his nonexistent arm muscles. Rita and I laughed.

"Let's go for lunch," Rita said. "We can devise some rules."

I wanted to do more than that. International relations, particularly when mixed with race and economics, get complicated. I looked at these well-meaning young people and wished we could somehow incorporate them into some kind of program with Bahia Street, one that would not infringe upon the program itself. One that would start with the premise that the person getting something out of this overseas experience was almost always the foreigner not the local people, to create some kind of program that would teach the infrastructures of equality, building upon what Rita and I had learned through Bahia Street. A program that would help Americans understand that they were not superior to others on the planet, that our ways of doing things were not inherently the correct ones, that we were all in this soup swimming together. These young people wanted to learn about inequality and social justice; they just needed someone to show them some realities outside what their lives had so far led them to believe. I had no idea how to set up such a program. Perhaps someday, I thought.

Although I didn't know how to set up the program I envisioned, Rita and I had decided to bring a small group of visitors, in a controlled setting, to see Bahia Street's work in Salvador. We would also take these visitors to see parts of Bahia they otherwise would not be able to visit—from shantytowns, so they could have a taste of the kinds of poverty in Bahia, to beautiful villages and beaches they would otherwise never find. The money we made from these trips would go to the Bahia Street program.

The first group was made up mostly of friends who had already been involved with Bahia Street in the States for some time: Phyllis, Meps and her husband Barry, and a few others. Rita and I planned to invite them to the end-of-year presentation that the girls gave each year to their parents and other community members. We figured the foreign visitors would then just be part of a bigger celebration and not have too much of an impact. In the meantime, Rita and I were racing around trying to get everything done before these visitors arrived.

Rita invited me to sit in on one of her end-of-the-year teacher evaluation meetings. Geldon had left Bahia Street because he wanted to continue his studies, and so Rita had hired Luciano as the new math teacher. Luciano lived in a Candomblé community, and had begun an educational center of his own with the support of his Mother of the community and based upon the model of Bahia Street. So far, they were teaching classes in math, science, and literacy to children in the neighborhood, and had a small library of donated books.

Luciano and the other teachers discussed a curriculum they were developing that would relate directly to the lives of the girls in Bahia Street. A problem with the general public school curriculum was that it was written for a middle-class life that bore no relationship to the reality of the girls. But creating an alternative, relevant curriculum was not as simple as it might have appeared, even for those who had grown up in these conditions themselves.

"I tried to write a math story problem relating to the lives of girls," Luciano said at the meeting, "This is what I wrote: if you spend 10 reais a month on rice, 10 reais a month on beans and 10 reais on vegetables, how much does a family spend a month on food?

"I gave this story problem to the girls and one of them wrote, 'In our household, we spend nothing in a month on food at all.'" Luciano looked up. "I am having to rethink my story problems."

"Can I take photos?" Meps asked.

We had just arrived at the Bahia Street Center for their celebration. I looked around and saw other people with cameras. "I think so," I said. "Let me ask Rita." I waved to Rita my query and she nodded. "Of course!" she shouted, holding up her own camera.

The day began with a breakfast of bread, cakes, and fruit prepared by the families of the girls. Rita showed a video they had all made about Bahia Street. This video had been part of a project to teach the girls about the power of media. Rita and Fio had encouraged them to make it on anything they wished and they had chosen Bahia Street. In the end, everyone thought this was a good idea anyway, since Rita and Fio were nervous about them running around the streets of Salvador with a video camera in their hands.

From the video, we moved on to a barbecue lunch. The place became more and more crowded as parents, other relatives, friends, and assorted community members arrived. The girls were beside themselves with excitement and nervousness. They were dressed to the hilt, their hair braided with shells and ribbons. Together with Edson, the Arts teacher, and Fio, they had written, produced, and were now going to perform a play. We, the audience, were all handed programs. The play was called *Vamos Colorir o Mundo* (Let's Color the World). The audience, seated on folding chairs and on the floor, quieted down. In the next room we could hear the girls shouting and their teachers telling them to get ready to start. Rita stood at the back of the room, camera in hand, trying not to look too nervous.

The first group of girls came out. They were dressed in brilliant-colored groups—yellow, red, orange, white, and black. It quickly became clear the colors were meant to represent different ethnicities or classes, symbolizing how arbitrary color and class discrimination can be. The scenes the girls had written dealt with their lives: of a young baby being left alone and dying, of drugs and death, race and discrimination. The presentation ended with some pagode samba dancing to local hit tunes.

I was so proud of these girls, I could hardly contain myself. I glanced back at Rita and she nodded at me, indicating "Pretty good, aren't they?" The parents and community screamed their approval; most were in tears.

After the performance, Edson spoke about the production of the play and his excitement about the girls' creativity. Fio followed. Then Rita. Then me. Then a cluster of girls approached Fio. "They want to say something, too," he said.

"How could we think these girls would let such an opportunity pass?" I heard one parent say to one of the teachers. They both laughed. One by one, various girls took their place center stage, some shy, others prancing, and each told how much her teachers, the program, and her new friends meant to her life.

Lastly, Nina (at eight years old the youngest girl, small and full of exuberance) took the stage. A natural performer, she thanked her teachers, Rita, and the program for teaching her to read, and also she told us, "I really like art." She held up a string of carnival beads we had been exchanging as symbols of friendship and said, "I want to thank the person whose support and kindness has made it possible for me to study and learn." She walked to the front row and hung the beads around her mother's neck. The audience cheered.

Rita, Fio, and I were standing at the back. Fio and Rita exchanged a meaningful glance. "She's not her mother," Fio said to me quietly. "Her mother died when she was very young, so her father took her to live with his father and then left. The grandfather had a young girlfriend at the time. The grandfather has since died and this woman is the girlfriend. She kind of got stuck with a child that had nothing to do with her."

"Nina's very fearful she'll leave her," Rita said. "Like everyone else in her life."

A few days later, Rita, Fio, and I were sharing our usual evening beer and sandwiches at Nelson's bar.

"Where was Christina?" I asked biting into my hot cheese and meat roll.

"You didn't tell her?" Fio asked Rita.

I put down my sandwich. "What?"

Rita sighed. "Christina's mother brought her in last week. Christina was all beat up. Her mother was dragging her by the hand. She pushed her in front of us. 'What are you going to tell them?' she said to Christina. Christina looked at the floor and then said in a very low voice, 'I want to leave Bahia Street. I don't like it anymore.'"

"What!?"

"Yeah," Fio said. "We couldn't do anything. Her mother's not going to let her come back."

"We did manage to get her into a room next door with the door shut for a minute," Rita said. "We told her that she could come back anytime, that Bahia Street would always be open for her."

"We told her we loved her," Fio said.

We sat in silence.

"She created a lot of the play that the other girls performed without her," Fio said. "Her mother wouldn't even let her come to that." He idly folded his napkin into a small square. "She's one I wish I could adopt," he said.

"At least Christina can now read, she passed the sixth grade," Rita said. "She understands about contraception and has more awareness of the world around her. But..." She lapsed into silence again. After a few moments, she said, "It's things like this that make doing Bahia Street so hard."

To a Mailing List of 560: May 12, 2003

Dear All,

Each year, Bahia Street grows stronger and more effective. With forty (!) girls this year, the price per girl is actually decreasing.

The building we had been renting was too small, so Rita moved the entire operation a block down the street to a larger building. It has space for two classrooms, a lunchroom, and an arts room. It is also much better ventilated than the last building. Salvador, as most of you know, is very hot, and the other building was often so stifling that study became impossible. We are still working to buy our own building. A building of our own would allow Bahia Street in Brazil to generate its own income and give security in so many ways.

We have twelve new girls, none of whom know how to read or how to study. Rita and the staff are doing what has become a skill for them— helping the new girls adapt to focusing on specific topics. Many of the girls also come with behavior problems. Interestingly, as the group as a whole has grown, the girls who are the core of Bahia Street help the new girls to adjust and feel secure. And this kind of friendship, from girls who have gone through exactly the same confusion the new girls feel, is part of what makes the entire environment of Bahia Street effective.

Our success rate overwhelms even Rita and me: again, all of the girls who took the end-of-year exam passed with grades of 80% or higher. Our teachers, all of whom (except the English teacher) are from the shantytowns or rural interior of Bahia themselves, say Bahia Street is a central inspiration of their lives. I would say that they are also an inspiration to us. Bahia Street now has fourteen full- and part-time staff members in Salvador including teachers, counselors, a nurse, an administrative assistant, a curriculum director, and Rita. When I see the incredible people Bahia Street has drawn to Rita's side, the dedication, compassion, intelligence, creativity, and street savvy these people bring, I am sometimes not sure what to say. Six years ago we started with ideas, a handshake, one donation, and one girl. It shows that we can make a difference in this world, that we are not powerless. Bahia Street is basically a small grassroots organization and this is what we have done and are doing. We are small, but we have strength. We have integrity.

The Chieftains have finished their songs on the stereo and a blue heron is crying on the lake. This is one of the most beautiful springs I can remember. The early rains brought vibrant green growth and the trees are holding their bloom for weeks. I am stretching my limbs, waking like a bear, sniffing and snorting, ready to pass into the scents of the warm air. The greatest joy of winter is late spring.

The days are getting longer, the dark of winter is past, the time of the tulip has come.

Warmest thoughts to you all,
Margaret

twenty-seven | sharing a life boat

"OK, do it."

"Do what?"

"Buy a building." I was on the phone to Rita.

"Where'd you get the money?"

"Meps and Barry. They sat down together and decided they could give Bahia Street an interest-free loan. So let's do it while the dollar is high."

"You'd better be sure on this," Rita said. "Because I think I know just the building."

It seemed I had barely hung up the phone and here I was in Salvador. Rita had made an offer on a building two days after my call. We decided, for a bevy of reasons relating to legalities and registration, to have Bahia Street in the United States legally own the building, which Bahia Street in Brazil would then rent from us. But this meant that Rita couldn't sign the final papers until I arrived.

This process for transferring of title from the original owner to Bahia Street was, however, incredibly complicated. It seemed that the transaction was being conducted by the nephew of the owner, herself an elderly woman. But, then it came out that the building actually belonged, legally, to the grandfather, now long dead. No one had bothered to transfer the building into the daughter's name. This kind of thing was common. The commonness of these kinds of lapses, and the familiarity with which they were dealt, did not lessen the red tape we had to negotiate. Rita hired someone, who then hired someone else, to make it possible for us to get through the corrupt city bureaucracy. Even so, Rita and I had spent most of the day and the day before in an office waiting for the one lawyer whose signature would make the transaction legal. Perhaps our agent didn't pay her enough. I heard the conversations of others when they spoke with her (we were all waiting in one big, ugly room while she, like some lazy queen spider, signed the papers she chose.) People kept giving the lawyer little presents and saying to her, "Oh, do stop by my house later for some cake." She always nodded and they set up a time. I wondered about the nature of this "cake," whether it was perhaps made of bank notes?

Finally, Rita told our agent that I had to return to my country the next day, and if we didn't get our signature, than he wouldn't get paid. She had, intelligently, only paid him a portion of his fee. So, he hustled and somehow made the lawyer set an actual appointment—she then only kept us waiting four hours before she deigned to see us.

So, now the building was ours, but I was nervous. It had a beautiful facade dating from the early nineteenth-century, but it was a total mess. It had been passed on in a single family, generation to generation, and no one seemed to have done any maintenance for a hundred years. We got a renovation grant from England by incredible good luck, but it was only 12,000 pounds. Rita said she was sure that would cover the costs of renovation. I hoped so. Rita was exhilarated about the whole thing, so I kept my mouth shut. We were going through the building with the architect in a few days. He had already seen it and said it was OK.

Rita and I had been spending long evenings talking. Last year, she had begun having panic attacks. Her heart would beat erratically, would race and not stop. Then she would get anxious and paranoid. It hit her first when she went to the World Social Forum in the southern Brazilian town of Porto Alegre. Rita had traveled little. She seemed so urbane, but she never had the money or opportunity to see much of anywhere except Salvador.

Her doctor gave her some kind of medicine for the panic attacks, told her to quit drinking alcohol, get more exercise, do meditation, and to take weekends off. She had done everything the doctor suggested. She also began seeing a therapist. Bahia Street was so stressful for her, let alone where she lived. A man had come to the front of her house the previous month and shot someone on the street right in front of Rita. Her niece had been sitting at the curb six feet away. The killing was a case of mistaken identity.

"Why can't these assassins be more professional and at least shoot the people they are paid to instead of some innocent bystander?" she had asked me rhetorically. The assassin was supposed to hit the father of the ten-year-old boy across the street, but he had shot a local mechanic instead. The father of the boy had now disappeared, and the boy was afraid to come out anymore. The neighbors were leaving food for him.

"I can't stand it much anymore," Rita said. "Things are getting worse and worse. Outside the center, this city is like a war zone; it is a war zone." It was the lived reality of the statistic that Brazil had the highest murder rate in the world. Friends of the Bahia Street girls kept getting killed. "I've always loved my neighborhood," Rita said, "but now I don't want to go home anymore."

She was spending most of her weekends in Arembepe. She had rented a room and had friends there. We went there when I first arrived. The room was very simple; we slept on mats on the floor, but we spent most of our time outside anyway. It was tranquil, and it was safe. She had around her the smell of the sea that she had known as a child. I worried about her. Rita ate healthy food, lots of fish and vegetables, but people who have been brought up poor in Salvador die young. Rita was in her forties. I got scared sometimes.

I lay in my hotel room a few days later with the fan on. I should run down to the sea, I thought, jump in, clear my brain, and let my stomach settle. But I couldn't. I had no energy. My stomach hurt.

Rita, Mario the architect, and I had inspected the building the previous day. We went into the neighbor's house and looked at it from above.

"Well," Mario said. "It's a good buy. It will have to be entirely rebuilt of course, but with the land at the back and its location, it's still a good buy."

"What do you mean, has to be rebuilt?" I asked. "You mean gutted and repaired."

"Well, more than that. You have to leave the facade since it's an historic building, but the rest will all have to come down. We'll have to start from scratch." He nodded while surveying the building. "That's good, really. You can make it what you want. Otherwise you never would have had the building you wanted, just a refurbished home, not a school."

I looked at Rita. "Did you know this? That the entire thing has to be rebuilt?"

Rita seemed unperturbed. "No, but I'm sure we can do it. Mario's right. This way we can get what we want."

"But Rita, there's the cost. Have you considered how much this will cost? How are we going to get the money?"

Rita laughed. "You worry too much. You got that wonderful grant. We'll figure out a way if we need more. That's how we do it in Bahia."

We then all trouped to Fio's nearby apartment where he had been preparing a goodbye fish dinner for me. He served the dinner on the roof, in the night breeze, with a view of the Salvador sky. I sat there a few minutes, watching the sky go from turquoise to cobalt in the rapid tropical twilight.

Later, I asked Mario if we could go downstairs so I could talk with him. "How much is this going to cost?" I asked.

"Well, we have to figure that out."

"Can you make even a rough estimate?"

"Of course. It's all based on engineering, on mathematical models of what, structurally, you'd need. Let's see…" He took out a pen and notebook and began making calculations. "First, you have to pay for the demolition. That's expensive. And you won't be able to start until after Carnival. Then it will be the rainy season, so you can't really start until June. The foundation. Steel structural beams. Cement. This is very rough you understand, based on the size of the area." He paused. "I'd say about a hundred thousand."

"A hundred thousand what? Reais or U.S. dollars?"

"Dollars."

I sat there. Mario laughed and went upstairs. When Rita came down, I called her to the window. "The rebuilding is going to cost a hundred thousand dollars. We don't have the money."

Rita laughed. "Why are you talking about this? This is your going away party! Come and eat the dinner Fio made. Have a drink."

"Rita, don't you get it? I cannot get this money. It's too much. We'll have a shambles. We're already in debt for the building itself. And we're supposed to come up with this ridiculous amount on top of paying that off? My board in the States will flip. I don't know what they'll do."

"You worry too much. We have the building. It's incredible. We'll figure something out."

"Rita, I don't think you quite get this. You're here, doing the program, but I'm having to come up with the money. The economy is terrible right now in the States. I see no way I can come up with this money."

"Margaret, relax. If I'd known you were talking with Mario about this, I'd have stopped you. He's a middle-class architect. He thinks in middle-class terms. We'll do it for less than half of what he's talking about. We'll go to the different vendors, get them to give us cheap deals, hire local people. In Bahia you have several prices for everything. If you deal with official people, they all take their cut. We won't do anything official. We'll make the building safe. We'll do a wonderful building, but it'll cost much less. You'll see. Now, relax. Forget about it. Come and enjoy Fio's dinner."

"Easy for you to say. You don't have to come up with the money or face my board."

I went upstairs, tried to eat Fio's dinner, tried to be polite to the other guests, tried to be civil to Rita. Then I came home to my hotel room and lay on the bed all night, unable to sleep. After what seemed an eternity, I watched the growing light of dawn.

I felt betrayed. I loved Rita. In the eleven years or so I had known her, she had only grown in my esteem, only gained my increasing respect as she devoted herself to this project. She had such vision and had created an incredible program that now functioned in a city where so much never did. She demanded teacher attendance in a society where teacher truancy was the norm. If a teacher didn't show up, she or Fio taught the classes. It was her bottom line that she never let the children down.

And now we had a partner in Fio. Bahia Street could hardly have a more intelligent and dedicated worker than Fio. Rita had known him for years; they'd been in theater together some twenty years before. Fio had been a well-known sculptor as well, but a few years before had almost died of spinal meningitis. The illness had left him physically frail, and he had slipped into a deep depression. Rita had somehow coaxed him into the job at Bahia Street. And there he'd come alive again. The girls had also changed with him, responding to his gentle, clear calm. When he smiled, he seemed almost to emit his own light. I had never believed in the concept of "unconditional love," but if it existed, Fio embodied it. Rita and I were harder, had more barriers, were perhaps more emotionally vulnerable.

I stood up and watched the sun rise. I again reflected on the reality that in the States almost no one had actually seen Bahia Street. Most had never even been to Brazil. Their trust was in me, the person they knew. I was the person who wrote the letters they read, who reported on the project in some faraway land. And now I'd screwed up. Our operating budget was now about $100,000 a year, not including the building. On top of that, we had the loan I had assured Meps and Barry we would pay off—and for which the U.S. board had legal responsibility.

I was convinced it wouldn't work. Something was going to crash.

Rita, her brother, Rubim and I were scheduled to go through the building the following day. Rubim was a general contractor. Why hadn't Rita told me this before? I wondered to myself. Why hadn't he inspected the buildings?

I tried to think, to be rational. I stopped at our usual cafe for a solitary cup of coffee, a medium with milk, so I could stall longer while drinking it. What would possibly be Rita's motives for not including this qualified person in our decision about the building? I stirred a bit of sugar into the very strong coffee. I didn't really want to admit that I understood Rita's actions, but I was also pretty sure I did. Rita had felt that the U.S. board would be happier if she had the place checked out by a middle-class person. In other words, Mario, not her brother. I also had to admit, regardless of the outcome and the trouble it had caused us now, that in that sentiment, she was probably right.

I finished my coffee, smiled at Reinaldo who asked me if I was feeling well, and went to face Rubim and the building.

"God in Heaven!" Rubim said as we stepped over rubble. "I'm not sure this place is safe enough to inspect. I often wonder how people live in these places. Rita, be careful who you let in here." We filed down the broken stairs to the lower floor. "Beautiful porticoes," Rubim said. "And the metal filigree. We'll take those down, restore them and use them in the new building. To give it the same wonderful feel this one has."

"How about demolition?" I asked. "How complicated will that be?

When would people be able to start? How much will it cost?"

"Did you hear what happened up the street?" Rita asked. "The building three houses up is in the process of being reconstructed itself. The family doing it doesn't have much money, so some family members are demolishing it while others live in the ruined back portion. Yesterday, an entire wall fell down. Three stories of wall just crashed. It would have killed everyone. But by some incredible luck, it happened while everyone was away for lunch. So, no one was hurt."

Rubim nodded. "That kind of thing happens a lot. It's because people don't know what they're doing. See." He walked over to a wall that edged the back of the building. "You can't just bash these walls out in these old buildings. They're fragile. You have to start at the top and back, slowly working your way toward the front and down. And when you want to demolish a wall like this, you have to cut it out in chunks, removing it piece by piece. Otherwise you weaken the entire structure."

"What about the demolition?" I asked. "How much do you think that will cost?"

"Well, I've got some skilled boys who generally work with me. Unless, Rita, you have someone else in mind. We could have my fellows lead the demolition, working together with local lads. My fellows work hard and they won't cost much. I, or someone, would just have to be continually on site to instruct them on what to do. My boys are pretty good anyway."

"What about the rainy season?"

"Well, my boys want work, so they'd begin now. Work until Carnival, then come back right after. They could finish it in about two months. You can't pour cement in the rain, but you can demolish stuff. My guys are from Salvador. They understand the rain."

"And the cost?"

"Oh, for demolition. Depends on what you can negotiate, but I'd say about 2,000 reais."

"So, about 800 dollars."

Rubim shrugged. "I don't know about the dollar. But you'd have to be careful with this building. Since you can't damage the front facade, all the debris, everything, will have to be taken out the front door in sacks. We're used to that. The street's too narrow to have a debris

container, so we'd have to get a truck come in, probably best at night."
He laughed.

"The neighbors," Rita said. "I'll have to talk to them."

"At night there won't be much traffic for us to block."

"So, Rubim," I said, "we have about 50,000 reais for the rebuilding, including demolition. That's it. Can we do anything reasonable with that?"

Rubim paused, surveying the building. "Well, sure. If Rita and I go out and buy all the materials ourselves, if we don't try to hire outsiders, if we work with people we know so we don't get ripped off. My guys generally work for about 25 reais a day. So, if we did all that, you could do the building for that. It wouldn't be fancy. We could just leave the walls cement for now and paint them some bright colors. Then we can put on the tile when you get more money. But, yeah, if we're careful, I think we can give Bahia Street a usable school."

Rita gave me a huge smile, one in which I saw no triumph or malice. "We'll do it, Margaret. I'll get Mario to give me the plans, and then I'll go to local people I know in the periphery to buy the materials. Maybe I can even get some of them donated. Fio can talk Mario into doing the plans for free."

"That's impressive if he can do that," Rubim said. "Middle-class people never do anything for free."

Rita nodded. "Mario's not a bad person. He's impressed with Bahia Street. And he adores Fio. They've known each other for years. He thinks Fio is a brilliant artist."

We moved to the open space at the back of the building, and Rita sat on a crumbling wall beside me. "Margaret, I've given much of the last six years to these girls. Of anyone in the world, you know I will not do anything that could possibly cause them harm. I've never had any biological children, but these girls, they're my children now. I know them. I was incredibly lucky, chance was with me, for me to finish school, go to university. If change is going to happen here in Brazil, if we blacks are ever going to get any power, we have to do it with education, with understanding. With our own building, we will be able to do so much. This project has my heart. If there's anything we in Bahia understand, it's how to survive. This project's the same. While I'm here, it will survive."

She took my hand. "I'm sorry Margaret, that I seemed cold the other night. It wasn't intentional. We had prepared this special meal for you. I wanted you to enjoy it. I know you have a huge burden finding the money. We have this money now. If we don't have any more, we can still do it. Don't forget, I'm here. I can collect this and that, get favors." She looked at me. "We're in this together. Bahia Street has everything I have."

Rubim's shadow crossed over our heads as he crunched through the rubble behind the building. "The original cistern's still here! Where they used to bring the water. It's in good condition. We can keep that, keep the building's history. And there're two trees back there! A palm and—what's that other tree? Rita, you know?"

Rita turned around. "A guava," she said. "Isn't it wonderful? Some real green. I thought we could make this back part into a garden. Use it to teach the girls about plants, biology, have them actually grow their own vegetables."

"Yeah," Rubim said. "I can see it. A little kiosk there at the back, what do you call it, a gazebo kind of thing. To give shade. You could even have classes out here."

Rita laughed. "That's what Fio said the minute he saw it."

"So," I said to Rubim, "you're going to be working on this with us, aren't you? Directing all this, making sure it goes right?"

Rubim looked at Rita. "Well." He sounded embarrassed. "Rita and I haven't discussed it. I just came to do an inspection for her. And because I like what Bahia Street's doing. I mean, I'd be happy to do it. I think I have time. But it's up to Rita. She might have someone else in mind...."

Rita laughed again. "You know you're the best, Rubim." She turned to me. "He signs off the permits to make sure buildings are correctly constructed, to make sure they're safe and don't fall down. So, he's pretty good. And he's my brother, so of course he's great." She stood up and brushed the dust from her pants. "We'll discuss it."

"Hmmm..." I said. "So, shall we go out for a beer—er, I mean a soda? To start the project off?"

Rita coughed as she negotiated the dust and broken stairway. "Perfect."

To a Mailing List of 580: October 20, 2003

Dear Donors, Friends, and Volunteers,

As I write this, the first stormy rains of autumn slap their notice against my office window. Their energy swirls through the buffeting wind and creates mottled reflections in graphite pools that sit cupped on the sidewalks and wooden dockways. I am still in shorts, but wearing a fleece and rain jacket, torn between nostalgia for this last summer and delight at the changing color and pungent new smells. With these first rains come the greening of the land.

So, the news from Salvador. We have bought a building! Rita found a suitable building on the same street as the current Bahia Street Center, and negotiations began.

This has been an experience. I have learned more about Brazilian law and real estate than I ever wanted to know. We had wonderful help both here and in Brazil with advice from lawyers, real estate brokers, and others familiar with the pitfalls of buying property in Brazil. In Brazil, one does not buy title insurance as one does in the United States. Rather, one hires someone to do title and other background research on the building. We found several misplaced papers, wrong names on contracts, etc., but had it all sorted and were waiting for the final document, until...the government workers went on strike. Then, of course, nothing got done until they went back to work again, which was only a short time ago. The final papers have now been delivered to Rita, however, and she has the keys. Now we only have to rebuild it into the Center we have dreamed about. I am a bit intimidated by all this, but Rita, Fio, the girls' caregivers, and other volunteers in Salvador are all excited to begin.

Last month, when I rang Rita at the Center, she sounded as though she were speaking in an echoing silence. Generally when I ring her, we have trouble hearing each other over all the noise of young girls shouting, running, playing, or whatever sounds come from a collection of forty girls. I immediately asked her what was going on, how come I could hear her so well. She laughed and began telling me about the children's protest in Salvador. The city of Salvador has recently raised the bus fare to R$1.50 for each ride. Two rides, for example, coming to and from school, now cost R$3.00. Since many people in Salvador earn about R$300 a month, this is a huge daily cost and means that many families will not be able to send their children to school.

So, the public school children took to the streets in protest. They spilled out of the schools and sat on major Salvador avenues. This included children from age ten on up. They brought commerce in Salvador to a dead halt. But, as of yet, the city administration has not agreed to give the school children a subsidy for their bus fare. The children are not giving up, though, and the mood in Salvador is that the government will have to negotiate with them eventually.

All this disruption has impeded the running of the Center. Several girls contacted Rita and said that although they would not be going to public school and were protesting, they wanted to come to the Center. Rita told them not to as they would have to walk (for many a walk of about five to ten miles each way). She worried about them wandering alone in unfamiliar neighborhoods with all the police and other activity. So the Center, like the public schools, has only been running on nonprotest days.

When I heard all this, I became confused and asked Rita what in the world she was doing there.

"I just needed to get some things done," she said. "So I came in."

"From your home? How did you get there?"

"I walked."

"But Rita, that is almost ten miles or something."

Rita laughed. "Well, I'll get fit and skinny."

I told her she was too dedicated.

On a bike ride recently arranged by one of our Bahia Street volunteers, I met Karima. Karima is Moroccan-French, speaks several languages (Spanish, French, English, Arabic, German, and Albanian—and she is already picking up Portuguese) and has extensive experience working with international non-profits in social justice. So, Bahia Street is lucky enough to have her now working with us. The timing could hardly be better; we are growing and need someone with this kind of experience. So, I welcome her to Bahia Street and look forward to you meeting her at our next event.

As I finish this, I am listening to Mongolian music that I collected some years ago in Inner Mongolia. It is a saudade kind of music, resonating well with the hollow thumps and slaps the wind carries off the water and under the dock here, offset by the quiet and warmth of a single lamp inside the office. My best to all of you. May this change of season bring you curious noses and intimacy.

um abraço,

Margaret

twenty-eight | heartbreak

"Did you know that the building would have to be rebuilt when you bought it?" James, one of my U.S. board members, asked.

"No." I could hardly believe this was happening. I had no idea what to do.

At the time we bought the building, the Bahia Street Board in the States consisted of five people: Joyce, by then my longest serving board member; Almuht, a sharp-minded realtor and leading member of the Brazilian community; Henry, a Rotarian and lawyer who had, *pro bono*, spent hours rewriting our by-laws and making sure our legal papers were in order; Mo, a general contractor and guitarist who also worked with "at-risk" young people; and James, a fairly new addition to the board, whom I had asked to join because he had strong local business ties and a good head for business methods. I liked them all. Some of them were my closest friends in Seattle. They had always given me good advice and support. I had never been political or "strategic" with my board, but had always told them my straight thoughts or reactions. Too late I realized this was a huge mistake, that being on a board was always political, no matter how much one might like its members. I had not allowed for the obvious fact that the board had never had the experiences in Brazil or the history there that I had.

I had just told the Board that we would not be refurbishing the building in Salvador; we would be rebuilding it. That this included demolition and would likely take at least a year.

"Did Rita know this?"

"No. But she understands how Bahia works. I don't think it makes so much difference to her. We have the building, that's the most important part. Now we just make it work for us."

"But this is going to take much more money than we have," Joyce said.

"They say no, that they can do something reasonable with what we already have."

"And how are we supposed to believe them?" Henry asked. "When they can't even determine if the building is sound? What about liability? We're incurring a huge amount more liability now than we would have before."

"I don't know that we are."

"That's the problem," James said. "You don't know. We should have someone there working on this who does."

"Rita knows what she's doing."

"She certainly didn't on the building," James said.

"She'll be working with her brother who's a general contractor. He's very knowledgeable."

"Wait, wait," Henry said. "Who said she could hire her brother? We own the building. We should be the ones who decide who she can hire. I would think hiring her brother is a very bad idea. Then we won't be able to control anything."

"In Brazil, it's better to work with close friends; relatives are best. You can trust relatives much more than you can others. And her brother is a very competent person."

"But we don't know that," Henry said. "I think at this point we need to get an outsider, someone who is credible, who has done projects that have a name that we can research. Then we hire them. That person would need to check all the finances before we release any more money."

"Actually, Margaret is right. In Brazil, the closer the relationship with a person working with you, the better." Almuht said. "Rita's brother is probably a decent choice."

"Liability is a big issue here," Henry said. "We owe money on this building. The loan is our responsibility as board members. We are legally responsible if all our meetings are not conducted correctly. Have we done everything in formal procedures here? No. I can answer that. I'm a lawyer. You don't understand the danger you have put yourselves in. We could be sued for thousands of dollars if something goes wrong on the building—we would all be legally responsible."

"Surely not," Mo said.

"I don't consider myself responsible for this loan," James said. "I will try to contribute, but I'm not going to make promises."

"And what about the lien I suggested we get?" Henry asked. "You never did that, did you, Margaret? You said it was too complicated to do internationally. Well, I consulted with a lawyer in São Paulo and he tells me that we can definitely do it. It would cost us about two or three thousand, but we can do it. And you never told us that. Also, remember that months ago I suggested one of my contacts, a middle-class Brazilian who lives here in the States, could check out the building. But you said no, Rita was director and she could handle it. Well, clearly she couldn't. If you hadn't ignored my suggestion, we wouldn't be having this problem."

"A middle-class outsider would not have understood the situation," I said. "They would not respect Rita. For them to be in Bahia, a person not of her choosing, would have undermined her standing. They would have been looking for a snappy, middle-class building. And that is not what Bahia Street is, nor what Bahia Street would build."

"All these idealist notions of yours, Margaret, are very nice, leaving control to the people in Brazil, but it doesn't work," James said. "We have final responsibility. We control the money. Rita may be fine for looking after little girls, but this is a much bigger project. She clearly doesn't know what she's doing."

"I'm responsible for all this," Henry said. "I understand the legal ramifications. As a lawyer, I am actually in more legal danger than the rest of you if we are not seen to be doing things correctly. I could be sued or worse." He paused. "So, my main concern is that Rita is just going ahead with the project right now, without our knowledge or control. We need to make clear to her that she can do nothing until we give the permission."

"The money for the reconstruction is actually coming from England," I said. "And the main concern they have is that it gets spent in a timely manner."

"But we own the building," James said.

"You seriously think we are liable?" Mo asked Henry. "Perhaps we could just ask Rita to give us a business plan. To itemize what they plan to do. We could just get periodic reports and make suggestions on them."

"We can have her making the reports," James said. "But it seems clear that we also need someone there looking over her shoulder, making sure she spends the funds correctly as we have dictated."

"Rita did not take a salary the first two years of Bahia Street," I said. "She has managed an incredible program with tiny funds. I don't think we can possibly think at this stage that she would misuse funds."

"We are not suggesting that she would misuse them, just that she doesn't know what she's doing." Henry tapped his paper with his pen. "You will ensure that she's not doing anything on the project, won't you, Margaret? That she has not begun demolition. Or even hired an architect? Because we will need to approve all these people first."

I said nothing.

"You aren't saying anything, Joyce," James said. "What is your opinion on all this? What do you think of us having to build a building now? Would you have agreed to borrow all this money if we had known that?"

Joyce shook her head. "I don't know what to say. I react to things in an emotional way. I'm in a kind of shock. I need to think about it."

"But really," James said. "You're on the board. We want to know what you think."

"No, no, I don't know what to say yet."

"Well, give us at least an impression of how you feel then. You've said nothing at all."

"I guess I feel betrayed," Joyce said.

I covered my eyes.

"Perhaps that's how we all feel," James said. "Margaret, you have never done anything this large before either. Starting this nonprofit was great. You have done a wonderful job, but now, when we are talking about this amount of money, we need someone else to oversee things in Brazil. I think we should get one of Henry's contacts to suggest someone to oversee the project." Henry nodded his approval.

"That won't work," I said. "It will just cost a huge amount, and Rita won't work under some middle-class person anyway."

"Well, if we had done this properly from the beginning," Henry said, "if you had listened to my suggestions, then you wouldn't have this mess."

"So, let's see who Henry can come up with," Mo said. "I would like to know the actual liability risk. And we also have to discuss how we are going to pay Meps and Barry back for their loan."

"The promissory note we have from them says we will have a lien," Henry said. "We really need to get it as soon as possible."

"I would think that if it is causing a problem," I said, "and is going to cost a lot of money, than Meps and Barry would be happy to remove that statement from the note. I doubt they want the responsibility of getting landed with some building in Brazil anyway. We have said we will pay them back. It's our word they trust."

"What we need is a lien," Henry said. "And we should have had it from the beginning."

Joyce gave me a ride home. We said little. Joyce had been my strong supporter for years, a person I'd gone to when I saw no way to proceed.

"You know, I didn't want to say anything," she said. "I'm not ready to know how I feel. I wish James hadn't pushed me."

I said nothing. As she pulled to the curb at the front of my house, she turned to me. "You know, I never told my husband when I agreed to this loan. I never thought about liability. I never quite understood that I'm legally responsible. We don't have much money. My husband would kill me if he knew I'd done this."

I looked at her as I opened the car door. In the reflected streetlight I saw tears in her eyes.

Then, although I didn't think this could happen, things with Bahia Street got worse. Henry contacted his person in São Paulo who, without seeing it, said the building would cost even more to rebuild than Mario's estimate. Henry's other contact said he could find someone to oversee the project, but a person who spoke English, which was what both Henry and James wanted, since they could not speak Portuguese. This would cost us about two thousand a month. It would use up all our money without our ever beginning the project. I called Rita and told her what was going on.

"Well, Mario's working on the plans already," she said. "You can tell them what you like. And I've hired three boys from down the road to clean the place up. We can't really start demolition until we can see what's in there. They should be done by the end of the month."

"I'm supposed to tell you not to do anything."

"Fine. So, you've told me. So what?" Rita paused. "Margaret, those big shots in São Paulo don't know anything about how we do business in Bahia. Your guys there in Seattle just don't think we can do any big project here unless we have some white male overseeing us, a white male who has close ties with the States so he can convince them, while he's cheating them the entire time, that he'll do things just like they would have done in the States. Well, that's just not going to happen."

"The board in the States actually owns the building, Rita. I didn't quite understand the implications of this when we set it up. As non-profits, Bahia Street in Brazil and Bahia Street in the States are legally separate entities—as I set them up so you could retain more secure control—but that separation is broken now because they really can control the building. They own it."

"Then if worse comes to worst, we just sell the building. We're running Bahia Street just fine now without it. We can figure out another way to buy one and not give them control at all." We were both silent for a moment. "You understand what they're trying to do, don't you, Margaret? These middle-aged white men on your board?"

"They're good people, Rita. They're just scared. Henry's being ethical, in his view as a U.S. lawyer."

"That's his problem. What they really want to do is take over Bahia Street. It happens all the time. Groups get started, people work very hard to get them successful, and then some newcomers to their boards decide they want to change the entire idea of the program, get the votes on their side, and just take over. I don't know about the States, but here, legally, the board can fire you."

"Here, too. But they wouldn't do that. You wouldn't work with anyone else anyway. You and I started this whole thing. None of them really understands anything about Bahia."

"So? Do you think they care? They understand their world. And all of Bahia Street falls apart. Well, that isn't going to happen. You set it up smart, Margaret. This is where your idea of the infrastructure works. You can just shut the Seattle office entirely if you have to. We sell the building and survive on the money from England. We can get Meps and Barry to help us, or your friend Bobbi from Australia who came last year."

"Right." My voice did not carry enthusiasm. "By the way, we got another grant from England."

"For the building?"

"No. For the photography project. Part of it is to build a photography lab so you can teach the kids photography."

Rita laughed. "Life's ironic, isn't it? This has been my dream forever, but now I can't even think about it."

Henry wanted us to have a meeting with his São Paulo contact, Walter, who seemed to spend half his time in São Paulo and half in Seattle. I wasn't clear what, exactly, Walter did, but it was something big in construction for companies like Monsanto. I doubted he could be a person I'd like or respect.

A week before the scheduled meeting, I arrived at the office to see Karima sitting on the sofa. Karima had become an indispensable volunteer. She treated Bahia Street with the dedication she would any job, and over the months had taken from my shoulders a huge amount of the increasingly heavy administrative load of managing the international aspect of Bahia Street. She'd recently become pregnant, and I could see her belly growing round already. She sat slumped, staring at the floor.

"Margaret," she said. "I've decided to quit."

"What?"

"Well, I came to this organization thinking it was a cool group, that it was actually doing something. I liked the people. Here I thought I could do something meaningful, work with a group that's actually making a difference." She paused and sighed. "But it's not like that anymore. You're depressed all the time. Your board is trying to destroy everything. All I hear is fighting and nothing gets done. You owe that loan, but no one's even thinking about how to repay it—and you have your first payment due next month. It makes me stressed. I just don't want to come here anymore."

I collapsed into a chair. Karima had changed my entire feeling about working in the office. She understood computers much better than me, she had set up a proper accounting system in the computer, taken over the database from Barry, handled most of the basic administration in about half the time it took me, and did it twice as well. Besides, I liked her. She had become a friend, someone who really understood what Bahia Street was about, someone with overseas experience, who didn't think the United States was the center of the known universe. If I lost her, I could never fight this board.

But, I wasn't fighting the board much anyway. Henry was very good at his rhetoric; he was a lawyer after all. My confidence wasn't so high. Without Karima, I would have to face the office each day completely alone. I didn't think I could do that.

As I looked at Karima, something snapped. I can't lose Karima, I thought. I have to do something. Desperation began to suffocate me like a shroud. I forced myself to stand.

"Karima, instead of you leaving now and going home, let's take a long walk in the Arboretum. It's a beautiful spring day. Tomorrow, quit or whatever you like, but today, just walk with me. Help me think this through. And we can talk about a lot of things."

Karima smiled and pushed herself to her feet. "Sounds like a good idea. I get a bit sick these days, but the walking will do me good."

So we walked and looked at the trees, still bare from winter, saw crocuses sprouting, new spring grass shooting up. I don't remember what we said, but by the time we returned to the office, my entire attitude had changed. I no longer felt depressed. I was annoyed at myself for having so easily lost track of why we were doing Bahia Street in the first place. What James had called my "idealism" was indeed the core of what we were doing. Bahia Street had been that way when he joined the board, and if he didn't like it, he would just have to leave.

I have to win this one, I thought. If I'm ruthless and make enemies, that's just the way it has to be. Despite our conflicts, I respected Henry. But there was no way he was going to convince the board to let his way of thinking take over Bahia Street. I was just not being very smart about all this; I was being too emotional.

And, I thought to myself, to be fair to the next board member who joined, I had to be very clear, and have our ideas of operation written down for them to read, that control of Bahia Street was in Brazil. Anyone on the board would just have to stretch themselves to understand that others can sometimes understand how to do things in their own countries better than Americans. I realized why another aspect of Bahia Street had been a success: the entire project was a process. These funds for the renovation were more than a building investment. They were an investment that included Rita, the Bahia Street staff, the families, the larger Salvador community who would be getting paid for working on the project, and our own education in Seattle about the realities of incorporating concepts of global equality into our international and local infrastructure. This road was never going to be easy, I realized. If it became easy, then we were no longer challenging the status quo.

To a Mailing List of 615: April 15, 2004

Dear All,

Raining, raining over the bounding main...I was going to jog to work today, but somehow the penetrating drizzle urged me toward the bus, and before I knew it, I was actually on the warm and dry bus heading to the office. Oh well, best intentions and all.

This letter is mostly news of Brazil since I recently returned from there. First the building.

The building is located in Salvador's central business district, near the current rented Bahia Street Center and one block from a major business street. This area of Salvador dates from colonial times and was originally a neighborhood for wealthy Portuguese. An adjoining neighborhood, known as Pelourinho, was later abandoned by its wealthy residents who moved to outlying suburbs in the 1900s. Poorer people moved in, the buildings were divided up into tenements, and, with no infrastructural maintenance, the buildings deteriorated. Beginning in the early 1990s, the local government realized the tourist potential of this neighborhood and, in a complicated and controversial move, evicted tenement residents and spent millions restoring the infrastructures and façades of Pelourinho buildings. This project was a resounding success for the government, and Pelourinho is now the major tourist point of Salvador.

This renewal has influenced private owners in adjoining areas including the street of the Bahia Street Center. This street is famous as the birthplace of one of Bahia's most beloved poets (Castro Alves) and boasts an early classic structure that is now a museum for sacred artifacts. Buildings along the street, which have stayed with families for generations, are now being bought and renovated. At the time of my visit, five buildings on this street alone were in the process of renovation. Because nearly all the buildings on this street date from the early to the mid-1800s, they are considered "historic" and the street-facing façades cannot be changed. They are also mostly constructed of plaster and wood, materials that tend to become infested with wood-eating bugs and deteriorate in the tropical climate. So, following the procedure of Pelourinho, these renovators are reinforcing the front facade, then gutting and reconstructing everything behind. Bahia Street will follow the same plan with the building we have bought.

So, now the exciting process of renovation commences. Rita is working with a local architect on plans that will best fit the Center's needs and is in the process of hiring a local contractor who will oversee the actual renovation. I will keep you informed of the progress.

Last year, UNICEF held a contest for Brazilian groups working on social projects. 1,834 groups from all over Brazil put in applications, from which UNICEF selected one hundred as the best in the country. Bahia Street was among this group. From this 100, they selected thirty semifinalists. Without internal contacts, Bahia Street was selected! We now have a big plaque as a semifinalist. The award says a great deal about the work of Bahia Street, and we are delighted to receive this recognition.

Some news on the girls:

Ire, the little girl who had what turned out to be a form of epilepsy and was unable to take her exams last year because she was sick, was able to get treatment, thanks in part to the correct diagnosis by a doctor in Seattle. This year she entered an exam that has a prize of a scholarship to an excellent private school in Salvador. Much to everyone's surprise and delight, she won the prize. This means she has left Bahia Street, but she visits periodically and seems happy in her new school.

In Rita's neighborhood a few days after my arrival, a fifteen-year-old boy was shot. He had gotten involved with drug selling and gangs, then tried to get out. Two gangs in the area were having a fight. One boy had shot another and wounded him, so the damaged gang had to take retribution. They arrived where the fifteen-year-old was with a friend and shot him dead. It didn't seem to matter that he was no longer in the gang; indeed, this seemed to encourage them to shoot him. The murdered boy was a good friend of two of the girls in Bahia Street, including Aninha. So, now both her father and one of her best friends have been shot and killed. She is coming to Bahia Street but is not talking to anyone, except Fio and Rita. Bahia Street desperately needs a psychologist to work with the girls. We had one for a bit, but she was too middle-class and didn't understand the reality of the girls' lives. I don't see how we can afford to hire another staff person, but definitely a good psychologist should be first in line.

Black Conscience Week occurred while I was in Salvador, so there were marches and talks and events which the girls attended. One of the girls, Maria, also had her birthday during that week. Maria was born in a small town in rural Bahia, one of eight children of several fathers. Shortly after her birth, her mother abandoned her, and she somehow survived, *mostly on the streets and by roaming the countryside. Eventually, when she was about six, she began working as a servant for people in the area, washing clothes, getting water, doing the hard work. But people considered her wild, almost feral, and mentally deranged. It was accepted that she could never learn to read or write. Her mother came back, and Maria went to live with her for a bit, but then her mother decided to come to Salvador and leave Maria in a house full of male quasi-relatives. It was clear to everyone in the area that she would be used and raped constantly in this situation. Someone contacted Rita and asked if she could help. Rita went to the village, met Maria (who wouldn't even look at her) and the mother. She convinced the mother to bring Maria with her to Salvador and enroll the girl in Bahia Street.*

Maria has now been in Bahia Street for one year. She can read and write, and it is clear that she is very intelligent. She lives with her mother, who essentially ignores her, and comes to Bahia Street in addition to attending public school. She still has grave emotional difficulties, but has become part of a group of Bahia Street girls her own age, and these girls like her very much. So, at the Black Consciousness event on her birthday, all the other girls of her group bounced up and started shouting happy birthday for her, then started chanting "Maria! Maria!." This caused quite a disturbance in the event proceedings, but being Bahia, the audience joined in, the event halted for a few moments to shout happy birthday to Maria, and then continued. It should be noted that the Bahia Street girls formed quite a large contingent and almost all the young people at the event. The other participants were delighted to see young African-Brazilians attending and were quite indulgent toward them. Maria was embarrassed but very pleased.

As regards Maria as well, it is amazing what decent food can do. She was tiny when she arrived, but now, after eating her good meal a day at Bahia Street and the snacks she gets there, she has shot up and is now a strong-looking and beautiful young girl. We shall see how she does this year, but everyone at Bahia Street is on her side.

So, I could go on for more pages, but I had better stop until the next letter. Don't get wet in this rain!

All the best—as always,

Margaret

twenty-nine | evolution

I was packing up the office for the night when James called. His timing could not have been worse, for him. I ripped into him with all I had thought about that day, leaving him little room on either side to speak.

"You sound like you're mad at me, Margaret. I like you. I don't want you mad at me. I just don't want you to go any further in what is clearly a serious mistake."

I phoned Joyce the next day and asked her out for a beer. I told her what Rita had said. I spoke with her about the difference she'd made to Bahia Street, of the investment all of us—her, Rita, myself, others—had made to accomplish what we had.

"I never wanted to say I felt betrayed," Joyce said. "I didn't really. I was just shocked. I was hurt, I guess. And James made me speak before I wanted to. I got scared. Although we've never met, I feel I know Rita. I think she and I are, in a deep way, very similar."

That night, when I got home, I telephoned Almuht. "Why don't you and Mo do a three-way conversation with Rita and Rubim?" I suggested. "I'll just stay out of the conversation completely. That way you can ask Rita any questions you want directly; you don't have to worry about my lack of knowledge about housing or construction. Both you and Mo know a lot more about that than I do. You can translate."

"What a great idea!" Almuht said. "I'd love to talk to Rita. And to see what her brother says."

Almuht and Mo telephoned Rita a few days later. I heard from Almuht first.

"Rita is fantastic!" she said. "She knows totally what she's doing. Anyone outside would be a disaster. You know that, I know that. Middle-class guys in Brazil would just treat Rita like some lowly person. They'd steal from us, make the entire thing much more expensive, and Rita would never work with them anyway."

A few minutes later, I heard from Mo. "Rubim is fantastic!" he said. "I wish I could work with him on the building. They still know all the classical construction methods there—stone masonry, the woodworking. I could learn a lot. He's such a great guy. It'd be fun just to hang out with him and chat about stuff. We got talking about all the different methods of construction between the States and Brazil, how permits work, all that. It's fascinating."

I smiled into the phone receiver. "I'm sure it is, Mo."

I felt manipulative. But I also asked myself why I'd never had board members talk with Rita directly. She could defend herself better than I could. By speaking on her behalf, I was, in a sense, diminishing her, suggesting that I was somehow more central. Her voice was the strong one here.

The day finally came for the lunch meeting with Henry's contact, Walter. James and Mo couldn't attend.

Walter arrived with a notebook, several folders, bright eyes, and dark curly hair. "Ah, so you're Margaret," he said when we met. He spoke in Portuguese. "I'm so pleased to meet you. Bahia Street seems like such a wonderful project. I want to visit it when I go to Salvador next."

"That'd be great." I smiled in spite of myself. His enthusiasm was infectious.

We ordered lunch from the counter and all sat down.

"So, explain to us the process of constructing a building in Brazil," Henry said.

"Sure." Walter took a few bites of his sandwich and spread out the folders he had brought. "Now, remember, I work for big companies; we do everything top drawer. We're talking millions of dollars, so a little school building is very different. But there are some aspects that are the same."

Everyone nodded. Almuht and Joyce opened their notebooks. I said nothing and waited. I wondered if my face reflected the burning bile that sat at the base of my throat.

"Your architect must be certified."

"He is," Almuht said. "They got someone named Mario who worked for Boeing and the Brazilian airline Varig."

"Great. Because in Brazil the architect does more than the plans. He makes the calculations with the structural engineer of what materials you'll need. They should also have a certified structural engineer."

Almuht checked her notes. "They do."

"But what about the general contractor?" Henry asked. "She wants to hire her brother for that."

"If her brother's a general contractor, then that's great," Walter said. "The general, in a small project like this, doesn't have to be certified, just—they have a term for it in Portuguese, 'established in the trade'— and if she can get her brother, all the better. At least then there's less of a chance he'll be cheating her. She knows where he lives."

"But how can you have control over that?" Henry asked. "If it's her brother, she could use the funds any way. Shouldn't we have a supervisor?"

Walter glanced in my direction. His eyes looked troubled. I realized that he sensed discord and wasn't sure how he should respond. Strange, I thought. It didn't appear as though Henry had talked with him at all about the board conflict, just invited him cold to give us some advice. He was only now sensing the political weight his words might carry.

"If you think you really need an outside supervisor, I suppose I can help you with that." Walter glanced quickly around the group. "But you have to trust the people you're working with in the end. I don't know who this general is, or what Rita's like, but if you can't trust them, then you're going to have problems regardless."

"And what about liability?" Joyce asked. "Can people there sue us?"

"I suppose so. People are always suing each other in Brazil. You can't avoid getting sued at some stage. But suing you here in the States? I doubt it. Especially not if you're working with Rita's brother. The laborers will likely be illiterate. They might do a local suit, but inter-national—no, I can't see it."

As we got ready to leave, Walter came over to shake my hand. He gave me an engaging, open smile.

"We should get together for coffee or lunch sometime," he said. "It'd be fun to talk about Brazil, about all kinds of things."

"I'd love to," I said, and to my surprise, I meant it. A lesson, I thought. Never prejudge anyone. Especially when you've made them into someone else's chess pawn in your own mental chess match.

"Thank you so much for taking the time to come," Joyce said to Walter. "I feel so much more comfortable about everything now. I appreciate your clarity in explaining things."

"Did you eat that entire huge sandwich?" Almuht teased him in

Portuguese. Walter patted his slim tummy, and they both laughed.

"Until the next meeting," Henry said. He gave me a civil smile. We both knew then that the tide had turned and that in any resolution regarding the building, the board, except possibly for him and James, would likely now vote with Rita. And partly because of the reassurance of his friend Walter. But I didn't feel elation. Instead, I felt saddened. I liked Henry. He had done a lot for us. I understood his side and, from his perspective, he was being responsible. I hated maneuvering against him. But this project had been with me too long. I'd put in too much time and, as Rita said, too much heart.

James rang a few days later. "I think I will have to quit the board," he said. "We have philosophical differences. You believe that in an international organization, everyone should just do as they think best. I believe such an organization has to be an umbrella, with one group working as the central overarching head, controlling all its projects."

"That's true, James. We disagree." I paused. "Thank you for contributing as you have to the board. And I hope we can still be friends."

"So do I," James said. "I like you."

After the day of our walk in the park, Karima officially quit, but continued to come to work, as dedicated as ever—and more pregnant by the day. She spent half her time sleeping on the couch and was impressively efficient with the rest of her time. She said she would go when the baby was born. Selfishly, I dreaded that day.

This was to be the day of the showdown board meeting. But, life is a shape-changer. Whenever I thought I recognized a pattern or direction, it would shift into something completely different.

Mo had e-mailed me earlier in the week to ask if he could chair the meeting, usually my job. He felt that the tension between Henry and me would make it difficult for us to get anything constructive accomplished. I happily handed over the reins. He sent out an e-mail detailing this to the entire board and asking for suggestions for the agenda. He didn't receive much, so he set the agenda for us to vote on whether we would give Rita liberty to direct the reconstruction of the building as she chose.

"Henry said at an earlier meeting that he just wanted us to properly vote on all this," Mo said, "that if he lost the vote he would go along with whatever the board wanted. I think he's honorable and will stick with his word."

"Yes," I said. "I think so, too. But I don't think he'll feel comfortable if it goes against him."

Henry had influenced me, however. I had never really thought about the legal ramifications of the board or our actions. I resolved to make this vote a legal, binding part of the permanent Bahia Street by-laws. If this challenge to our infrastructure of equality had happened now, it could happen again. Also, I thought, we have to get moving fast on raising the money to repay Meps and Barry's loan.

As Karima and I were printing the agenda, the phone rang.

"Hello, Margaret. This is Chris from Portland."

"Oh, hello. How're you doing?" Chris was a donor who I had only met a few times. He found us through our website and loved both what we did and the letters I wrote. He was in his late twenties or early thirties and had made several generous donations over the last few years.

"I'm all right." He paused. "Margaret, I'm in a position right now where I'd like to make a larger donation to Bahia Street. If I were to do this, what do you most need? Where would my donation be the most help?"

I smiled to myself. "Well, Chris. We have this loan for the building we bought. We have a grant to refurbish the building, but we have to repay the loan on top of raising the funds for the daily running of the Center. Any contribution you could make toward paying off that loan would be incredibly appreciated."

"How much is the loan?"

I told him.

"Well." He paused. I waited. "I think I could probably pay that off."

I sat down. "The entire thing?"

"Well, yeah. Actually why don't we just round it up a few thousand and give you the extra to help with the refurbishment when the other money runs out?"

"You're giving funds to repay the entire loan?" I realized I sounded stupefied and unprofessional.

"Yeah, yeah, we can do that. I'll talk to my brother—he'll be going into this with me—and my financial advisor on whether I should send one check or two or just order a money transfer. But yeah, I'm sure I can get you the funds by the end of the week."

I tried to control the lump closing my throat. I coughed, hoping this would make my voice sound normal. "Um, Chris, that's incredible. I'm not sure you know how much this means, particularly right now. Um, well, thank you."

"I really support Bahia Street. I'm very impressed with what you all are accomplishing. This is a way I can contribute to making social change in the world. And I do know that what I give you here will make a difference."

I took a deep breath and tried to pull myself together. "In November, we're having the opening for the new building in Salvador," I said. "If you and your brother would like to come, I'm sure everyone there would be delighted to meet you. Then you could see exactly where your money went."

Chris laughed. "I'd love that. And I'll bet my brother would as well. My father had always dreamed of owning a building or a hotel in Bahia. Perhaps this way, we'll be fulfilling, in a certain way his dream."

"That's wonderful." A tear slid over the edge of my eye. I quickly wiped it away. "Rita's sending me photos of the building reconstruction as it progresses. I can send you copies of these if you like."

"Oh." Chris sounded genuinely surprised and delighted. "If it's not imposing. I don't want to intrude on private Bahia Street information, but I'd love to see those."

"No, no Chris. You would not be intruding."

I put down the phone and sat for a long moment in an anesthetized, suspended cocoon, swinging, swinging, amid a silence that blocked out cold wind or noise.

Karima had stopped working and was sitting watching me. "He's going to pay off the entire loan?"

"More. Extra for the reconstruction as well as the loan."

"That's a lot of money."

"Yeah."

Karima pushed herself to her feet. "Allah be praised," she said. "Miracles happen."

Just before the meeting, I checked my e-mails for a final time.

There was one from Henry. "I will not be attending the meeting," he wrote. "Nor any meetings in the future. I feel I must leave the board because I have ethical differences with the way business is being conducted. Henry."

The irony slapped me full in the face: on the same day Henry decided to quit we no longer had the loan that made him so nervous. But the nervousness was not really about the loan. It was about control and fear of the unknown. And, for Henry, being a lawyer, he had real liability issues the rest of us didn't have. Also, neither Henry nor James had any real idea of what went on in Bahia. Nor did the rest of the board for that matter, with the possible exception of Almuht. From this interaction, I had learned—again. I had let the board think I really controlled what went on in Bahia. I came back with my happy reports and all seemed to go well. I never really foregrounded the fundamental principle of Bahia Street's success—that Bahia Street USA was not the top controlling umbrella, that Bahia Street Bahia was legally, and in practice, the core power of the organization. It was my mistake. I needed to write a position paper explaining the principles we had developed for Bahia Street. It was complicated because the understanding of what we were doing had come gradually, over years of experience. When Joyce had joined the board, I hadn't been clear enough in my own head to explain these principles. It had been a process of learning, by both Rita and me.

I heard what sounded like Mo's step outside. I smiled, anticipating his warmth and his laugh. I would take this incredible group of friends out for a beer. My toasts would also stretch a half a globe away to include Rita. My love for her almost hurt sometimes.

To a Mailing List of 750: September 18, 2004

Dear All,

I am sitting at the office with the cool scent of fall rains blowing across my shoulder. As I begin this, my thoughts keep turning to the story of the fellow who chopped off his arm to save his own life, then rappelled down a cliff, one-armed, and walked out to meet his rescuers. I just heard him on the radio because only six months after this event, and with only one arm now, he has already completed a book of his experiences. That kind of determination is awe-inspiring. If we aren't careful, it can make the rest of us feel small in comparison.

But then, let us reflect upon the incredible things we each do in our lives. One thing that resonated with me when this fellow was talking was his feeling of being contained within a greater force, that when the rescue team met him he had only about a half an hour more before he would have lost enough blood to cause a heart attack; the timing was so perfect that he himself felt overwhelmed. And when he returned to the place of the accident, he saw the meeting of both his birth and his death.

I, of course, reflect upon Bahia Street. That it began seven years ago with only a thought between two friends and that it has become part of a larger force, of the people and energies that have made it so much more than the two minds that originally conceived it. So many times, Bahia Street almost collapsed in the early stages and then surprising connections went right to allow it to grow. This force I am talking about includes all of you who are reading this and who have helped in your varied ways over the years. When I think of that, I become awestruck again, of what beauty and strength can come from determination and collective energy. A "thank you" doesn't quite work in this case, more a feeling of balance in what we are doing together.

So, with that, let me tell you the news. I will be going to Bahia in November and will return with more details, but I am delighted to report that reconstruction of the building is progressing well. Skilled and semi-skilled workers rebuilt the foundation, digging the deep holes for the girders by hand. Then, still entirely by hand, they placed the girders and poured the foundation cement. Upon this was laid the internal infrastructure for the entire building. Support beams for the first floor have now also been hung and the floor for the first story poured.

Rains slowed this process, but the rainy season has now finished, and we can expect sunny weather for the rest of the construction. The next phase will be to refurbish the front façade of the building and secure it, a necessary move since the interior of the building will now begin to contain more expensive portable materials. Then work will begin on completing the first floor, then the second, on up to the top. Rita explained that by proceeding in this manner, if the project runs out of money, Bahia Street will still have a usable building that can slowly be completed as we obtain funds while holding classes, etc., downstairs.

I would like to emphasize that this entire process is being organized, overseen, and executed by African-Brazilians, nearly all of them from the shantytowns of Salvador. These are the people whom Bahia Street serves. Part of the effect of this building project is that it is giving employment to shantytown residents. Such legal employment is scarce in these neighborhoods where residents must generally turn to informal or illegal activities to survive. The wages Bahia Street pays to the workers on this building are giving this group of men respectable work and money, which they can use to feed their families.

The work is even more powerful because those directing the project are members of their own community, people who they can admire and use as role models. Although Bahia Street is doing this work because we need a new Center, the process of the reconstruction is also providing an important service in itself.

So, it is now the next day from when I began this letter. On my bike ride here, I sniffed the scents of autumn, a crisp edge to the warmth of the morning sun. As I left the house at seven thirty, the sun was barely above the horizon. We are moving toward winter, a time of tempestuous storms, rain, wind, and the intimacy of indoor warmth. I wish you all strength and good will through this season of change.

abraços

Margaret

thirty | resting on the wings of a butterfly

I sat on the couch in the office looking at Depression K406. Depression K406 didn't say much and had a leering grin. I called him, "No Exit." Beside him sat his fat companion. I didn't know his companion's name. He just blocked out the sunlight.

No Exit. What was my plan when Bahia Street reached this stage? The building was going great. Rita was sending me photos. It had been demolished in less than two months and now they had laid the foundation. In Seattle, we had just had our biggest fundraiser of the year, a summer Brazilian Harvest Festival. Everyone had a great time. The most talented Brazilian and Brazilian-style musicians in the area participated. Long time volunteers pulled everything together. We had a silent auction organized by an experienced volunteer. Food was donated and organized by a professional chef.

I was gratified. I was honored. And I had to force myself to do every tiny piece of organization.

I was tired of it. I wanted to go hiking, do some interesting research, some fun writing. The meager funds I had been able to put aside when I quit my teaching job were long gone. I was tired of buying all my clothes at second hand shops and never going out to eat. I should have been saving money for my older years, and I had nothing. I had been living on $15,000 or less for years now, and it wasn't working any more. I wanted to go on kayak trips, to do something that engaged my mind. I wanted out.

But there was no way out.

Grant writing. I always hated grant writing. I was not bad at it. I'd done it for years, long before we started Bahia Street. I'd funded most of my research through grants. But then, it was a necessary, ugly task leading to a delightful end. **Now it was the whole.** My skills now focused on taking complex situations and ideas and reducing them to simplistic bullet points that a reader, who knew nothing about the subject, could understand by skimming a one-page review. My job now was to tailor an application to fit the funders' desires without compromising what we actually did at Bahia Street. I could now write what the funders wanted, and not actually lie about where their money would go. I spent my time resisting the temptation to convince Rita to change the program in Brazil to something that had less relevance there just because a certain idea was trendy and more likely to get funding.

Something had to happen. I couldn't continue. I was hollow. With this attitude I would never inspire. I felt like a cheap sales promoter. More and more people kept describing me as "noble," presenting an image of sacrifice they could only watch and never hope to achieve. I didn't like that image. I didn't do this for noble reasons; for political commitment, yes, but the mantle of noble was too heavy. I wanted to prance around in a swimsuit or light down ski coat. My house needed so much work, it was falling apart and I had no money to repair it.

I wanted to leave, to go live in Europe or Canada. I didn't care. I just wanted out.

I traveled to Alaska for two weeks, spent the time hiking in high alpine meadows and coastal forest, encountered a moose, camped with the door (not the mosquito netting) of my tent open to an endless light that compromised to twilight for the shortest of time. I didn't think about Bahia Street. I didn't think much about anything. I did crossword puzzles. I met strangers and learned about their lives.

When I returned, I rang Nancy. I didn't know her well, but she had been a long-time supporter of Bahia Street. She was vice president of the Seattle World Affairs Council. Over the past seven years, she had developed a very successful global education program in the local schools. She also had had two children and finished a Master's degree in Public Administration. I wanted to ask her for advice, to see if she might be interested in some joint project. I wasn't sure what.

"I'd love to do something," she said. "When I have time. I just quit my job, but I've already applied for a job at the university. In Southeast Asian studies."

She seemed a shoo-in for the job. I was convinced she'd be hired. But when I called a week later, her husband told me that no, they'd hired an equally qualified Filipino man. Nancy is white. Hard luck for Nancy, but I probably would have made the same decision myself. I tried hard to sound sad for Nancy, but I'm not sure I succeeded. She wanted a job with an internationally-oriented nonprofit. In Seattle these were very few and far between. I had no idea what I could offer her at Bahia Street—certainly not a third of the salary she had received before, but maybe she and I together could create something.

And that is exactly what we did. I put forward some ideas, and she exploded them to triple the size and scope I had envisioned. We explored the idea of an educational program in Bahia to teach people about NGO management and global inequality. The program would make people aware of how they could be activists here in the States in order to change our collective relationship with the world. We'd coordinate work placements with Brazilian nonprofits, where half the fee would go directly to assist the local nonprofit and the other half to a new project to provide legal, infrastructural, and fiscal advice to these groups. We'd commission a series of forums tied to the overseas programs. We could set up programs with universities to take students to Bahia and teach them about a host of international issues. I had the contacts and standing to get the programs certified and to lure my friends from around the world to teach for us. Nancy had the experience and understanding to actually set up such huge ideas.

I presented the concept to the board, coaching them in private first so they wouldn't have to face surprises in front of others. I told them that this would require an amendment to expand the parameters of our nonprofit status. They all asked good questions and gave the project their total support. They seemed energized in a way I hadn't seen at Bahia Street for a year. I rang Rita and told her about it. She grasped immediately the political aims and gave her support.

"It's the next phase," she said. "We've been teaching Brazilians to be activists. Now we can begin to teach Americans the same thing."

I never feel I have left Brazil until I hit U.S. soil. On this return flight from Salvador via São Paulo and Dallas, I'd been speaking only Portuguese. I'd chatted with the airline staff, the fellow sitting beside me who was a salesman from Rio, and the woman across the aisle who was a journalist from Fortaleza. We shared drinks, stories of our lives, often in much more intimate detail than we would tell a close friend. We would likely never see each other again, and that gave us the freedom to reveal things for which we might otherwise be held accountable.

I realize that what I miss most when I leave Brazil is the laughter. Brazilians taught me that laughter is one of the strongest companions we have. In every interaction—with a bank teller, sitting on a bus, standing in line at the grocery store—mundane moments can become a delight. With laughter, pain, and hardship comes the organic substance of a reality we all share. With shared laughter comes compassion.

"Fio was just in the hospital for another attack of his spinal meningitis condition," Rita told me on the last night of my visit. We were sitting together drinking fruit juice and sparkling water—pretending it was beer. We'd decided to go to a special bar in Barra, down by the sea. I watched the reflection of the moon across the water, a trail of light that frothed into iridescent mist as it hit the foam of the waves. I turned to Rita, question in my eyes. "No, he's OK," she said.

We sat silent for some time. Barra was a mixed middle-class neighborhood where many tourists stayed. At the table beside us, a man in his fifties shared a table with two beautiful men who looked to be in their late teens or early twenties.

"Of course you can take a walk with one of us," one of the young men said in broken English.

Rita looked at me.

"Negotiations," I explained.

Rita nodded and smiled. "Hope our older gentleman is not so stupid as to go."

I laughed. "We shall see."

"So, you were telling me that Henry is coming to Bahia in a few months with some Rotarians?" Rita asked.

"Yeah. He came and talked with me. He asked me for advice on the trip."

"That took courage."

I nodded. "I have respect for Henry. I'm glad he did it. We were supposed to meet for coffee, but it stretched into lunch."

Rita smiled. "Well, I'm pleased he's coming, so he can see for himself what we've done. I think he'll be proud."

"Yeah. I think he is already. And James, the other fellow who was against the building?" Rita nodded. "He has now asked his Rotary club to give us funds to furbish the new building. He really supports us now. I guess things just got confused for awhile."

"We're getting old," Rita said.

"Maybe you are. I certainly am not."

"That's what the fellow beside us thinks." We both snickered. "You're older than me, aren't you, Margaret?"

"Last time I checked. Don't think it's changed. You can console yourself with that, you will always be younger than me."

"We have to think about who can take over Bahia Street—after us, I mean."

"Yeah. I've thought about that. Nancy seems very good, in a few years perhaps. If not her, I feel confident now that someone will come along. For you it's harder."

"Perhaps. Fio can't do it. Perhaps one of the girls, when they get through university, would like to come back."

"Yeah." The tourist at the next table rose with the younger of his companions, the other remained seated. I looked at Rita.

"Silly, silly man," she said. She paused. "You could come live in Arembepe. You should buy a small place on the beach there, before the dollar drops any more."

"That's a nice fantasy. I don't know what I'll do when it comes time for me to pass Bahia Street on to someone else, my excuse for coming here all the time. My heart is divided now."

Rita laughed. "Your heart may be divided, but your soul is here."

The waiter arrived with another bottle of water for us. The young man at the next table picked up the older fellow's backpack, which he had inexplicably left at the table, stood up, nodded to the waiter, and walked out.

"*Oi ai*," Rita said. The waiter raised his eyebrows, poured us each some water from the bottle.

"Bahia, Bahia," I said. We watched the moon. A group of young men played soccer on the firm sand near the waves. Someone down the street began beating out a samba on a tabletop, and others joined in complicated, perfectly timed polyrhythms on metal and wood.

"We've done something good," Rita said.

"I think so." I swallowed the last of my water. "We've known each other almost fifteen years, you realize that, Rita?"

"And still friends." Rita laughed and poured half her water into my glass for a toast. "To friendship," she said, raising her glass.

"To friendship." We laughed again as we saw tears in each other's eyes.

"Excuse me." The waiter stood beside our table with our check. "You can pay up front, if you're ready." We looked at him, startled. "The gentleman and his friend are returning. The older gentleman may want to call the police and he may want you to get involved..."

"Of course." Rita took the check. "Thank you." I fished some bills from my pocket and handed them to the waiter as a tip.

"The waiter, of course, saw nothing," Rita said as we paid our bill. "No."

As we walked into the street we began to giggle, a releasing giggle that simmered, spurted, and could not be contained. "We are terrible," I stammered. "We are mean, horrible people."

"No, no," Rita said. "He'll be all right. It'll be part of his Tales of Bahia when he gets home. And anyway, you're not laughing at him, you're just laughing."

I looked at Rita's beloved face reflected in the street lamp and felt tears again. I laughed a different kind of laugh. "You're right," I said. "I'm just laughing."

To a Mailing List of 800: March 18, 2005

Dear All,

I have been walking in the Arboretum. It is more beautiful than I have ever seen it. The cherry trees, the magnolia, everything in flower. I stand under a canopy of scent and color, the light somehow changing texture as it filters through this haze of bloom. And inside me, a peaceful exhilaration stands. Part of this exhilaration is the intense beauty of our natural world, but part is because of two milestones Bahia Street has reached.

At the beginning of March, with the start of this Bahia school year, Bahia Street in Salvador moved into the new Center. Rita e-mailed me a notice all in capitals. "CALL ME!" she wrote. "CELEBRATE!" Bahia Street will no longer be renting a space in Salvador. We are operating from our own building, bought last year and reconstructed by Rita, the staff, construction crew, volunteers, and neighbors in Salvador.

Of course, the building still needs work. The original plans are for a four-story building and we now have a two-story one (which is still larger than the space we were renting before). The walls are rough but painted bright colors. There seems to be a problem with the phone connection going into the building, so the phone is somehow connected outside. This means that right now everyone has to go into the street to talk on the phone.

Such annoyances, however, are small. As a symbol—and reality—of accomplishment and power, this achievement is huge. It is a milestone we can celebrate together. Toast yourselves tonight and perhaps we will feel each other's energy.

The second milestone is very close to my heart. As all of you know, the aim of Bahia Street is to provide young women and girls in Brazil an opportunity for a quality education that will allow them to pass the university exam and have a chance for professional equality. Since we start with young girls, this is a long-term goal. The difficulties the girls face in terms of malnutrition, violence, and psychological problems that stem from living in such poverty, just to mention a few, are horrific by any standards.

Juliana was the first girl to enter the Bahia Street program. We had almost no money at the time and little infrastructure. Everyone said our aims were idealistic and unlikely to succeed. Juliana, however, wanted to try. She told everyone in her neighborhood, and us at Bahia Street, that she wanted to be a doctor. Her neighbors laughed at her.

That was eight years ago. This year Juliana took the Brazilian university exam and, on her first try, she passed. She has now been accepted to university. As if this were not enough, the university chose her for one of the five scholarships it awarded this year.

No one is laughing at Juliana now.

So, I leave you with only joyful news. We need these bright spots in our turbulent world. Cherish that you have chosen to be part of it. Hold your delight close and share it with friends.

Shared joy makes us strong.

abraços,

Margaret

ACKNOWLEDGEMENTS

This list of friends who have contributed in various ways to this book is inadequate and represents only a small number of those involved. The Wenner-Gren Foundation for Anthropological Research gave me the first grant that made this entire journey possible. I am grateful to all the people who have helped and guided me in Bahia, many of whom appear in the pages of this volume. Naming just a few include the Santos family, Cecilia McCallum, Jair, Zeze, Lazaro, Jogo de Dentro, Lula, Curioso, and Luzia. During the creating of Bahia Street, I have also been guided and supported by many people—some of whom also appear in this book. In particular, I would like to mention the first Bahia Street Board, Margaret Schulte, Pat Ingressia, Eduardo Mendonça, and Mark and Carol Salkind, and our first sustaining contributors Alex Uxbridge, Ina Whitlock, Michael and Beret Kischner, Betsy Willson, and Roger Clark. To all of our other donors and volunteers—far too many to list—you have made Bahia Street possible. Susie De Paolis has spent invaluable hours managing the Bahia Street Trust. Bobbi Ballas, Robert Barclay, Gus Stewart, and Henry Schulte read early versions of the manuscript and made comments that I found greatly helpful. Early versions of various encounters from Part One of the book appeared in the Clam Cove Report of Vashon Island. My editor, Ashley Shelby was invaluable, guiding me to transform the manuscript into a strong, readable narrative. Bryan Blondeau and Kyra Freestar very kindly inputted my handwritten edits into the computer manuscript, Melanie Wyffels proofread the Portuguese. Margaret Schulte helped with the last minute editing, and the staff at Cold Tree Press transformed my manuscript into the beautiful book you now see. Nancy Bacon gave me her much-appreciated, pragmatic, and practical support, and conceived this book's title. Sarah Odedina offered me her invaluable advice. James Eng gave me his quiet confidence throughout. And without Rita, this book would have had no reason to exist.

Printed in the United States
217135BV00001B/2/A